Living the Christian Life in Today's World

Living the Christian Life in Today's World

A Conversation between Mennonite World Conference and the Seventh-day Adventist Church

June 28-July 1, 2011 – Silver Spring, Maryland, USA
May 28-31, 2012 – Basel, Switzerland

Participants from Mennonite World Conference were: Robert J Suderman (Canada); Valerie G Rempel (United States); Henk Stenvers (The Netherlands); Patricia Urueña Barbosa (Colombia); Danisa Ndlovu (Zimbabwe); and Thomas R Yoder Neufeld (Canada).

Participants from the Seventh-day Adventist Church were: William Johnsson (Australia); John Graz (France/Switzerland); Bert Beach (United States); Gary Councell (United States), Denis Fortin (Canada); Peter Landless (South Africa); and Teresa Reeve (Canada).

Carol E Rasmussen, Editor and Production Manager
William G Johnsson, Consulting Editor
Robert John Suderman, Consulting Editor
Lindsay Sormin, Book Designer

The authors assume full responsibility for the accuracy of all facts
and quotations as cited in this book.

Copyright ©2014 by:

Public Affairs and Religious Liberty Department
General Conference of Seventh-day Adventists
12501 Old Columbia Pike
Silver Spring MD 20904 USA

And by: Mennonite World Conference

ISBN: 978-0-692-02116-3

Preface

In 2011 and 2012 representatives of the General Conference of Seventh-day Adventists and of the Mennonite World Conference met together for official conversations. In many respects the meetings proved to be a journey of mutual discovery.

The history of Mennonites stretches back 500 years, that of Adventists only about 160 years. Mennonites arose out of the religious ferment of the 16th century, Adventists out of the Great Second Awakening in the United States in the 1830s and 1840s.

Adventists and Mennonites have had frequent contacts during the past 40 years, particularly through their participation in the annual meetings of the Christian World Communions. These periodic encounters, along with other contacts, gradually led to the conviction on both sides that an official conversation might be both instructive and valuable.

From the outset of discussions leading to the conversation, it was understood that organic union was not the objective. Rather, the exchange of ideas would provide an opportunity for learning about each other's history, beliefs and values, clarifying misunderstandings and removing stereotypes. Out of the discussion, therefore, might emerge areas where Mennonites and Adventists can cooperate in selected areas of mutual concern.

Participants in the conversation quickly realized that they share much in common. They desire to recover the authenticity and passion of the New Testament church, they have a similar understanding of Christian history, and they are strongly committed to be followers of Jesus in their personal lives and in their corporate witness to the world.

The theme of the conversations was "Living the Christian Life in Today's World." Discussion proceeded by way of prepared papers which, while theological in nature, endeavored to show the practical outworking in the life of the community.

This book gathers together, with slight editing, all the papers presented in the two rounds of conversation. It also includes a summary statement that was agreed upon by participants at the conclusion of the meetings. This statement includes recommendations for ongoing cooperation.

The papers represent the thinking of individual participants: they are not official documents of either the Seventh-day Adventist Church or of the Mennonite World Conference.

The two years of conversation were characterized by Christian fellowship and mutuality of purpose. To God be the glory!

William G Johnsson
General Conference
of Seventh-day Adventists

Robert J Suderman
Mennonite World
Conference

Table of Contents

FIRST
MEETING

Anabaptist Overview

Patricia Urueña Barbosa

The grace and peace of our God be with you. We, as representatives of Anabaptist churches, are more than pleased to participate in this initiative of dialogue and approach with the Seventh-day Adventist Church. This is an historic date when we meet to share the beliefs and practices from our own Anabaptist identity, and learn from the wisdom and Christian practices of our brothers and sisters from the Seventh-day Adventist Church.

The 21st century demands these types of contacts between churches that are committed to justice, peace and nonviolence. We celebrate that the Word of God, the saving grace of Christ, the Christian faith, and the mission entrusted to us by Jesus to witness to the world of His incarnation, teachings, and redemptive and transformative power bring us together. We also celebrate, as part of the Anabaptists, the Christian commitment to peace, conscientious objection to mandatory military service, and the practice of nonviolence as a basis for the ethics of the Christian life. We want to learn from the Adventist Church about your commitment to evangelization, discipleship, comprehensive health care, ecological concerns and ethical decision-making as a global church.

In this context, the following historical approach aims to deepen knowledge and mutual understanding, where we can identify the common historical roots, the principles and reasons for our faith and practices. We desire to continue encouraging ourselves to be witnesses to the Gospel of Christ so that, guided by the Holy Spirit, we move forward in building unity among Christians and mutual cooperation in the mission of the churches in the world.

History and Principles of the Anabaptist Radical Reformation

Both the Protestant Reformation and the Catholic Contra-Reformation are well known by the majority of those interested in the history of the Church. However, parallel to the Protestant Reformation was another movement: the Anabaptist movement or Radical Reformation, as a reaction to both classical Protestantism and Catholicism.

From the Radical Reformation originated the Mennonites, Hut-terites, Amish, and some groups of Brethren, such as the Mennonite Brethren, the Church of the Brethren, and the Brethren in Christ. The present-day Baptist denominations also can claim significant roots in the Anabaptist movement of the 16th century.

Before we approach the history and Anabaptist principles, it is necessary to consider some things that took place in the Church which preceded the Reformation and set its course:

Change of attitude toward Scriptures: Through the development of the hierarchy, the Bible began to lose its place as the only authority for the Church.

Growing importance of tradition: For example, if something was practiced and believed in the Church, it came to be considered a rule, even though it had no biblical basis.

The Bible was beyond the reach of ordinary Christians: To avoid misinterpretations, it was taught that only the Church (or leaders) could interpret the Bible correctly. The result was that most Christians knew little about the Bible.

Change in the way that baptism and other practices in the Church were understood: The New Testament calls on the Church to practice the baptism of those who confess Christ as Lord and Savior, that is, "the baptism of believers." With the influence of

Constantine on the Church, the understanding changed from "the baptism of believers" to "the baptism of infants," without a personal confession of faith.

Over time people started to believe that this practice of baptism had a sacramental value. In other words, the Church began to teach that these ceremonies had power in their own right (in a magical sense). It was taught that baptism was the spiritual regeneration; through baptism a person became a Christian. By this concept the Church could baptize infants without a confession of personal faith. Through the very act of baptism, they said, a person gained a new life.

Also over the years came other non-biblical ideas. As a result of the traditional practice of prayer to Mary and the saints, the value of making the sign of the cross and the prayers for the dead began to gain acceptance.

Change in the practice of the Holy life: When Christianity became the official religion of the Empire the practice of the Christian life ceased to be an option and became an imposition. If everyone had to be a Christian through force, it was no longer a matter of personal decision and it was thus impossible to maintain a high standard of living in holiness. So it was expected that the leaders were saints, but not the laity.

Also there were many abuses in the Church due to the prevailing immorality among the clergy, the lack of apostolic zeal in the majority of the bishops, the ignorance of the clergy, the despotism of the popes, and the sale of indulgences, all of which caused people to distrust the Church hierarchy.

Movements seeking the reform of the Church: Through the centuries before the Protestant Reformation, many movements and protests stood against the above-mentioned harmful changes. Many leaders and supporters of such movements were persecuted, imprisoned and executed by the leaders of the Roman Catholic Church.

Some of the most influential leaders were the following:

```
              313              1054           1517
                              Orthodox       Reformation
              Roman          Church
              Catholic
  30          Church
Resurrection

Montanism   Monasticism    Albigensians  Wycliffe Huss Anabapt.
       Donatism                   Waldensians
```

Pedro Valdo (French, 1170) advocated a simple lifestyle of not amassing wealth, nonresistance, love, and nonviolence to put an end to the conflict.

John Wycliffe (English, 1329) considered Scripture as essential to the life of the Christian and the Church, looked for a way to return to the rules of the New Testament, criticized some doctrines and practices of the Church, and considered the Papacy as the Antichrist.

John Huss (Czechoslovakia, 1371), disciple of Wycliffe, accused the popes of their mistakes in public. These leaders, and other no less important Bible experts, were willing to give their lives for the truth of the Gospel, so much so that some were excommunicated, imprisoned, and burned at the stake.

The people and movements that paved the way for the Reformation also helped pave the way for the Anabaptists. Anabaptism is impossible to understand without linking its development with these movements. Despite the numerous movements, it was not until the time of Martin Luther that attempts to reform had a permanent impact on the Church of Jesus Christ and the society at the time.

The Reformation of the Church

In addition to the traditional thesis there are two theses for analyzing the Reformation of the Church: the nationalist political thesis and the economic thesis.

The traditional thesis: As we saw, the alleged abuses by the

Church were the prevailing immorality among the clergy, the lack of apostolic zeal in the majority of the bishops, the ignorance of the clergy, the despotism of the popes, the sale of indulgences, etc. Due to the above, mistrust by the faithful grew toward the Church as an institution. Because of this regrettable situation within the Church, reform was necessary.

The political and nationalist thesis: When Luther wrote in 1521: "I was born for the service of the Germans," and later, "I do not seek my interest, but the happiness of all Germany," it clearly marked the Reformation as a political action. Also Luther received support from the German princes which was decisive for the success of the Reformation. This was not scandalous because it was a world in which politics and religion were closely linked.

"Appeal to the Christian Nobility of the German nation," written by Luther, was a success because it appealed to the Germanic nationalist sentiment against Roman interference (as also happened in England with Henry VIII). The religious reforms used the nationalist sentiment which was one of the best allies in carrying out the reforms effectively.

The economic thesis: the Reformation was, in addition to being a religious event, a manifestation of the social and national economic turmoil. The Reformation itself was the product of a form of economy that was imposed on the world after the Middle Ages.

In this regard, Luther was considered as the instigator of the revolt of the peasants. Martin Luther came from humble beginnings and, using language of the people, led the oppressed masses against their oppressors. The same Luther originally encouraged the peasants in a revolt against the German Princes, but for a short time. Then Luther obtained the support of the Princes and urged the Princes to suppress the peasants without mercy.

Thomas Müntzer was the leader of the Anabaptist revolution. The figure of Thomas Müntzer embodied the "plebeian revolutionary" willing to carry out a revolution. The apocalyptic vision of Müntzer, whose desire to establish the Kingdom of the Saints and start a new social and religious order which eliminates any form of private property and social classes, swept away thousands of poor peasants who had nothing to lose except their poverty. This is how on June 15, 1525, the Müntzer troops were wiped out by the forces of the Protestant Prince Philip of Hesse and the Catholic George of Saxony. Müntzer was captured, tortured, and executed.

However, in general, today the Reformation is considered a process of religious conversion which led to the division of the Church in the 16th century. Along with the Protestant Reformation was another reform movement, the Anabaptists who were persecuted by the Protestants and the Catholic Church alike.

The Radical Reformation or Anabaptist Movement

Anabaptist Movement: Anabaptism was a movement of Church reform which occurred in the 16th century, whose roots are embedded in the religious, social, economic and political systems of most of Europe.

Anabaptism was the result of the work of the Protestant Reformers, the Bible studies conducted by humanists, social unrest, the exploitation of the masses, anti-clericalism and a deep and unsatisfied spiritual hunger among all the people, most of which were convinced that the end of the world was imminent.

Radical Reformation: The intent of the Radical Reformation was that the Church would go back to its roots, to the teaching and practice of the early Church. It was also seen as "conservative" by returning to the sources, purifying Christianity, restoring its original character, rejecting the trend of the Church and State to be one. It arose as a reaction to both classical Protestantism and Catholicism.

Anabaptism: "Ana," meaning "again." Anabaptism literally means "re-baptized," although it was a term that also identified all who were subversive.

The Origins of Anabaptism: The origins of the main currents that formed the 16th century Anabaptist family were found in the Swiss, central and southern German, the Moravian communities and Dutch Anabaptists.

The Anabaptist movement arose during the time of the Reformation and was an effort to "complete the Reformation." Anabaptist leaders were in agreement that reform of the Church was needed but they were not satisfied with the changes made by the other reformers. They wanted the Reformation to continue beyond those efforts. They insisted on returning to the model of the New Testament and carrying out reforms to succeed in this objective.

Among the many changes that had begun, the Anabaptists wanted to set up a Free Church that was not linked with any government or any state. The first Anabaptists emerged in Zurich, Switzerland, as a part of the Reformation begun by Zwingli.

The mood of the young leaders: When Zwingli began the Reformation in Zurich in 1522 he attracted many people who agreed with his desire to return to the model of the New Testament. Among them were two young people, Conrad Grebel and Felix Mantz, who supported Zwingli but disagreed with his caution. In October 1523, Zwingli made his first proposal to remove the mass. When at that time the City Council said no, Zwingli submitted to its decision. This sparked a protest among these young leaders. They were convinced that the Church should be independent of the State. With this began the division between Zwingli and young leaders.

At that time, two treatises written by a German reformer, Thomas Müntzer, fell into the hands of Grebel. He and his colleagues read and studied them with great dedication. In September 1524, he wrote a long letter to his new friend and brother, Thomas. In the letter Grebel provided a careful and thoughtful vision of the Free Church.

The letter from Grebel: The letter established the basic beliefs of Grebel and his colleagues. The main themes in the introduction of the letter include:
- The fall of the Church from its original purity
- The evil of sacramentalism
- The lack of spirituality among the members of the Church
- The error of not promoting a life strictly according to the principles of the New Testament
- The need to base faith doctrines only upon the Scriptures

In the main body of the letter Grebel strongly defended the following:
- The importance of preaching the Word of God. He agreed

with Zwingli in rejecting fixed patterns of liturgical singing in worship.

- No liturgical observance of the Lord's Supper. Only the biblical words, common bread and wine should be used. The Minister should not wear special clothes for this occasion. The Lord's Supper is not a sacrament. Grebel called it "Supper of the Unit." It has to be frequently observed with love and joy. Those who wish to participate should experience a fraternal life.
- A faithful Church, disciplined with radical obedience to the Word. It is exercised with prayer, fasting and following the rule of Christ as taught in Matthew 18:15.
- A Ministry sustained by its own congregation and not by funds from other sources such as the State.
- A simple house of meetings, without sculptures or paintings, where Christians gather to listen to the Word of God. We must avoid works of art that may become objects of veneration.
- A Church that operates on the principle of suffering, Christlike love. War is rejected completely.
- The baptism of water that is rich in symbolism: in Christ our sins are washed away. In Christ we are transformed internally. In the act of baptism, we show publicly our faith in the Lord Jesus Christ. We indicate that now we have "died" to sin and will walk in newness of life.
- Saved status of infants, based on the Bible, without the need of faith and baptism. The water of baptism is only for adult believers.

The diverse procedure among the Anabaptists: Despite being Zwinglian in its origins, Anabaptism could very easily and quickly—by its non-official nature, unrecognized by the State, and its clandestine situation—integrate people from various orders such as the Franciscan, Waldensian and Moravian orders, and also people from mystical and spiritualist backgrounds which were given to ecstasy. Others, without being officially part of the movement, were identified as Anabaptists by its critics or by historians. Thus the term became, independent of its literal meaning, a designation for any religious nonconformist.

The great debate in Zurich: Grebel and his companions were critical of Zwingli for allowing the City Council to stop the Reformation in Zurich. However, they did not withdraw abruptly from the Zwinglian movement. They rather hoped that Zwingli would allow the Word and the Spirit of God to lead the renewal of the State Church in Zurich.

In December 1524, and in January 1525, Zwingli met with Grebel and tried to get his support. But they were unable to reach an agreement. Their beliefs were too far apart. Then, a week later, on January 17, 1525, they had a public debate in front of the City Council. Zwingli was supported by his colleagues Leo Jud and Henry Engelhard. For his part, Grebel was advised by Felix Mantz and Wilhelm Reublin. Apparently the subject of the debate was baptism: Zwingli spoke in favor of baptism for infants and Grebel insisted that only adult believers should be baptized. But ultimately it was about the nature of the Church: would it be the Church of all the people (State Church) or the Church of only believers (Free Church).

Zwingli wanted to receive the approval of the authorities for the reform of the Church. Grebel considered that the State had absolutely nothing to do with the theology and practices of the Church of Christ. The Council adopted Zwingli's position at the end and exiled parents who delayed more than eight days the baptism of their newborn children.

Born of the Free Church: Grebel and his circle were very disgusted with the procedure of the City Council and the anti-biblical union between the Church and civil authorities. However, they remained in the State Church until Saturday, January 21, 1525. On that day the Council ordered that Grebel and Mantz cease to offer Bible study sessions as was their practice.

That same Saturday night, January 21, 1525, the Grebel group met to seek advice and pray in the light of the delicate situation. A new member joined the circle: an ex-priest called George Cajacob, or "Blaurock." As they reflected on their desperate situation, fear took hold of their hearts, so they fell to their knees and asked God for his guidance.

At the end of the prayer, George Cajacob begged Grebel to baptize him and Grebel agreed. Others, then, asked new Brother George that he re-baptize them, which he did with pleasure. Grebel was now free to depart from the official Church as it rejected him and collaborated with the State to prohibit his ministry and to exile those who refused to obey their anti-biblical orders. "The brothers" (as they called each other) were forced to separate from the State Church and established a church which they considered to be biblical, separated from the State and practicing the baptism of believers. From the perspective of the Anabaptists it was the most revolutionary event of the Reformation.

Persecution and extension of the movement: Both in the conception of the Catholics and of the Protestants the Church-State relationship was considered indivisible. Therefore, any deviation in this relationship was seen as a violation or offense. From there broke out a great persecution of this new group for alleged heresy and sedition, as well as its missionary zeal. Twenty-four were imprisoned; and on March 16, 1525, an exile was declared for all Anabaptists, so they had to leave Zurich.

Later, Grebel, Mantz and Blaurock were sentenced to life in prison, but they escaped. Grebel died at 28 years of age as a result of an epidemic in 1526. Felix Mantz was arrested, imprisoned and sentenced to die by drowning with his hands and feet tied, in 1526. For his part, Blaurock was tortured and burned in 1527.

The persecution then forced the Anabaptists to flee Zurich. From there they began to preach the Gospel everywhere in Waldshut, Bern, Basel, Strasburg and other surrounding areas, all despite persecution and suffering.

Leaders: The leaders of the movement in its extension into Europe must include:

- **Michael Satler,** who had a deep relationship with the poor peasants of his region and convened a congress of Anabaptist leaders in 1527 in the village of Schleitheim from which came the "Schleitheim Agreement."

- **Balthasar Hubmaier,** who wrote "The Baptism of Believers," the first important paper about the Anabaptist concept of baptism.
- **Hans Denck,** who taught that "No one can know Christ truly if he does not follow him in life," a saying that has become famous within the Anabaptist movement.
- **Hans Hut,** who emphasized the second coming of Christ, the importance of suffering for the cause of Christ and living in community.
- In the Netherlands stand out brothers **Obbe and Dirk Philips** and the ex-priest **Menno Simons,** who arguably was the person most deeply influential in the Anabaptist movement and for whom the Mennonites are named and are identified as the pacifist wing of Anabaptism. After his conversion, Menno actively supported the development of the Anabaptist movement in the Netherlands by traveling and writing. His writings include "The Christian Baptism" (1529), "The Foundation of Christian Doctrine" (1540), and "True Christian Faith" (1541). He affirmed the radical vision for the Free Church of believers, the important role of the Church as the center of Christian life, the ideals of practical holiness, based on the model of Christ, faith manifested in behavior, acts, and love and peace.
- Also, women deserve to be remembered as reforming pioneers. Anabaptist women were called to repent and to accept God's will and water baptism as their highest commitment. They were called and empowered by the Spirit to a "new life" of discipleship and these were reflected in their martyrdom. A third or more of all Anabaptist martyrs were women. Anabaptist communities were radically egalitarian in practice, offering full and equal participation to women and men as well as to peasants and aristocrats. Anabaptist development opened up many more possibilities for direct participation and leadership of women than was the "patriarchal social norm" in the 16th century. Women exercised remarkable informal leadership in proselytization, Bible reading (in

some cases), in "unofficial" teaching and preaching, in hymn writing, and in prophetic utterance (in the early movement). **Agnes Linck** and **Margaret Hottinger** from the early Swiss movement exercised a charismatic leadership. **Margaret Hellwart** was very active in persuading other women to join the movement. The underground communication of the Anabaptist message routinely was carried forward by women, within their circles of family, friendship, and acquaintance. In German communities, the active roles of leadership and teaching taken by several remarkable women were notable, among them **Anna Marpeck, Helena von Freyberg, Magdalena von Pappenheim**, and others.

Common features of the movement: As we noted above, it was a movement composed of people of various origins and with a variety of theological positions. However, the movement as a whole could be initially characterized by the following features:

- **Holy Spirit experience:** strong emphasis on the activity of the Holy Spirit. The Holy Spirit led people to repentance, faith, water baptism, and a new life. Also, there could not be a true reading of the Scripture without the inner work of the living Spirit of God. At different times in different parts of the Anabaptist movement, this strong spiritual emphasis led to extra-biblical revelations, dreams, and visions, granted alike to women and men.

- **Concept of salvation:** The only faith that saves will be a living faith that expresses itself in action in the world. True faith will obey the commands of Scripture, especially the command to teach and then baptize those who have believed (adults), living a new life as disciples of Christ, which at times led Anabaptist men and women to radical social action, as well as martyrdom.

- **Critique of power:** The Catholic Christianity inherited from the medieval period was characterized by the alliance between religion and power. The bishops were princes and landlords. There were personal and institutional links between the politics, economy, and the Church. The Protestant

Reformation in its early days criticized the alliance between wealth, religion, and the kings. However, in the formative years from 1522 to 1525, the reformers decided to support their respective governments. And the result was that Protestantism remained and wanted to be the State Church and the Radical Reformation rejected this alliance.

- **Sense of suffering:** The world of the 16th century did not tolerate neutrality. For this reason the alliance between religion and power could not be broken but would cause persecution. The Radical Reformation was characterized by the acceptance of suffering. This was based on the thoughts of Luther and Zwingli.

- **Search for authenticity:** Along with the rejection of religion linked to power was the concern for personal authenticity of faith, personal experience and responsible commitment. Infant baptism, regardless of the theological considerations in its favor, became symbolic of an automatic faith, imposed, conformist, superficial and inauthentic. Anabaptists instituted baptism of believers as a confession of faith and as a way to enter into the community of believers, that is, the local church. Also Anabaptists understood the Lord's Supper to be a memorial or remembrance of Christ's death and sacrifice, a feeding by faith in Christ. The Lord's Supper was also a closed supper, open only to those who had accepted baptism and had thus committed themselves to church discipline.

- **Voluntary and visible community:** The visible community, different from society in general, was part of the common vision of the Radicals. For the Radicals the only force that could rule the community was the Christian testimony. One of the central deeds expected of Anabaptist believers was radical economic sharing, the visible sign of one's commitment to the community, the Body of Christ on earth. Economic sharing was understood not only as living in communities but also as caring for the poor, the widows, and the orphans.

- **Missionary vision of a global approach:** A small community, bearer of a message ignored by the world, tends to perceive its duty to do mission. The reform that was accepted by the State had local influence. Meanwhile the Radicals, because of their rejection of surrounding Christendom, were socially and intellectually free to have a universal approach. Rather than rely on the powers of the State, its message could dare to compete with ideas in a pluralistic world.

Although Anabaptists share the basic doctrines of Protestantism, they emphasize the baptism of believers, separation of Church and State, a simple lifestyle, nonviolence, congregational discipline, community discernment in decision-making, and celebration of the Lord's Supper as a commemorative event of the work of Christ.

Bibliography

Harold Bender and John Horsh, *Menno Simons, su vida y sus escritos*, Traducido al castellano por Carmen Palomeque, (Scottdale, Pennsylvania: Herald Press, 1979).

Cornelius J Dyck, *An Introduction to Mennonite History: A Popular History of the Anabaptists and the Mennonites*, (Scottdale, Pennsylvania: Herald Press, 1993).

William Estep, *The Anabaptist Story: An Introduction to Sixteenth-century Anabaptism*, (Grand Rapids, Michigan: W B Eerdmans, 1996).

Raúl Garcia, *Soy Cristiano, Evangélico, Anabautista, Una interpretación de la Reforma Religiosa Radical del Siglo XVI*, (Bogotá: CLARA, 1991).

C Arnold Synder and Linda A Huebert Hecht, editors, *Profiles of Anabaptist Women: Sixteenth-Century Reforming Pioneers*, (Waterloo, Ontario: Canadian Corporation for Studies in Religion, Wilfrid Laurier University Press, 1996).

John Howard Yoder, compiler, *Textos escogidos de la Reforma Radical*, (Buenos Aires: La Aurora, 1973).

A Profile of Seventh-day Adventists

William G Johnsson

The Heart of Seventh-day Adventism

Every Christian denomination has certain passages of Scripture that, mediated through her tradition, express her *raison d'être*. For the Seventh-day Adventist Church, probably no word from the Lord is more significant or has played a greater role in her history than Revelation 14:6, 7: "Then I saw another angel flying in midair, and he had the eternal gospel to proclaim to those who live on the earth—to every nation, tribe, language and people. He said in a loud voice, 'Fear God and give him glory, because the hour of his judgment has come. Worship him who made the heavens, the earth, the sea and the springs of water'"—Rev 14:6, 7 (NIV).

First, it is an apocalyptic message. The book of Revelation, along with Daniel, has played a significant role in Adventism. The focus of apocalyptic, the end of all things in the second coming of Jesus, has been enshrined in the very name Seventh-day *Adventist*. Adventists are a people of apocalyptic, with all the New Testament ethos, expectation, possibilities, and potential for problems that apocalyptic brings.

Yet the *heart* of Revelation 14:6, 7 is the "eternal gospel." Adventists hold to the orthodox doctrines of the Trinity, the deity of Christ, and salvation only through His merits. If apocalyptic shapes the presentation of the Adventist message, the heart of that message is the good news common to mainline Christian bodies.

The passage calls men and women to put God first. It proclaims Him Creator of heaven and earth, Lord of all. It sets Him forth as the Judge of the living and the dead. It calls for a life lived, as John Milton put it, "as ever in my great taskmaster's eye." And these ideas are precious to Seventh-day Adventists. Adventists are a people of high ethical concerns. Doctrine is important for them, but practice even more so. They set forth God and His character, and uphold His Ten Commandment law. Out of that concern—to make God and His claims first in the life—arises their most distinctive practice and the other part of their name, *Seventh-day* Adventist.

Finally, Revelation 14:6, 7 sets forth a mission. Its vision is the world for Christ—the world with all its races and peoples and languages and marvelous human diversity bowing before His throne, a world where the ancient hostilities and alienations of race, color, language, sex, status, profession, and innate prejudices have been abolished by the Cross of Christ. So, while the Seventh-day Adventist Church is still comparatively small with about 20 million baptized members (all those who associate themselves with the church probably number 25-30 million), she is extraordinary in her worldwide thrust. She is the most widespread Protestant denomination: she is rooted in more than 200 countries. She is also one of the fastest growing, adding about one million members each year in recent years.

In capsule form, then, Revelation 14:6, 7 captures the spirit of Adventism. But whence came this movement? What are her roots in history and Christian thought? What are her distinctive teachings, and what is the basis for them? And, especially in these times, what issues and problems confront the Seventh-day Adventist Church? Finally, what is the relationship of the church to other Christian bodies and to the ecumenical movement? We shall explore these matters, of necessity briefly, in this chapter.

The Roots of Adventism

As an organized denomination, Seventh-day Adventism is a young church. She rose out of the eschatological expectation of the 19th century; she was formally organized only in 1863. The roots of Adventism, however, reach back much further—to the Reformation and even to the church of the New Testament.

The early 19th century witnessed an upsurge in millennial anticipation on a broad front. Christian writers and preachers such as Edward Irving in England, Joseph Wolff, "missionary to the world," and Manuel de Lacunza in South American proclaimed the near return of Jesus Christ. They pointed to fulfillment of biblical prophecies and in some cases advanced calculations based on biblical numbers.

In North America the Advent revival was spearheaded by a farmer-turned-preacher, the Baptist William Miller. Basing his calculations on the time prophecies of Daniel 8 and 9, Miller preached the imminent return of Jesus—first in 1843, then in 1844.

The preaching of Miller and others associated with him attracted widespread interest. It also aroused opposition from the established churches, and some of those who espoused Miller's ideas found themselves disfellowshipped. Among them were a young man, James White, and a teenage girl, later to become his wife, Ellen Harmon.

The last date set by the Millerites for the return of Christ was October 22, 1844. The Advent believers prepared, prayed, and waited—first in joyful expectation, then with troubled hearts as the hours ticked by. Of course, the night passed without incident; their hopes to see their returning Lord were dashed.

With the failure of the October 22 date the Millerite movement fell into disarray. It fractured into several groups, some still trying to set specific dates for the return of Jesus, others abandoning all date-setting. Many of those erstwhile followers of Miller's teachings concluded that the whole movement had been misguided and abandoned it.

Yet this unpromising soil was to provide the origin of the Seventh-day Adventist Church. One of these small Adventist groups, under the influence of a Seventh-day Baptist, adopted the seventh-day Sabbath. The believers attached to this group also reinterpreted the events of October 22, 1844 and eventually (in 1860) adopted the name Seventh-day Adventist.

While the story of their 19th century origins is important and well known to most Seventh-day Adventists, they see their identity on a larger canvas. In their obedience to Scripture they see themselves as heirs of the Reformation, with beliefs and practices that stem from both the German-Swiss side and the Anabaptists.

Many of the pioneers of the Adventist church were cast out of their parent churches for following what they believed to be the teachings of the Bible. Likewise, the Seventh-day Sabbath is not an easy doctrine—it cuts across possibilities for work and pleasure. Nevertheless, Seventh-day Adventists hold that it is clearly taught in the Scriptures, and they seek to follow the teachings of the Word. Among Adventists, the tradition accumulated by Christians over the centuries has been, and continues to be, largely deemphasized; there is a transparency, a directness, in coming to the Scriptures. Luther's rallying cry of *sola scriptura* is their watchword also.

The Adventist self-understanding tends to leap across the centuries, alighting for a time in the period of the Reformation and then taking a giant bound to the church of the New Testament. Here above all Adventists find justification for their distinctive doctrines. Apocalyptic, of course, is prominent: as Ernst Käsemann observed in a ground-breaking essay some years ago, apocalyptic is the cradle of New Testament theology. Here in the New Testament, Adventists also find Jesus, the Lord of the Sabbath, the Savior of humanity, who Himself kept the seventh day and by word and example endeavored to place it in its correct setting.

Thus, the way Adventists understand their history differs in significant measure from the way some church historians would write it. The historian usually focuses on the 19th century American milieu with its millennial expectation; Adventist will include this history but will draw links with the Reformation and especially with the New Testament church.

The Role of Doctrine

From her beginnings, doctrine has been important to the Seventh-day Adventist Church. Doctrine gave rise to the movement; doctrine is enshrined in the very name.

Adventists are uncomfortable with efforts to enshrine doctrine in creedal form, however. When in the early years some leaders attempted to formally state the doctrines of the church, the reply in essence was that the *Bible* is our creed. The Adventists wished to retain an openness to the leading of the Holy Spirit in interpreting Scripture: they talked about "new light" that the Lord might have for His people.

So observers of Adventism notice an apparent contradiction. On one hand, they find a heavy emphasis on doctrine—doctrinal sermons, Bible studies, widespread Bible reading and knowledge among clergy and laity—but on the other hand, strong resistance to formal doctrinal statements, a rugged individualism and diversity in the expression of doctrine, and reluctance to set up grounds for disfellowshipping people on the basis of doctrinal formulations. (To this day grounds for disfellowshipping tend to be more practical than doctrinal.)

Inevitably, doctrinal formulations, more and more formal, became necessary. The church of only a few thousand members has grown into a worldwide body of some 20 million. The church owns and operates more than 100 colleges and universities, plus hundreds of healthcare facilities. She emphasizes higher education, and as far as the educational level of her membership is concerned, she ranks toward the top among denominations. Doctrinal statements of Seventh-day Adventism therefore must reflect the growing sophistication of the church.

The relatively short history of the Seventh-day Adventist Church shows significant development in the understanding and articulation of doctrine. Among the early Adventists the term "present truth" (derived from 2 Peter 1:12) enshrined a key idea—that this movement would seek to be led by the Holy Spirit and be open to embrace new understandings as He might direct.

Adventist understanding of doctrine today is encapsulated in the Fundamental Beliefs, which number 28. We should notice the preamble to this statement of beliefs and also the first article. In the preamble we see enshrined the concern that Adventists shall remain open to ongoing understandings of Scripture as the Spirit may lead. And the very first article sets forth the Scriptures as the basis for Adventist teachings:

"Seventh-day Adventists accept the Bible as their only creed and hold certain fundamental beliefs to be the teaching of the Holy Scriptures. These beliefs, as set forth here, constitute the church's understanding and expression of the teaching of Scripture. Revision of these statements may be expected at a General Conference session when the church is led by the Holy Spirit to a fuller understanding of Bible truth or finds better language in which to express the teachings of God's Holy Word."

"The Holy Scriptures

"The Holy Scriptures, Old and New Testaments, are the written Word of God, given by divine inspiration through holy men of God who spoke and wrote as they were moved by the Holy Spirit. In this Word, God has committed to man the knowledge necessary for salvation. The Holy Scriptures are the infallible revelation of His will. They are the standard of character, the test of experience, the authoritative revealer of doctrines, and the trustworthy record of God's acts in history (2 Peter 1:20, 21; 2 Tim. 3:16, 17; Ps. 119:105; Prov. 30:5, 6; Isa. 8:20; John 17:17; 1 Thess. 2:13; Heb. 4:12)."

The doctrines addressed in the 28 Fundamental Beliefs are as follows:

1. The Holy Scriptures
2. The Trinity
3. The Father
4. The Son
5. The Holy Spirit
6. Creation
7. The Nature of Man

8. The Great Controversy between Christ and Satan
9. The Life, Death, and Resurrection of Christ
10. The Experience of Salvation
11. Growing in Christ
12. The Church
13. The Remnant and its Mission
14. Unity in the Body of Christ
15. Baptism
16. The Lord's Supper
17. Spiritual Gifts and Ministries
18. The Gift of Prophecy
19. The Law of God
20. The Sabbath
21. Stewardship
22. Christian Behavior
23. Marriage and the Family
24. Christ's Ministry in the Heavenly Sanctuary
25. The Second Coming of Christ
26. Death and Resurrection
27. The Millennium and the End of Sin
28. The New Earth

These articles can be changed only at a world conference/council of the church, which convenes every five years. At the 2005 council, a new fundamental belief was added—"Growing in Christ." This article, which sets forth Jesus' victory over demonic forces and meaninglessness, arose out of mission needs of the global church.

As we look over the 28 statements of Adventist doctrine, we are led to three conclusions: 1) The articles that are first and form the basis for the remainder, namely articles dealing with the Trinity, the person of Christ, and salvation, conform to orthodox Christian understanding. 2) Not one of the articles is absolutely unique to the Seventh-day Adventist Church. Even a fundamental belief such as no. 24, dealing with the ministry of Christ in the heavenly sanctuary and the pre-Advent judgment, clearly belongs in traditions setting forth the heavenly work of Christ and the final judgment. 3) If we are to speak of uniqueness concerning Adventist doctrine, then, it is in the *configuration* of doctrines rather than in individual beliefs.

A person who has grasped the doctrines of a particular denomination, however, has only just begun to understand it. Just as important, and perhaps more so, is its ethos.

The Ethos of Seventh-day Adventism

What makes an Adventist "tick," as it were? Most Adventists would agree with the following, although they might change the order:

1. *Mission.* Seventh-day Adventists are the most widespread of Protestant denominations. Though the church was cradled in North America, less than six percent of the membership today resides there. South America, Inter-America, Africa, and the Pacific Rim each have more Adventists than the church in North America. Further, Adventism is growing fast, worldwide. And with few exceptions Adventist growth has come about by a process of individual conversions rather than mass movements into the church.

Adventist publications continually keep before the people the worldwide work of the church. Thinking and planning are on a global scale.

Adventists give generously to support the worldwide work of the church in her various phases. The church encourages tithing and many members return to the treasury a tenth of their net income. In addition, members give offerings for local projects and also give to specific projects for advancing the church overseas.

Many Adventists give themselves in support of the world mission. The church continues to send out many missionaries; although, as national churches have become better established, missionary patterns have changed. Every year hundreds of young people volunteer a year of overseas service as student missionaries, while many retired Adventists help in overseas assignments on a short-term basis.

Adventists seek to carry on the mission of Jesus in these times. Thus, while evangelism, teaching, and witness feature prominently, the church seeks to lift and help people in their brokenness, regardless of whether or not those helped become members of the church. The Adventist Development and Relief Agency (ADRA) is a major player on the world scene, distributing food to the hungry and clothing to the naked, assisting when disasters strike, and also drilling wells, educating mothers in baby care and nutrition, helping poor farmers become self-sufficient, ministering to those with AIDs and so on. Likewise, Adventists own and operate a large healthcare system worldwide (see below).

2. *The prophetic gift.* Seventh-day Adventists believe that the New Testament teaching concerning spiritual gifts was not restricted to the apostolic age; they further believe that the gift of prophecy was specifically manifested in the ministry and writings of one of their pioneers, Ellen G White.

During a long and fruitful ministry, Ellen White (1827-1915) counseled, preached, taught, traveled, and wrote extensively. Although she at no time assumed a formal administrative role or was ordained as a minister, her counsels were highly regarded and helped shape the growing church. She was a prolific writer, with almost 25 million words, and her writings continue to be a point of reference and a source of inspirational material for Seventh-day Adventists.

Ellen White herself refused to take any position that would raise her writings to the level of Scripture. She continually upheld the Bible as the only rule of faith and action, the judge and test of all other revelations. The Seventh-day Adventist Church in general, while esteeming her writings highly, has looked to the Bible alone for its doctrine and practice.

Thus, in Adventism one will find an institution unique among Christian denominations—the Ellen G White Estate. This estate, administered by a board of trustees, employs a small group of scholars who specialize in the Ellen G White corpus. The estate fosters the dissemination of Ellen White's writings throughout the world church.

But the church in her publications and preaching continues to underscore the primacy and canonicity of Scripture. The 28 fundamental beliefs appeal to Scripture alone. Confession of belief in Ellen White's prophetic role is not made a test of fellowship.

Although occasionally some Adventists would raise Ellen White's writings to the level of Scripture, just as others would dismiss them summarily, the path of Adventism has been to value highly the writings but to keep them subordinate to Scripture.

3. *Health.* Seventh-day Adventists own and operate some 60 healthcare facilities in North America. With assets of billions of dollars, this is a large private network. Worldwide the church owns and operates about 400 health-related facilities, some very large.

The church became involved in quality healthcare early in its history. By the turn of the century its institution in Battle Creek, Michigan, was famous nationally and internationally. Today its Loma Linda University in southern California, which specializes in health sciences, has become a leading research center for the medical sciences. With breakthroughs such as infant heart transplants ("Baby Fae") and the world's first proton-beam treatment for cancer, Loma Linda has attracted widespread media coverage.

In addition, the church owns and operates a network of health food factories around the world. In Australia and New Zealand Adventist products hold the lion's share of the breakfast cereal market.

The church also vigorously promotes public health. She runs clinics on how to stop smoking, alcohol rehabilitation centers, weight control programs, stress clinics, and so on. A phalanx of public health workers fan out from the School of Public Health of Loma Linda University and serve the church or governments in a variety of situations, including the developing world.

Adventists themselves tend to be more conscious about health matters than the average Christian. Adventists do not smoke or drink, and the church advocates a vegetarian diet. Adventists, with their higher life expectancies, have been the subject of many demographic studies.

Why this interest in health matters? The story goes back to the founding days of the movement, and is too long to tell here. The main elements in the story are the counsels of Ellen White, the charismatic influence of Dr John Harvey Kellogg—the founder of Battle Creek Sanitarium—and W K Kellogg, developer of the Kellogg empire in breakfast cereals.

And there is a theological factor. Adventist health practices do not arise out of an ascetic concern—rather, Adventists teach a holistic view of man—nor are the particular health practices a way of "earning" salvation for Adventists. Instead, the Adventist health message springs from a desire to do all to the glory of God, to present the body as a living sacrifice for the Lord's service, and to be in the best of health in order to be mentally alert and spiritually attuned. Body, soul, spirit—Adventists seek to use all for the advancement of the kingdom.

4. *Education.* Adventists operate one of the largest school systems in the world (about 6,000 schools). The church encourages members to send their children to a network of elementary, secondary, and tertiary schools. Many children born into Adventist homes receive at least part of their education in an Adventist environment.

5. *Diversity and unity.* With members from more than 200 nations, the Seventh-day Adventist Church is incredibly diversified. She is a gathering of the nations, of the races, of the languages, of the occupations, and of the social strata of the world.

Yet there is a high degree of unity. Adventists are one in hope (the Second Coming), practice (the Sabbath, abstinence from alcohol and tobacco, concern for ethical living), vision (the worldwide mission), doctrine (the 28 fundamentals), and church polity.

Adventist Polity

Seventh-day Adventists are known for the effectiveness of the administrative, financial, and promotional church organization they have developed. Organization, however, developed slowly and uncertainly—the early Adventists feared any form of centralized church order and government. Belief and practice were their basic considerations.

Adventist church polity follows a representative system, with both Presbyterian and Congregational elements. This form of church government recognizes that the authority in the church is vested in the membership and moves upward, not downward. Leadership derives its authority and responsibilities from this constituency. Executive responsibilities are delegated to representative bodies and leaders. One level of ordination to the ministry prevails. Local elders and deacons receive a different form of ordination. The local church has distinct prerogatives of its own, such as dealing with church membership and electing local church officers.[1]

Among Seventh-day Adventists, the representative form of government operates in four steps, from the individual believer to the worldwide organization:

1. The church is the united body of individual believers.

2. The local conference or field is the united body of churches in a state, province, or other local territory.

3. The union conference is a united body of conferences, missions, sections, or local fields within a larger geographical territory.

4. The General Conference or general body embraces the church as an organization worldwide through the unions. The unions are the constituent units of the General Conference organizations and send delegates to its world session.

The general organization operates through divisional sections of the world field. At present the church has 13 fully operational divisions. They are set up and function as sections of the General Conference. Working arrangements by officially adopted policies between the general office near Washington DC and the divisional offices assign certain responsibilities to the division organization and reserve others to the general office representing the world body. A world budget covers the operation of the General Conference and its divisions. Thus the General Conference is the organization of the total church and is, when meeting in session with delegates from the world field (as it does every five years), the highest authority in the organized church. Between world sessions the executive committee of the General Conference, except in matters reserved for the session that are clearly outlined by policy, is the highest authority among Seventh-day Adventists.

The Seventh-day Adventist Church and her conferences (on all three conference levels) function on a committee system, final authority between sessions of the constituency being vested in the executive committee. The committee has policy-making, executive, and oversight functions.

The church also has organized "departments" and "services" at the various levels of organization. Department directors give leadership to program planning and field promotion; their duties generally are not executive. Examples of departments: education, public affairs and religious liberty, publishing, children's ministries; of services: auditing services.

Problems and Issues

The rapid expansion of the church and her increasingly international character bring attendant problems. Among them are the following:

1. *Growth of the Church.* The church is growing rapidly, with the fastest growth occurring in developing countries—especially in Inter-America, South America, and Africa. The racial makeup of the church has changed drastically, with the "mission lands" coming into their own.

Development of strong Adventist churches on the various continents with national leadership has led to a new situation for the church. Councils of the church have undergone a transition: the church no longer is dominated by white, largely North American, leadership. Questions of racial justice and the distribution of financial resources seem likely to become increasingly acute.

The years ahead will severely test Adventism's unity, up to now a characteristic feature of the movement.

2. *The Role of Women.* Although at its inception Adventism had among its leaders a woman of towering influence in the person of Ellen White, and although, especially during the first 50 years, women occupied leading positions of administration, such as treasurer of the General Conference, the Seventh-day Adventist Church to this point has not ordained women to the gospel ministry.

The issue is sensitive and emotionally charged. It came to a head in North America, where for the past 30 years women have served in some capacity in pastoral ministry. Women have been accepted into the ministerial program of the church's theological seminary, and now perform all the key functions of ministry, including officiating at baptism, at the Lord's Supper, and at weddings.

The church in North America opened the door to the ordination of women as elders of local churches in 1974. Ten years later this provision was extended to the world church. As far back as 1881 a General Conference session considered the ordination of women to the gospel ministry. At that time the resolution favoring ordination was referred to the General Conference Committee (which consisted of three men!) and was never heard from again.

During the 1980s, with some women entering the Adventist ministry and many being ordained as local church elders, the issue came to the front burner. High level commissions that included all divisions of the world church gave women's ordination intensive study in 1985, 1988 and 1989. The 1985 General Conference Session, meeting in New Orleans, took up the matter but reached no definitive decision. In 1990, the next session, held in Indianapolis, witnessed major debate over the issue. Delegates voted that, while Adventists have not reached a consensus concerning the theological soundness of ordaining women, because of the lack of widespread support, the church does not approve the ordination of women to the gospel ministry. The same session, however, amended the *Church Manual* to permit women ministers to baptize and officiate at marriage ceremonies.

Thus, the Church now has scores of women currently serving in ministry, including a pastor of a large congregation with male assistants, and in some regions of the world church pressure is building for change. The General Conference has set up a large committee to study both the theology of ordination and the issue of ordination of women to the gospel ministry; recommendations in both areas are to be brought to the next world assembly, which convenes in 2015.

3. *Doctrinal Debate.* During the early 1980s, the Seventh-day Adventist Church, especially in North America and Australia, went through a period of theological debate and some dissension. At issue were the Church's beliefs concerning the ministry of Christ in the heavenly sanctuary, the pre-Advent judgment, and the role and authority of the writings of Ellen White.

While the subsequent years have not brought significant new debate, Adventists in general retain a lively concern for theology.

The issues frequently heard involve areas of longstanding contention among Christians—Christ's human nature and Christian "perfection." A small but vocal minority continues to urge the ideal of sinless perfection; they do not have the support of church leaders, however. Currently the doctrine of creation is a topic of considerable interest, with study and debate among the church's theologians and scientists.

4. *The Adventist Identity.* In the modern era all Christians at times struggle with their distinctive identity as followers of Jesus Christ. In Adventism the struggle assumes particular forms.

The passing of time—this brings questions and tensions for Adventists today, just as it did for Adventists in the first and second centuries. How shall we live in this world, especially since we believe that Jesus Christ is to return to it in person? This question is ever present for Adventists. It becomes more acute as the number of professionals and highly educated members grows each year. And how can the forefathers' vision be transferred to the next generation? This question, stated in different forms and also troubling to other Christians, concerns many Adventists today.

The current General Conference administration, elected at the world council meeting in Atlanta in 2010, is leading the world Church in a call for revival and reformation. With emphases on prayer, Bible study, and expectation of the Second Coming, it seeks to bring Adventists back to their roots.

Ecumenical Relations

Seventh-day Adventists believe that God is working through many agencies, certainly far more than can be provided by the Seventh-day Adventist Church. The *General Conference Working Policy* states: "We recognize every agency that lifts up Christ before men as a part of the divine plan for the evangelization of the world."[2]

For this reason Adventists rejoice in the advancement of God's kingdom by every means that He provides. They enter into fellowship with other Christians (and they practice open communion); they rejoice in the opportunities of dialogue such as that provided by the Conference of Secretaries of the Christian World Communions.

At the same time, however, Adventists have a sense of destiny. They believe that in a certain sense they are a prophetic movement: God through them in particular has a message to give to the world, a message calling men and women to worship Him, to put Him first, to accept the eternal gospel, to make the Scriptures the foundation of their life.

This sense of destiny can lead to pride and arrogance. It can lead to triumphalism and a narrow exclusivism. At times Adventists have fallen into these traps. But it has also given Adventism a sharp identity, a clear self-understanding, a magnificent vision. It has helped make it a dynamic movement for the preaching of the gospel and the transformation of society.

Because of their unique self-understanding, Seventh-day Adventists have not formally joined the organized ecumenical movement. While they desire and seek fellowship and cooperation with other men and women of faith, they do not wish to be restricted—in doctrine, but especially in mission.

At the local level, Adventists enter into organized relationships with such bodies as ministerial associations or fraternals, local church organizations, Bible study groups, groups or networks to study community needs and help solve local problems, and so on.

With regard to the various councils of churches (national, regional, world), Adventists generally limit their participation to that of observers or consultants. For instance, Adventist theologians have served on the Faith and Order Commission of the World Council of Churches.

Adventists frequently enter into discussions with representatives of other Christian bodies. Among these contacts, bilateral conversations or dialogues have been conducted:
- with the World Evangelical Alliance
- with the Church of God (Seventh-day)
- with the Reformed Ecumenical Synod
- with the Salvation Army
- with the Assemblies of Yahweh
- with the Lutheran World Federation. A series of bilateral

conversations (1994-1998) led to a consensus statement and the publication of all the papers presented.[3]

- with the World Alliance of Reformed Churches

Only God knows those who are His. Certainly the church is far wider and greater than the body of Adventism, which, although growing fast, is still but a speck amid the millions of humanity. Adventists are grateful for what the Lord has done for them, challenged by the task to which they feel He has called them, and eager to be about His business. But they realize that they are but a small part of the larger body of Christ.

Adventism has made its share of mistakes. At times it has been narrow, too small in its thinking. At times it has turned its back on the cry of suffering, desperate humanity. At times it has so sought to exalt the importance of God's law that the Lawgiver, who is the Savior, was obscured.

But although the work has been enfeebled and defective, compassed about as it is by our common humanity, God has been marvelously gracious to the Seventh-day Adventist Church.

Through her He has helped make known the everlasting gospel to millions; He has disseminated information about healthful living that has been a blessing to millions of others; He has set up institutions that have saved millions of lives and given others a chance to stretch their minds and to rise socially.

As a Seventh-day Adventist I rejoice in what God has done and give Him the praise. To God Be the glory!

ENDNOTES

[1] W R Beach and B B Beach, *Pattern for Progress*, (Washington DC: Review and Herald Publishing Association, 1985).

[2] *General Conference Working Policy*, O 75.

[3] B B Beach and Sven G Oppegaard (eds), *Lutherans and Adventists in Conversation*, (General Conference of Seventh-day Adventists and The Lutheran World Federation, 2000).

Reflections on Salvation, Healing, Health and Ecology

Henk Stenvers

SALVATION

Introduction

During the Mennonite World Conference of 2003 in Bula-wayo, Zimbabwe I met two beautiful young girls, members of the Brethren in Christ Church in Zimbabwe. We talked about our lives and countries, the normal way of getting to know each other. The next day we accidently met again. And one of the girls asked me: "When were you saved?" And to be honest, I needed some time to think of an answer. The notion of being saved clearly had a totally different meaning for her in her context than it had for me.

She, growing up in an African country, where poverty and violence and uncertainty about the future are very present aspects of people's daily lives, where Christianity is one of many religions, where paganism is still very present in the culture, and where becoming a Christian is in a missionary context a real and new choice. For her the moment of Baptism was really a big, life-changing experience.

But for me, coming from Europe with its long history of Christianity—where Christianity is still the prominent religion—and having grown up in a family that has been Mennonite since the 16th century, being baptized was not really a life-changing event. Nevertheless, also for me, it was a choice, not for a new life but for a familiar and well-trodden path. That also is growing out of fashion these days. It is significant that only one of my two sisters is baptized and my elder brother also chose not to be baptized. In the beginning of the 1970s it was seen more and more as an exception if one chose to be baptized. Secularisation was already very strong in the Netherlands.

I made a conscious and positive choice. But it didn't mean that my life changed. I was already doing youth work at the congregation in Amsterdam and I had followed a few years of Bible school. So life went on as usual. The only difference was that I was allowed to take part in the Communion.

Coming from a family of medical professionals, I was trained as a doctor and worked for about 20 years in the medical field, for the most part as a general practitioner. For me the real life change came in 2001 when I decided to apply for the job of general secretary of the Dutch Mennonite Conference. It is a challenge to work as a non-theologian in such a function in the church and, on the other hand, it is a typical possibility for a Mennonite.

This little story shows how the way we experience faith and the different aspects of faith is very much dependent on the context in which we live. Though salvation is a very real concept for this girl in Zimbabwe, it is a much more theoretical issue in my country where we discuss or disagree with or even struggle to regain its essence and meaning in our changing world. For the Dutch Mennonites, at least, there is no authority from dogma or confession that can help us. It is the congregation as the hermeneutical community where the Word is being interpreted while praying for the inspiration of the Holy Spirit.

Historical Aspects[1]

When we look at the historical development of Anabaptist thinking about salvation we must consider that in the early years of Anabaptism, in the 16th century, there were many different groups with different views (if any) on theological questions. Although we have to keep this in mind we can discern certain similarities in the way these groups reject the medieval Church and with the other Reformers agree on the understanding of salvation. With the reformers they emphasise that salvation comes only by grace through faith (*sola fide*).

Although the Anabaptists agreed with the reformers about salvation through grace they criticised the Lutheran and later Calvinistic fruitlessness in their understanding of faith and emphasised the connection between salvation and sanctification.

Conrad Grebel and his brethren wrote to Thomas Muntzer in 1524: "...the same way so even today everyone wants to be saved by hypocritical faith, without fruits of faith, without the baptism of trial and testing, without hope and love, without true Christian practices, and wants to remain in all the old ways of personal vices .... We were also in the same aberration because we were only hearers and readers of the evangelical preachers who are responsible for all this error as our sins deserved...."[2]

If coming to faith does not have any effect on the way we live, then this faith is not complete. This search for a visible change in the life of the faithful was reason for disagreement with the other reformers.

Hans Denck (1495-1527)

According to Hans Denck, contemporary of Grebel and Müntzer, God's Grace is in the soul of everyone through the cross. It is the expression of God's graceful approach to mankind, through Christ. In Christ man has been shown an example that is to be followed in turning from sin and so becoming receptive to the Grace and Spirit of God. Faith grows out of the grace that God has laid down in the soul through the death of Christ on the cross. Man has been given an example that he should follow (*imitaitio Christi*).

It makes him renounce sin so that the heart becomes "empty" and becomes receptive for God's Grace and Spirit. This is the only way the human will becomes equal to God's will and the broken relation between God and man is restored. Through the gracious approach from God to man in Christ is the free will of man freed from the imprisonment of sin.

For Denck, justification is "not a forensic judgement from God on man. It is a process in which human life is bettered from deep within. Justification is rightification."[3]

Balthasar Hubmaier (1480?-1528)

Hubmaier takes the same stand: Faith without works is dead faith. Faith must show itself in the love for God and fellow man. (See James 2:17; Gal 5:13-14.)

Where other Protestants defend the *Sola Fide* principle, Hubmaier claims that if the free will is denied God cannot judge man for his sins. God would then condemn the sinner for something that he is not responsible for. That would make Him a terrible God. But it is not simply free will like with Erasmus.

The soul becomes free only through God's grace: in Christ sin is defeated. In the Word of God the Spirit frees the human spirit and heals the soul. But if the soul now sins again it is fully responsible.

Menno Simons (1496-1561)

For Menno Simons there is a very clear distinction between the old life and the new life in Christ. The new life obeys the Word of God and leaves no space for a distinction between word and deed. The goal is a visible, pure and holy Church of believers and followers of Christ. In this one can detect an intense longing for renewal and holiness. But this leads, with Menno also, almost inevitably to a severe moralism—a strictness and a certain rigour that can only be explained by the turbulence and fear of his early 16th century venture when so many people thought the world was falling apart and there was no hope for the church in its medieval state.

For Menno and his followers, faith and works are deeply interrelated. They cannot be separated. Failing in good works is an indication of a failing faith and vice versa. It is the unity of a Christian way of life that is at stake.

On the other hand: the reconciliation in Christ is for Menno the premise for the freedom of man to choose for good works. "Behold, kind reader, thus we do not seek our salvation in works, words or sacraments, as do the learned, although they blame us therefore, but we seek them alone in Christ Jesus and in no other means in heaven or earth."[4]

Around 1640, J G Loef painted *The Ship of the Church*, probably used for Jesuit educational purposes. It shows the crucified Christ up on the mast and it expresses the hope of salvation for the faithful on the Day of Judgment. The journey of the ship over the oceans of life is a hazardous one. It is not easy to steer clear of the rocks. She has only just passed Cape Pride and there the heretics were shipwrecked.

Among the heretics that attack the ship is Menno Simons. He raises his hand without a sword but with what might well be the *Fundamentenboeck.* [5]

The painting seems to want to say: Salvation is only to be found inside the ship of the church, by means of the sacraments, provided by the ordained priest to shepherd the faithful from the cradle to the grave. It is the only place of refuge....[6]

But not according to Menno. For him the ship was sinking, overloaded by the pope and prelates of whom he writes that they are unbelieving, proud, vain and disobedient,[7] but also overloaded by sin. The ship was sinking fast, penitence would not save it. Not in a world that was in turmoil, not in a sea that was so dangerously wild. So it was time to leave the ship of the traditional church and seek refuge in the lifesaving boat of the true congregation.

But to be saved, baptism was not enough. One has to repent, take on a new life, confess faith, testify to the new birth and enter into the obedience of Christ.

The destination of the lifeboat is the safe haven of eternal life and the kingdom of God. For navigation, there is the landmark of the cross to hold on to and live up to. Being part of the crew calls for teamwork. Discipline and discipleship are necessary requirements for a crew of such a small boat to prevent capsizing and to bring the boat safely to port. The boat is also a rescue vessel, to pick up souls on the way. At that time the Mennonite lifeboats were the only alternative to the giant sinking ship. The other alternative was swimming alone. Menno was convinced that it was impossible to manage and persevere alone.[8]

Summary of History

All the early Anabaptists agreed that salvation starts with God's graceful act in Jesus Christ. The Anabaptists believe that men are saved by the grace of God and not by their own good works. God's grace cannot be fulfilled without man, but man has to accept the gift of grace out of free will. The already existing grace of God creates the opportunity for the voluntary confession of faith as the answer. The expression of this connection of grace and free choice is the believers' baptism. Faith, works and confession cannot be separated. Good works are not the fruit of faith but the visible expression of faith.

This makes the doctrine of predestination impossible. If God works in man through the Holy Spirit, then man must be able to answer in faith. This asks for a conscious choice. Mennonites acknowledge God's greatness, but still man has personal freedom and responsibility. The Calvinists sometimes make God too big and man too small. Our challenge is not to make the mistake to make man too big—so important that he has to do it all alone and ends up sitting tired at the side of the road because life is hard. Believing then becomes a burden.

Justification and sanctification are two dogmatic labels that basically refer to one process of regeneration and renewal and transformation that reshapes persons, communities and eventually the world around us. In this way it is apt to quote the unexpected source, Margaret Mead: *Never doubt that a small group of thoughtful, committed citizens can change the world. Indeed, it is the only thing that ever has.*

According to the theologian Hans Jurgen Goertz the Anabaptists have not made an addition to the faith doctrine of the Reformation, but have renewed this doctrine, pointing towards God's power and Spirit to renew our lives and His world.

Present Views

Looking at the present views of Mennonites and Anabaptists on salvation, it is important to bring to attention once again that the context in which the different congregations and conferences live leads to different views. The emphasis on the free choice of mankind to confess his/her faith and the strong emphasis on the individual and the movement character of the Mennonite faith is one of the reasons that there are many different interpretations of the theological topics. The manifest importance of theological questions and the consequences for the daily life in the congregations varies locally.

Since the beginning of the Anabaptist movement salvation, sanctification showing in works is more prominent than theological discussion. It has always been more of a people's faith than one of theologians or synods. Even the way of thinking of the early Anabaptists is not to be found in very thick theological works, but to be extracted from letters, discussions, articles and, of course, confessions. The first confession, the *Schleitheim Articles* in 1527, was followed by many, many others; for example, the *Dordrecht Confession* of 1632, or the *Ris Confession* of 1766, or the Mennonite Church's confession *Christian Fundamentals* of 1921. These confessions always describe how the people who wrote them thought about their faith. They have no creedal value like the *Nicean Creed* or, for the Dutch Reformed, the *Confession of the Dortse Synod* in 1618-1619, or the *Augsburg Confession* of 1530 for the Lutherans. For Mennonites the confessions are not God-given unchangeable holy words, but human attempts to find words to describe their faith.

Confessions serve the church by building a foundation for unity within and among Mennonite and other Christian churches. Thus the new found unity between the Mennonite Church and the General Conference Mennonite Church in North America was reason to write a new confession: The *Confession of Faith in a Mennonite Perspective*. But as stated in the introduction of this confession, written statement should support but not replace the lived witness of faith. And confessions give an updated interpretation of belief and practice in the midst of changing times.[9]

Exemplary is the fact that Mennonite World Conference started a process in 2003 in Bulawayo to search for what Mennonites all over the world share in their faith. This has led to ten statements that we call *Shared Convictions*. It was repeatedly stated during the process of formulating that the *Shared Convictions* do not have the pretence of being a worldwide confession.[10]

We can safely state that within the Mennonite world the theological interpretation differs. We cherish this! We are in favour of unity in diversity! It is a wonderful variety, and it offers great opportunities to learn and grow in life and faith! But taking this into account, we can still discern Mennonite views.

Common is the view that accepting faith is a personal voluntary decision. Whether that is a crisis conversion or the gradual nurturing followed by the decision to make a commitment. God, the Spirit, leads people in different ways (once-born and twice-born). Salvation is not acquired automatically because we are born into a Christian family or grow up in the church.[11] Although it is an individual decision to accept God's grace, we are saved in a community. The church is the context of salvation.[12] This is in contrast to other Protestants, and especially evangelical churches, where the emphasis is much more that of the individual relationship with Christ.

In the community of the congregation or the wider church divisions, there is healing as persons of every human grouping are reconciled and united.[13] In this healing community people learn together, celebrate and share. The congregation inspires and gives resources and endurance to be disciples in a violent and secular world.

"The experience of God through the Holy Spirit, prayer, Scripture and the church community empowers us and teaches us to follow Christ. To follow Christ means discipleship. That means nonconformity with the world. True faith in Christ means willingness to do the will of God rather than wilful pursuit of personal happiness... seeking first the reign of God in simplicity rather than pursuing materialism... acting in peace and justice, rather than with violence or military means... giving first loyalty to God's kingdom, rather than to any nation-state or ethnic group... honest affirmation of the truth rather than reliance on oaths... performing deeds of compassion and reconciliation... instead of letting sin rule over us."[14]

Augsburger describes in his book *Dissident Discipleship* (2006)[15] seven practices or principles that can enlighten us more when we talk about this Mennonite spirituality and the practise of living. Augsburger describes this Mennonite Spirituality as a *tri-polar spirituality*. The spirituality of personal transformation, the inner journey, the experience of divine encounter, the God-ward journey, the relation of integrity and solidarity with the neighbour, and the co-human journey are interdependent. No single one is fully valid apart from the other two. No single one can be truly experienced without the other two; no two can be extracted as primary or as actually present without all three.[16]

Tri-polar spirituality, with its radical commitment to God-above-and-beyond-all yet God-for-us, and its daily practise of God-with-us-and-between-us-all, appreciates the neighbour in Christian love no matter the crises of threat and violence or the call of the nation-state to contradict the will of God on earth.[17]

This tri-polar spirituality leads to the seven practices:

1. Radical Attachment

Radical attachment to Jesus is not believing something about Jesus, or believing in Jesus, but believing Jesus (in discipleship) and believing in what Jesus believed (in imitation).

2. Stubborn Loyalty

Stubborn loyalty to the community of the Spirit is joining the circle around Jesus as the primary social location where we learn to act towards all others as, in reality, we act towards Jesus.

3. Tenacious Serenity

Tenacious Serenity is the quality of yielded fortitude, of surrendered steadfastness that stays the course, commits the soul and relinquishes the self to what is truly good, what is ultimately prized, what is the will of God. *Gelassenheit* is a strange mix of surrender, patience and stubbornness, living in resistance and surrender, God-trust and serenity, even if things go differently, living as one.

4. Habitual Humility

Habitual humility is the primary evidence, the undeniable sign of Christian discipleship. Humility is sincere concern for the good of others balanced with simple gratitude for the gift of one's self, shown in a genuine willingness to serve the neighbour and heard in the gentle laughter of self-effacing humour.

5. Resolute Nonviolence

Resolute nonviolence is the true evidence of love for neighbour, enemy or persecutor. To believe what Jesus believed is to practice active, nonviolent concern for the welfare of the other in all circumstances

6. Concrete Service

Concrete service is the practise of serving Christ by serving the neighbour. Service is not about me, but about the one being served. Serving others is voluntary, inner-directed, sometimes naïve, and truly collaborative.

7. Authentic Witness

Authentic witness is the practise of genuine presence, with sensitivity to, modelling for, and then sharing with others about one's deepest beliefs, values and hopes.

Dissident Discipleship is the practise of reverse theology—not the worship of sovereignty, lordship, almighty power, total dominance, or utter and final control, but worship of opposites.

Salvation means to modern Mennonites essentially the same as to the early Anabaptists: accepting God's always present offer of grace, laying down the sinful life and starting anew through baptism in the community of disciples. Although the way people express discipleship differs according to the different context in which they live, they have the same foundation of their acting in faith. The one foundation that for Menno also was his guide for life: *For no one can lay any foundation other than the one already laid, which is Jesus Christ* (1 Cor 3:11). The congregation built on this foundation, called to be part of the body of Christ, to be His hands and feet, living in and witnessing of His peace—that is what it is all about. That is our salvation.

HEALING

The Healing Community of the Congregation

On a Personal Level

The earlier mentioned seven practices that Augsburger discerns imply that being a healing community is one of the things the congregation and the bigger faith community, the church, strives for: Healing in the sense of making whole on the personal or organisational level.

The congregation is, or should be, in itself a healing community. In the congregation people are not judged by social class, colour of skin, gender, sexual preference, political stand or whatever. The congregation is united around the Word, around the foundation of Jesus Christ, in peace and witness. Of course there are different talents but those are to be used to serve, not to exercise power of the one over the other. The service of the chairperson is essentially of the same value as the service of the cleaners. One cannot function without the other.

There is shared care in difficult stages in life and shared joy in happy times. These beautiful principles do not always prevent conflict. History shows that Mennonites are also good in having fights. The many church divisions in Mennonite conferences in the past are sobering examples of the impatience Mennonites can have with their brothers and sisters who have other views. And those other views are not always, or even often not, about theological questions but about money or the way life rules should be interpreted.

One topic of the discussions, especially in the past, was the question of banning and shunning. Theoretically, banning was to be an act of love. To go back to the life boat as a picture of the congregation, a person who was banned was put overboard, but not without a net to be drawn into the boat again when he or she repented. One was put aside temporarily until he or she saw the error of their way. Then one was lovingly welcomed into the community again and the relationship was healed. Much of the discussion between the early Anabaptists was about how far banning and shunning should go. There is an example of the pastor who went so far as to ban his whole congregation except for his wife. That is not an example of a healing community. The practise of banning and shunning is hardly practised anymore, especially in Europe. In some Amish communities, of course also from Anabaptist origin, the ban is still used.

In the Mennonite congregation a free person can stand up straight on the foundation without being bound by dogmas or repressing life rules.

As a Community with Other Churches

Being a healing community in itself is also a commitment and challenge to strive for healing relationships with other communities. Good examples are the dialogue of Mennonite World Conference with the Roman Catholic Church. The dialogue started with healing of memories where there was an open interchange of stories of persecution and suffering. This made it possible to search for what the Roman Catholics and Mennonites have in common. And although there are many, many differences the common dedication and search for peace was found to be a shared topic. The report about the dialogue was named *Called Together to be Peacemakers*.

The dialogue with the Lutheran World Federation was even more of a healing process. It led to the official excuses of the Lutherans for the persecution that followed the condemnations of Anabaptists in the *Augsburger Confession* of 1530. This was humbly accepted and followed by penitence about the many times Mennonites have verbally put the Lutherans down. The symbol of foot washing was used to celebrate this healing.

As a Community in the World

What we learn in the community can be practised in the world around us—healing activities in the sense of bringing peace and restoring relations. Bringing peace without force, such as the so-called peace operations of NATO or UN troops—is about letting people get to know each other on a personal basis or learning other ways of conflict handling or being present like the Christian Peacemakers. It is about helping when necessary and possible, like MCC, and it is about education and training like so many missions and other organisations engage in.

Inspired by the community and sent by the congregation, Mennonites go into conflict areas; for example, the Dutch Diet Koster who is working in the occupied territory in Israel. She has a children's home where she helps Palestinian children and organises meetings between children from Israel and from Palestine so they get to know each other. In that way slowly understanding can grow.

Another example is the Christian Peacemaker teams that go into conflict areas to stand next to victims and to become peace-witnesses. And there is the Indonesian group from the poor GITJ conference that went to help after the tsunami. They helped everyone who crossed their path, regardless of their religion. That caused curiosity from an orthodox Islamic organisation that asked for the religion first. Now the two organisations are in contact and work together.

In the Netherlands we organise courses in mediation techniques and non-violent communication. Nowadays congregations offer these courses to all kinds of organisations in their local community, such as childcare organisations, social health organisations and schools.

HEALTH

It is virtually impossible to find Mennonite literature that focuses on health. The general Mennonite principles of discipleship and the earlier mentioned practices make it probable that Mennonites in general will want to work towards a society where health and healthcare are reachable for everyone. The body as the Temple of God is also a concept that is not strange to Mennonites or Brethren in Christ, although also here there are big regional differences. This meant that many Mennonites and Brethren would refrain from smoking or drinking alcohol. Nowadays the social use of alcohol is not frowned upon anymore in many communities. Smoking is, but the reasons are more social than theological.

Mennonite Church USA published a resolution in 2003 that focuses on healthcare access for all persons and the way congregations can be advocates. The resolution states: "As Anabaptists we understand that following Jesus means a daily responsibility to practise what we believe. We believe in Justice and self-responsibility because we are accountable for our actions.... We believe that being a good steward of our health is not just seeking treatment for our acute and chronic illnesses, but attending to our spiritual, mental, emotional, and physical well-being. We believe in working together to provide mutual support for each other, and to support community needs beyond ourselves."[18]

The resolution not only advocates a broader and abstract idea about healthcare access. There is also attention to how the congregations can work towards health. "Each congregation will be engaged in healthcare advocacy and counsel for their members who desire it." And very practical: "Our potlucks will no longer look like an invitation to a heart attack.... We will promote wellness of the whole person, and create healing environments which integrate treatment for the body, mind, emotions, spirit, and soul."

This holistic approach means that the congregation strives for *shalom* for each person. Most Mennonites will thus see health as more than the absence of illness. A healthy person is whole in the sense that he is at peace with himself, with his body and with others and that he is free to make his own choices in life. In that sense even a person who is suffering from a disease can be healthy.

A society where there is a great difference between, for example, rich and poor, women and men, or young and old, or where there is no equal access to care is not a healthy society.

A healing community like the congregation creates an environment where people can be healthy in body and mind and where there is care for the people who are ill.

ECOLOGY

Another topic that has everything to do with a healthy society and stewardship is ecology. As with health, ecology is also not a very popular subject among writers about the Mennonites. Luckily the *Mennonite Encyclopaedia*, and especially the online version, helps here.

The subject of ecology became popular in the second half of the last century when scientists realised themselves what an enormous impact the human species has on the rest of nature. Human population ecology deals with problems like famine, pollution, disease and even with violence associated with overpopulation pressures.

The response to the ecology movement was different among the different Mennonites.

Many Mennonite farmers in the USA resented the curbs on the use of pesticides. On the other hand, Mennonites reacted quickly and compassionately to urgent calls for food, rejecting the idea that only people and countries which had a good chance of continued survival should be helped. Mennonite Central Committee started many food programs all around the world.

In Europe came a strong ecology movement. Many Mennonites joined this movement. Sustainability in use of sources, or in our financial investments, "green energy," and recycling are topics that are important for many Mennonites and congregations.

The ecology crisis has also created a new appreciation for the simple life. The worldwide success among Mennonites of the book *Living More with Less* illustrates this.[19] In this book simple living was promoted as a way to "cherish the natural order."[20]

As a result of the ecology movement, caring for the earth and fighting hunger and poverty have become very much part of the way Mennonites give hands and feet to discipleship and stewardship for all of God's creation.

A few examples: In the *Menno*, a one-time magazine we published in 2011, we portrayed a Frysian farmer. He does not use any artificial fertiliser and he has cows in what we call a walking stable where they can lie in real hay. His motivation is not only environmental. He does not want to provide unequal competition for the farmers in the third world.

Goshen College and also Elkhart Seminary have decided to let part of their grounds grow naturally. That means less mowing, less use of fertilisers, and less use of energy.

In Kitchener MCC started a Blue box project where chemical waste was collected separately and the project was finally adopted by the town.

There are projects that promote local shopping for food. In Elkhart, Indiana, Mennonites started a project in poor neighbourhoods where vegetables were planted or sowed in public patches of ground, to be used for free by the people living there.

To summarize: The decision to take more care of the environment has been for the most part the choice of the local congregation or even groups or individuals within the congregation. What we share is the conviction that we as disciples have to be careful with the environment and adapt our behaviour to lessen the damage to our world.

ENDNOTES

[1] For the historical part of these reflections I made extensive use of an article by Fernando Enns, *Das Rechtfertigungsgeschehen in der Interpretation de Mennoniten*; in: *Von Gott angenommen – in Christus verwandelt. Die Rechtferigungslehre im multilateralen ökumenischen Dialog*, hg. Von U Swarat, J Oeldemann, D Heller. Frankfurt/M: Lembeck 2006, 155-176.

[2] Letter from Conrad Grebel to Thomas Müntzer (1524) from *The Sources of Swiss Anabaptism: The Grebel Letters and Related Documents*, edited by Leland Harder, 1985.

[3] Hans-Jürgen Goertz, *Die Taufer: Geschichte und Deutung*, (München: C H Beck, 1988), 69.

[4] Menno Simons, *A Fundamental and Clear Confession of the Poor* in *Complete Writings of Menno Simons* (CWMS) (Elkhart, Indiana: John F Funk, 1871).

[5] Gerke J J van Hiele, *The Sea, the Ship, and the Lifeboats, Discipleship in the Life and Times of Menno Simons*. In Alle Hoekema and Roelof Kuitse (editors) *Discipleship in Context*, occasional papers #18, (Elkhart, Indiana: Institute of Mennonite Studies), 9.

[6] *The Sea, the Ship* 10.

[7] CWMS *Fundamentenboeck*.

[8] *The Sea, the Ship* 15-19.

[9] *Confession of Faith in a Mennonite Perspective*, Published by arrangement with the General Board of the General Conference Mennonite Church and Mennonite Church General Board, (Scottdale, Pennsylvania: Herald Press, 1995) 8.

[10] *Shared Convictions* adopted by Mennonite World Conference General Council, March 15, 2003.

[11] *Confession of Faith* 37.

[12] Ibid 38.

[13] Ibid 39.

[14] Ibid 65.

[15] David Augsburger, *Dissident Discipleship*, (Grand Rapids, Michigan: Brazos Press, 2006).

[16] *Dissident Discipleship* 14.

[17] Ibid 15.

[18] Mennonite Church USA, *Health Care Access Resolution*, 2003, 3.

[19] Doris Janzen Longacre, *Living More With Less*, (Scottdale, Pennsylvania: Herald Press, 1980).

[20] *Living More With Less* 42.

The More Abundant Life: Some Adventist Views on Health, Healing and Wellness

Peter N Landless

The interaction between behavior and outcome, cause and effect, compliance and reward was debated even before the founding of Christianity. The disciples questioned Jesus regarding the man who had been blind from birth: "Rabbi, who sinned, this man or his parents, that he was born blind?" (John 9:2).[1] Jesus' answer reprimanded the curious, and possibly judgmental, disciples. "Neither this man nor his parents sinned," said Jesus, "but this happened so that the work of God may be displayed in his life" (vs 3).

Is behavior, then, not important? What about the injunction of Paul: "So whether you eat or drink or whatever you do, do it all for the glory of God. Do not cause anyone to stumble" (1 Cor 10:31-32). And didn't Jesus Himself also encourage His disciples to reveal their love for Him by a distinct code of conduct? "If you love Me, you will obey what I command" (John 14:15). "Whoever has My commands and obeys them, he is the one who loves Me" (vs 21).

How easy it is to emphasize the behavioral aspects of Christian living and debate the details of what we should eat, drink, wear, read, listen to...and so forth. The Pharisees, of course, were the archetypical model of this form of religion, and practiced the behavioral approach to the extent of praying on the street corners. Yet Jesus brings immediate perspective in terms of a legalistic self-improvement (aggrandizement) program: "For I tell you that unless your righteousness surpasses that of the Pharisees and the teachers of the law, you will certainly not enter the kingdom of heaven" (Matt 5:20).

Was Paul, who was such a learned protagonist of righteousness by works prior to his Damascus Road revelation (when he was still Saul), clinging to the behavioral life-buoy when he wrote, "So whether you eat or drink or whatever you do, do it all for the glory of God"? Certainly not, and the key disclaimer to salvation through behavior is embodied in the words "to the glory of God." Not only in this instance does Paul resonate the teaching of Jesus as described in John 9,[2] but on at least three occasions Paul refers to the human body as the temple of God and that His Spirit lives in that temple.[3] Jesus referred to His own body when He said, "Destroy this temple and I will raise it up again in three days! ...But the temple He had spoken of was His body" (John 2:19, 21).

Paul further expands on this theme with these words: "You are not your own; you are bought at a price. Therefore, honor God with your bodies" (1 Cor 6:19-20). Because of the precious blood that was spilled in our stead, we are exhorted to pay homage to God in how we treat our bodies, and also in what we eat, drink, and in all our behavior, to glorify our Creator and Savior. This injunction includes intention, attitude, and actions. Jesus informs this state by a condition which is, in fact, an empowerment. This way of life will be possible, when based on a living relationship with Him and bonded in love. Through knowledge of Him, we will learn to love Him; as we freely love Him, we will find ourselves compelled to serve Him. All aspects of behavior and being will then be under His control.

Toward the end of his life, John addresses Gaius the elder: "Dear friend, I pray that you may enjoy good health and that all may go well with you, even as your soul is getting along well" (1 John 2). John implies that physical well-being may influence spirituality, and vice-versa. He had witnessed the activities of Jesus involving the whole person. Perhaps, as John walked on the sea shore of Patmos, he relived the indescribable fellowship of an early-morning breakfast of fish and bread prepared by the nail-pierced hands of his Savior. He may further have reminisced, with tender recollection, Jesus' empathetic attention to detail after raising Jairus' daughter from the dead, and when He, the Bread of Life, "told them to give her something to eat" (Mark 5:43). No doubt he remembered, too, the miraculous feeding of thousands, where Jesus again revealed His concern for people's physical well-being.

Jesus' involvement with the whole person is prosaically described in the opening paragraphs of *The Ministry of Healing*: "Our Lord Jesus Christ came to this world as the unwearied servant of man's necessity. He 'took our infirmities and bore our sicknesses,' that He might minister to every need of humanity (Matt 8:17). The burden of wretchedness and sin He came to remove. It was His mission to bring to men complete restoration; He came to give them health and peace and perfection of character."[4]

Jesus spent much time in healing the sick. Matthew reports that "Jesus went throughout Galilee, teaching in their synagogues, preaching the good news of the Kingdom, and healing every disease and sickness among the people" (Matt 4:23). Single-handedly, the Great Physician practiced and demonstrated the spirituality of health and blended healing, teaching, praying and preaching. Our Savior pressed on, saying, "...we must do the works of him who sent me" (John 9:4).

The healings performed by Jesus addressed body, mind and spirit. He healed not only physical maladies but addressed the forgiveness of sin and relief from guilt. He affirmed faith and the very approaches that brought the needy one to Him. He advised changes in life values and admonished those healed to turn away from sin.

Jesus emphasized the importance of wholeness. He recognized the vital interaction of body, mind and spirit. It was only toward the latter quarter of the twentieth century that the World Health Organization emphasized this concept and concluded that the definition of health is not only the absence of physical disease, but that mental and emotional well-being are essential to wellness. This is an emphasis reflected in the Old Testament: "...fear the Lord your God as long as you live by keeping all His decrees and commands...and so that you may enjoy long life" (Deut 6:2).

Jesus subsequently reinforces this wholeness of purpose required in loving God: "Love the Lord your God with all your heart and with all your mind and with all your strength" (Mark 12:30). In the latter exhortation, there is a graphic description of all facets of our being and behavior. This is a theme reflected in other places, where Jesus' ministry is recorded.[5] The concept of loving and caring for others is connected to this commandment and introduces the importance of social support in wholeness and well-being: "Love your neighbor as yourself" (Mark 12:13). Modern science is showing that people who practice religious beliefs and also are involved with the welfare of others have enhanced immune function.[6] Religious involvement and spirituality have been associated with a decrease in cardiovascular disease and hypertension, improved mental health, and less depression and anxiety, substance abuse, and suicide.[7]

Even among the foremost researchers on spirituality and health, there are varying definitions of spirituality. Harold Koenig refers to spirituality as "the personal quest for understanding answers to ultimate questions about life, about meaning, and about relationship to the sacred or transcendent, which may (or may not) lead to or arise from the development of religious rituals and the formation of community."[8]

A more succinct and less unwieldy description of spirituality is "the opening of every part of life to the presence of God."[9] This latter working definition encompasses body, soul, heart, mind and strength comprehensively.

Wholeness in Brokenness

At creation there was perfection and wholeness. Since sin, this perfection has been eroded, and many suffer physically, mentally, and spiritually. Job—despite all his mental, physical, emotional and spiritual struggles—"did not sin by charging God" (Job 1:22). Paul pleaded three times for his particular thorn in the flesh to be removed, but instead of physical healing of his "brokenness," he received a special kind of wholeness: "My grace is sufficient for you," he was told by the Lord, "for My power is made perfect in weakness" (2 Cor 12:9). No wonder Paul could say, "For when I am weak, then I am strong" (verse 10). This encouragement is particularly meaningful to those who, despite faith, prayer, and medical intervention, still suffer with chronic diseases. Paul here reflects the spirituality which opens every part of life to the presence of God; this same spirituality has been seen in various people: Fanny Crosby, who—though blind—wrote of a wonderful assurance and friendship in Jesus; Helen Keller, who overcame the obstacles of blindness and deafness—not through healing—but by achieving wholeness in brokenness; Joni Eareckson-Tada, who continues to thank God for her quadriplegia, and sings His praises and reaches out to the disabled. These and so many others reflect wholeness in Christ despite brokenness of body.

Eating and drinking healthfully, exercise, moderation, modesty, etc., do not *of themselves* achieve wholeness. God's strength is made perfect in weakness. This is providential, so that we cannot boast in our own strength or works; it helps us to remember that physical health, although desirable, is a means to an end, not the end in itself. This is where the Pharisees of Jesus' day, and their modern-day counterparts, falter and fail.

Christ's promise, "I am come that they might have life, and that they might have it more abundantly" (John 10:10) can still be a reality even among the most physically broken. Health is not a rite of passage in this life. As important as wellness is, Jesus emphasized an important balance: "Do not be afraid of those who kill the body but cannot kill the soul" (Matt 10:38).

God's Instructions on Health

Early in the Old Testament, God saw fit to give His people instructions on healthful living, including diet, cleansing and sexual behavior. The Levitical laws were to be preventive and distinctive. Jesus, in His sojourn on earth, healed physical and mental diseases and linked forgiveness of sin with well-being and abundant life, placing emphasis on emotional and mental health as well.

As early as 1863, Ellen White counseled the fledgling Seventh-day Adventist Church on healthful living. The outstanding feature of her initial message was the "relation between physical welfare and spiritual health, or holiness."[10] Throughout her life, she was the channel of information which fashioned the church's philosophy and emphasis on health. Long before medical evidence emerged on the extreme dangers of smoking, Ellen White spoke out strongly on this and other issues, including the use of alcohol and poisonous medications such as arsenicals and mercury-based drugs. The drinking of tea and coffee, and use of stimulants, was very strongly discouraged, as—ultimately—was the use of flesh food. She promoted a lacto-ovo vegetarian diet as the optimal diet. In addition, the use of fresh, clean water (inside and out), clean air, adequate exercise and rest, temperance, faith, appropriate sunshine exposure, integrity and social support were strongly encouraged. These principles still form the foundation of our health education and practice. Presently, the health message and initiatives of the Seventh-day Adventist Church are based on biblical, Spirit of Prophecy, and evidence-based principles.

Time magazine[11] reported the positive outcome of the first Adventist Health Study, describing the results as the "Adventist Advantage."[12] There was significant reduction in most cancers and cirrhosis of the liver. Subsequent studies have shown a significant increase in longevity in those living the Adventist lifestyle. The results of metanalyses have been so compelling that $19 million has been allocated to conduct Adventist Health Study II, with a special emphasis on the differences in malignancies between Adventists and the general population.

Further international attention was focused on the Adventist health emphasis in the November 2005 issue of *National Geographic*, which focused on the "secrets of living longer."[13]

Currently, the second Adventist Health Study (AHS-2) is being conducted. The first Adventist Health Study took place in California, comparing the health of Seventh-day Adventists and non-Seventh-day Adventists. This showed the advantages alluded to already, but also the significantly prolonged life expectancy of between 7 to 9 years. AHS-2 has enrolled 95,000 participants throughout the USA and Canada and has a special focus on diversity and a substudy on spirituality and health. This initiative is progressing well and the results should be available in the next two to three years. Already, there are interesting preliminary results emerging.

More important than living a few years longer is Jesus' injunction to "do the works of him who sent me" (John 9:4). God has given us, through varied sources, consistent guidance on how we can be healthy, happy and holy. The health and wellness is to be channeled into His service as conduits of His grace to a broken world with no strings attached. The benefits accrue to the servant and those served. We are, indeed, blessed to live in a time when science continues and confirms the instructions given. History and the universe will judge us on how we apply the knowledge and benefits.

"Have faith in the Lord your God, and you will be upheld; have faith in His prophets and you will be successful" (2 Chron 20:20).

ENDNOTES

[1] All texts quoted are from the New International Version unless otherwise noted.

[2] "That the work of God may be displayed, i.e. God be glorified."

[3] See 1 Corinthians 3:16; 6:19, 2 Corinthians 6:16.

[4] Ellen G White, *The Ministry of Healing*, (Boise, Idaho: Pacific Press Publishing Association), 17.

[5] See Matt 22:37; Luke 10:27.

[6] Paul S Mueller, MD; David J Plevak, MD; Teresa A Rummans, MD, Mayo Clinic

Proc., 2001; 76:1225-1235.

[7] Mueller 1225-1235.

[8] Harold G Koenig, Michael E McCullough, David Larson, *Handbook of Religion and Health*, (Oxford University Press, 2001).

[9] Benjamin C Maxson, "The Missing Connection," *Dynamic Steward*, October-December 2003, vol 7, no 4.

[10] D E Robinson, *The Story of Our Health Message*, (Nashville, Tennessee: Southern Publishing Association, 1965).

[11] *Time* magazine, October 28, 1966.

[12] Gary E Fraser, *Diet, Life Expectancy, and Chronic Disease: Studies of Seventh-day Adventists and Other Vegetarians*, (Oxford University Press, 2003).

[13] Dan Buettner, "The Secrets of Long Life," *National Geographic*, November 2005.

Reflections on Foundational Anabaptist Understandings of Discipleship, Non-Conformity and Ethics

Valerie G Rempel

arold S Bender, writing in the *Mennonite Quarterly Review*, described "the concept of discipleship as the most characteristic, most central, most essential and regulative concept in Anabaptist thought," the thing that "largely determines all else."[1] It is a statement that begs to be argued with:

- What about the new birth that leads to salvation,
- believer's baptism as entry into the community of faith,

- the concept of the church as a covenant community "without spot or wrinkle"—a church separate from the state around it,
- the understanding of the Lord's supper as a memorial meal eaten with brothers and sisters in the faith, or
- the radical reading of the gospels which propels the community to practices of love and nonresistance?

Surely these rightfully belong to any conversation about the radical 16th century movement under discussion today.

Still, Bender's strong statement has merit. This is because in an Anabaptist framework,

- Salvation is understood as regeneration that is evidenced in the believer's daily life,
- Adult or believer's baptism is made upon a confession of faith that is proved by one's daily life,
- The pure and undefiled church is a visible witness to the transformative power of the Holy Spirit in the lives of true believers,
- The Lord's Supper is to be observed only if one's relationships are in right order, and
- Love and nonresistance speak to a radical living out of the ethics of Jesus.

Discipleship is central because it is inextricably linked to the way Anabaptists understand salvation. More than just forgiveness of sins, salvation is understood to bring about a genuine new birth. This "newness of life" is expected to be demonstrated in the life of the believer as one's entire being comes under the Lordship of Christ.

Nachfolge Christi

For Anabaptists, the concept of discipleship is often captured in a German phrase, *Nachfolge Christi*, understood as "following after Jesus." *Nachfolge* is usually translated as *imitation* or *emulation*. For example, the devotional work by Thomas a' Kempis, *The Imitation of Christ*, is, in its German form, *Nachfolge Christi*. For Anabaptists, however, the phrase carries a slightly different nuance that is usually translated as "following Jesus." This is not in its more precise definition referring to succession, but in the sense of following the way of Jesus. "Following after Jesus," calls to mind the group of men and women who gathered around Jesus as disciples, who literally followed after Jesus during His time on earth. To be a disciple is to learn from Jesus, to follow Jesus in life and death. Gareth Hewett writes that "following Jesus is not just a geographical exercise; it is a way of life. It is an attitude of mind and heart, it is taking up a cross, it is being a servant."[2]

For believers who embrace this understanding, Jesus becomes the pattern for a new way of living. J Lawrence Burkholder notes that "discipleship involves a return to what is considered the earliest and therefore the normative form of Christianity... [and] Christ's message becomes the message of the disciple."[3] This is true for both the individual and the church. What does it mean to follow after Jesus? To quote H S Bender once more, it is "simply the bringing of the whole of life under the Lordship of Christ, and the transformation of this life, both personal and social, after His image."[4]

For early Anabaptists, discipleship was inevitably linked to suffering and persecution. A true disciple of Jesus followed Him to the cross, if necessary. Indeed, many early Anabaptists were martyred because of their then radical views about baptism, the separation of church and state, and their refusal to bear arms. But beyond a physical martyrdom, the believer was expected to die to self. Another German word, *Gelassenheit*, meaning "yieldedness," spoke to the attitude of the Christian. A true Christian yielded first to the Lordship of Christ, but then sought to cultivate that spirit of yieldedness in relationship to the covenant community and, if necessary, to those who would persecute them.

Because early Anabaptists took the Bible so seriously, they conceived of the Christian life as a disciplined life. It was not intended to be showy or to be preoccupied with personal comfort, wealth or status. The life of a disciple was to be a holy life. This has often been expressed both in personal piety but also in a separation from the world. Ironically, early Anabaptists were routinely praised for the quality or apparent godliness of their lives even as they were hunted down and killed.

In the same way that Jesus gathered a group of disciples, Anabaptists have assumed that discipleship has a communal aspect. It is expected that following Jesus will shape relationships within the community of faith and it assumes a common journey. One does not travel alone. This is variously expressed in a commitment to church discipline and efforts to corporately fulfill the great commission.[5]

As already noted, this concept of discipleship oriented the believer to the life of Jesus. That meant that the qualities Jesus exhibited—humility, compassion for those sick or in need, care of the outsider, a refusal to retaliate when harmed, a dedication to God—all of these were qualities to be cultivated in the believer. Discipleship was inevitably connected to ethics because the character of one's life was understood to be a reflection of the change that had happened in the believer.

Discipleship, understood as following after Jesus, was not unique to the Anabaptist experience although it did take on particular importance within the tradition. Scholars have pointed to links with late medieval monasticism, describing it as "a kind of Protestantized late Medieval spirituality."[6] The focus on right living as a visible demonstration of the change that has occurred is echoed in pietism and Wesleyan holiness, as well.

The "Middle Path"

Early Anabaptists shared with other 16th century reformers the necessity of repentance for sins and the acceptance by faith of the salvation offered through Christ's atoning work on the cross. Like Luther, Zwingli and Calvin, they rejected the sacraments as the means to salvation. They differed, however, in their understanding of how that grace worked. For Anabaptists, God's grace was freely available to all rather than an elected few and was at work so that people could choose Jesus. This had implications for the nature of the redeemed life, as well. Luther continued to see humankind as corrupted. For him, that strengthened the role of grace. Early Anabaptists, however, had a more optimistic view of humankind and of redemption. For them, conversion was a genuine new birth that made possible a new way of living. Indeed, it not only made it possible but essentially required it as an act of obedience.

This is the "middle path" spoken of by the early radical, Michael Sattler.

"Verily, blessed be he who remains on the middle path, who turns aside neither to the work-righteous. . . preaching works in such a way that they think no more about faith, and wish to neither see nor hear anything about faith, that it is necessary for salvation, so that all their works are like wild plums, i.e., ceremonies without faith. Nor to the side of the scribes, who although they have forsaken works, then turn aside to the right, and teach in the name of 'gospel' a faith without works, and take the poor obedient Christ... as their satisfaction, but will not hear what he says, Luke 9: 'Come, follow me.'"[7]

This middle path linked genuine faith to good works in the manner referred to in the book of James.

"What good is it, my brothers and sisters, if someone claims to have faith but has no deeds? Can such faith save them? Suppose a brother or a sister is without clothes and daily food. If one of you says to them, 'Go in peace; keep warm and well fed,' but does nothing about their physical needs, what good is it? In the same way, faith by itself, if it is not accompanied by action, is dead. But someone will say, 'You have faith; I have deeds.' Show me your faith without deeds, and I will show you my faith by my deeds."[8]

Luther wanted to reject the book of James which he viewed as dangerously close to righteousness by works. The early Anabaptists read it quite differently. For them, James describes the character of the Christian life. As the former priest, Menno Simons, put it,

"True evangelical faith is of such a nature that it cannot lay dormant; but manifests itself in all righteousness and works of love; it dies unto flesh and blood; destroys all forbidden lusts and desires; cordially seeks, serves and fears God; clothes the naked; feeds the hungry; consoles the afflicted; shelters the miserable; aids and consoles all the oppressed; returns good for evil; serves those that injure it; prays for those that persecute it; teaches, admonishes and reproves with the Word of the Lord; seeks that which is lost; binds up that which is wounded; heals that which is diseased and saves that which is sound. The persecution, suffering and anxiety which befalls it for the sake of the truth of the Lord, is to it a glorious joy and consolation."[9]

If James laid out the relationship between faith and works, it was (and is) the gospel accounts that most shape an Anabaptist understanding of discipleship. In addition to the model that Jesus provides in the collected stories about Him, we find His own words, especially in the Sermon on the Mount, to be critical for helping us understand what the Christian life looks like.

"Going in the Opposite Direction"

Henry J Schmidt, another North American Mennonite, wrote that "the call to 'take up your cross' is an invitation to find our identity, our value system, our new lifestyle in full identification with Jesus Christ. Biblical discipleship always calls us to conformity to Christ and to nonconformity to the world."[10] For Schmidt, this call to nonconformity is found in Jesus' words at the end of the Sermon on the Mount when, in Matthew 7, he speaks of the narrow gate versus the wide, the narrow road versus the broad, of being in the minority versus the majority. "But where is the narrow road?" Schmidt writes. "Someone has suggested the narrow road is located in the middle of the broad road, but going in the opposite direction."[11]

This struggle to go in the opposite direction, to live a life conformed to Christ rather than the world, has been an important part of our understanding of discipleship. The biblical text seems clear: "Do not conform to the pattern of this world, but be transformed by the renewing of your mind. Then you will be able to test and approve what God's will is—his good, pleasing and perfect will"—Rom 12:2, NIV. But what nonconformity means and how it is expressed has varied from time to time and from group to group.

One of the factors that shaped an Anabaptist understanding of what the Christian life looks like is found in the two-kingdom theology that developed early in Anabaptist thought. As Anabaptists read the Bible, it was clear that there was the kingdom of heaven, already breaking in on earth, and the kingdom of darkness. One was either standing in the light or had joined oneself to the world (the dark). Again, the New Testament provided lots of language to describe this otherness. Jesus' followers are described as strangers, aliens, citizens of a different kingdom, called to be in the world but not of the world.

Steven M Nolt points to the *Schleitheim Confession* (1527) and its strong language when he quotes, "there is nothing else in all the world and all creation than good or evil, believing and unbelieving, darkness and light, the world and those who are [come] out of the world, God's temple and idols, Christ and Belial, and none will have part with the other."[12] Or to quote the Bible once again, "Do not be yoked together with unbelievers. For what do righteousness and wickedness have in common? Or what fellowship can light have with darkness?"[13]

Early Anabaptists saw a very clear distinction between the two worlds. Political realities also helped make clear the distinction as many were persecuted and even martyred. Nonconformity was expressed in separating church and state, in refusing to bear arms, in rejecting oaths, in the practice of mutual aid and in the simplicity of their lives. Over time, the concept of nonconformity began to take on particular nuances and practices in the various groups of Mennonites that emerged.[14]

Swiss and Southern German Anabaptists came to North America in the early 18th century. Here, in a "friendlier social environment," it became increasingly difficult to see the line between the church and the world.[15] Most Anabaptists refused to bear arms and many resisted involvement in any political concerns. In addition, the biblical admonition to keep from being "unequally yoked" was extended beyond marriage to business relationships, as well. Socially, anything that required an oath or membership in a society other than the church was frowned on. Other practices were less distinguishable from those in the pietistic or holiness traditions.

Nonconformity was often expressed in a separation from the wider culture which included amusements, drinking alcohol, swearing, belonging to clubs, etc. It was also expected that Christians would live simply and that this would be evidenced in their dress as well as their homes and furnishings.

Over time, the matter of clothing served as a particularly visible symbol of nonconformity. While agreeing on the need for simple clothing that did not follow the world or fashion, various groups differed in the degree to which they mandated particular clothing styles. Again, while agreeing on the need for modesty, there were different understandings about the need for head coverings or a particular religious uniform. As communities increasingly interacted with the larger culture via media consumption, education and urbanization, attempts were made to call communities to maintain or even adopt plain clothes. These provided a visible boundary marker and there was much pressure to conform to this outward symbol of nonconformity. Eventually, some groups abandoned what could be viewed as dress codes, though they still maintained a commitment to nonconformity and, frequently, a commitment to a simple lifestyle.

Steven Nolt has observed the way in which nonconformity increasingly became redefined. Initially exhibited in a reluctance to engage in worldly affairs, some Mennonite communities created their own institutions that paralleled the larger culture. In essence, Mennonites created an educational and economic subculture that allowed them to stay separate from the world but engage in practices that looked a great deal like the world.[16]

The experience of Dutch and Northern German Mennonites was somewhat different. A significant contingent moved to the Vistula Delta of Poland, then migrated to southern Russia at the invitation of Catherine the Great around 1789. By the time they arrived in southern Russia their communities were closing. As historian P M Friesen described it, the colony structure put in place in Russia meant that "they now lived in closed civil communities and jurisdictional districts in which they not only could, *but were forced to* perform the considerable, though menial, police and judicial tasks of that time."[17] In this context the community functioned as a kind of self-governing island within the larger political realm. What did it now mean to separate church and state? What did it mean to be in the world but not of it?

This was further complicated because what constituted "simple living" had never been agreed on. The Dutch had had a fair degree of wealth. Many established prosperous farms and businesses in Prussia and would eventually become financially successful again in Southern Russia where they became excellent farmers, built large factories, established schools, and built estates. In that context, nonconformity became increasingly linked to personal piety as it was shaped by the pietism and revivalism of the 19th century, movements which also made their way into southern Russia. When many of them eventually immigrated to the United States, and later to Canada and South America, they did so without the history of "plain clothes" that had characterized other parts of the Mennonite world. For many descendants of this branch, assimilation into the wider culture tended to happen fairly rapidly.

From a sociological view, nonconformity, especially in its visible markers, has functioned as a kind of boundary that helped maintain distinct communities. Mennonite culture was retained, in part, through the tradition of language, food, family relationships, patterns of worship, music, and the expectations within the community of what constituted right living. Over time, these have been variously used or disregarded by different groups of Anabaptists. The growth of the church around the world has also shifted some of the traditional emphases as new Mennonites and Brethren in Christ interpret the biblical text in their own contexts.

Today, nonconformity takes various routes. In some quarters there is still an emphasis on simple living as exhibited in simple or even plain clothing or simple, wholesome food.[18] This does not necessarily mean a rejection of all parts of culture, e.g., education, technology, etc, but moves the church toward an attitude of stewardship in the use of these resources. In other parts of the church, nonconformity is couched in the broader language of resisting Christendom where nonconformity is spoken of as resisting the culture's messages when and where they conflict with Christian values.

Advocates of this language tend to speak of loyalties or allegiances. Again, the two-kingdom theology that has been so present in the tradition is used as a way of defining proper citizenship. One's loyalty belongs to the Kingdom of God and that will rightly shape attitudes and behaviors.

Conclusion

The disciple of Christ seeks to live by the ethics of the New Testament. He or she is guided by the example of Jesus and takes seriously the exhortation offered in the Sermon on the Mount. Increasingly, Anabaptists find themselves engaging in the world, translating that biblical ethic into work for justice, healing and hope. Mennonites have also become institution builders—denominational structures have been developed, schools, retirement homes, mental health hospitals, and other health and human service organizations have been developed. Relief work through Mennonite Central Committee or Mennonite Disaster Service serves as an expression of the message of peace and reconciliation. This, too, is seen as an alternative witness that seeks to extend the kingdom of God.

ENDNOTES
[1] Harold S Bender, "The Anabaptist Theology of Discipleship," *Mennonite Quarterly Review*, no 24, January 1950, 27.
[2] Quoted in J Nelson Kraybill, *On the Pilgrim Way: Conversations on Christian Discipleship*, (Scottdale, Pennsylvania: Herald Press, 1999), 40.
[3] J Lawrence Burkholder, "The Anabaptist Vision of Discipleship," *The Recovery of the Anabaptist Vision: A Sixtieth Anniversary Tribute to Harold S. Bender*, Guy F Hershberger, editor, (Scottdale, Pennsylvania: Herald Press, 1957), 136.
[4] Bender 29.
[5] Harold S Bender, "Discipleship," *The Mennonite Encyclopedia: A Comprehensive Reference Work on the Anabaptist-Mennonite Movement*, Vol IV, O-Z Supplement. Bender writes that "Major aspects of the concept include: (1) Holy living; (2) suffering in the spirit of Christ, bearing the cross; (3) the practice of love and nonresistance; (4) separation from the world of sin and evil; (5) full brotherhood in the church; (6) obedience to the great commission; (7) a disciplined church; (8) rejection of the use of power by the Christ (e.g., state offices)." See also Harold S

Bender and Harry Huebner, "Discipleship," *Global Anabaptist Mennonite Ency-clopedia Online*, 1989, Web 26 June 2011. http://www.gameo.org/encyclopedia/contents/D5788ME.html. GAMEO continues to list these as the core concepts. It should be noted, however, that various groups would interpret these differently. For example, Anabaptists have held public office at local, state or provincial and even national levels. Various groups differ on their understanding of what it means to live separately from the world and there has been erosion in the commitment to love and nonresistance.

[6] See, for example, the conversation between C Arnold Snyder and Adolf Ens in "Discussion of Arnold Snyder's Paper: Keywords Relating to Discipleship in the Thought of Menno Simons," *Discipleship in Context: Papers Read at the Menno Simons 5000 International Symposium*, (Elspeet, Netherlands, 1996); Alle Hoekema and Roelf Kuitse, editors, *Occasional Papers* #18 (Elkhart, Indiana: Institute of Mennonite Studies, 1997), 114.

[7] "Michael Sattler, 'On the Satisfaction of Christ,' before 1530, Legacy, 115-116" in *Anabaptism in Outline: Selected Primary Sources*, Walter Klaassen, Editor, (Scottsdale, Pennsylvania: Herald Press, 1981), 57.

[8] James 2:14-19, NIV.

[9] Excerpted from *The Complete Works of Menno Simon* (Elkhart, Indiana, 1871), 246. http://www.mennosimons.net/newlife.html. Accessed June 24, 2011.

[10] Henry J Schmidt, editor, "Conversion, Discipleship and Social Change," *Conversion: Doorway to Discipleship*, (Hillsboro, Kansas: The Board of Christian Literature of the General Conference of Mennonite Brethren Churches, 1980), 112.

[11] Schmidt 112.

[12] Quoted in Steven M Nolt, "Reinterpreting Nonconformity: Mennonite and Brethren Thought and Practice," *Anabaptist Currents: History in Conversation with the Present*, Carl F Bowman and Stephen L Longenecker, Editors, Forum for Religious Studies, Bridgewater College, Bridgewater, Virginia (Rockland, Maine: Penobscot Press), 184.

[13] 2 Corinthians 6:14, NIV.

[14] "Nonconformity," *The Mennonite Encyclopedia: A Comprehensive Reference Work on the Anabaptist-Mennonite Movement*, Vol III, I-N Supplement, h.s.b.

[15] Nolt 185.

[16] See Nolt's astute comments in "Reinterpreting Nonconformity."

[17] Peter M Friesen, *The Mennonite Brotherhood in Russia (1789-1910)*, revised edition, translated by J B Toews, et al (Fresno, California: Board of Christian Literature, General Conference of Mennonite Brethren Churches, 1980), 92, italics mine.

[18] Doris Janzen Longacre's books, *More with Less* (1975, 2000) and *Living More With Less* (1980, 2010) are popular guidebooks toward a simple lifestyle.

Ordinances of the Church

Patricia Urueña Barbosa

More important than determining the most appropriate word—either *ordinance* or *sacrament*—removing the sacrament from the medieval sense of priest-centered and "magic" is to theologically renew the term and find it more meaningful and responsible. For Mennonites, ordinances are practices that have biblical and theological foundations. They are instructions or commands that are assigned by Jesus and give identity to the church.

The purpose of the constant practice of the church's ordinances is to shape the believer's character in the image and likeness of Christ. It does so by God's grace and is based on deep convictions of faith. These practices are necessary to find concrete ways of expressing Christian ethics. These ways are found in the decisions and activities of daily living, not only as individuals but also as a church. The ordinances serve fallen, broken, and hurt humanity and they are good news because they confront the selfish, individualistic, unjust, and oppressive practices in the world. They are good news that call us and commit us to participate actively in the healing and reconciliation that God desires for the world.

There are three practices that are inseparable in the church: Baptism, the Lord's Supper, and foot washing.

Believer's Baptism

Baptism is administered to those who have consciously repented and amended their lives and believe that Christ has died for their sins and who request baptism for themselves. Infants, therefore, are not to be baptized.

In the Old Testament the ritual of washing was done to symbolize the cleansing of sins and the desire to continue walking with God. This was the background for the practice of John's baptism. John the Baptist began his ministry with the baptism of repentance together with the proclamation of the coming Kingdom of God (Matt 3:1-8). Jesus, at the beginning of His ministry, was baptized by John (Matt 3:13-15) and Jesus' disciples baptized new believers during Jesus' ministry (John 4:1-2). The baptism came after repentance and it denotes the action of the Holy Spirit (Acts 2:28).

From a biblical perspective, baptism means: forgiveness of sins (Acts 2:38), participation in the death and resurrection of Christ (Rom 6:1-4), and death to sin and walking in newness of life through our union with Christ (Rom 6:1-4; Col 2:9-15). It is a symbol of washing received through Christ's blood (Acts 22:16) and new birth by water and the Spirit (John 3:5); it is a new creation in order that all human division is overcome (Gal 3:26-29; Eph 4:5); it is salvation and enables us to have a clear conscience (1 Peter 3: 21); it is a commitment of believers to each other (Acts 2:41-47; 1 Cor 12:12,13).

Over time, the Catholic Church came to regard the sacrament of baptism as necessary for salvation in order to counteract the effects of original sin. In the case of adults, it cleansed the sins committed so far. Baptism was part of the concept of Christendom: the person was born as a Roman citizen and was baptized as a Catholic Christian, ensuring both the socio-political unity and the soul's salvation. Baptism is God's vehicle of grace and it must be administered early. The Anabaptists of the 16th century, like other subsequent churches, rejected the sacramental vision of Catholicism. They rejected baptizing infants and began the practice of rebaptizing believers. It was done in their homes or rivers, returning to the radical meaning of Christian baptism. This is what happened on January 21, 1525, when a group of radical adults gathered in Zurich, Switzerland, and performed the first rebaptism of adults in the Anabaptist movement. This was done behind closed doors and in secret because of persecution.

They earned the nickname of the re-baptized, or Anabaptists, because of this practice. Rebaptism was something qualitatively new in Christian history and a reform that was revolutionary, socially, politically and religiously, in that time. As a consequence of the practice of rebaptism, the Anabaptists were persecuted and tortured and suffered martyrdom. Baptism, for the Anabaptists, defined their lifestyle and the concept of Christian life, church, and the regenerating experience of the Holy Spirit. Based on 1 John 5:6-8, Anabaptists considered three kinds of baptism:

1.   The baptism of the Spirit creates regeneration and enables people to walk in Christ's resurrection. The person receives the spiritual resources necessary in order to live a Christian life. The believer's life becomes a "walk in the Spirit" (Rom 6:4; Gal 5:16, 22-25), not as a mere mystical experience, but in terms of social virtues such as love, joy, peace, patience, kindness, generosity, faithfulness, gentleness and self-control (Gal 5:22-23).

2.   Water baptism symbolizes the recognition of this experience of regeneration brought about by the Spirit of God (John 3:3-5) and the commitment that a person acquires with God and the community of believers (Acts 2:41-47; Eph 4:1-13). It is the community of believers that has seen the real fruit of the Spirit of God in the life of the person and provides the baptism. It is a public act that symbolizes that one has repented of one's sins, is ready to enter into the fellowship of Christ's body, and is willing to follow Christ in daily discipleship through the power of the Holy Spirit. For these reasons baptism acquires its full biblical meaning in community.

3.   The baptism of blood derives from the previous two practices. The disciples of Christ experience suffering and persecution from the world because of their commitment to the Lord (Matt 5:11-12; 24:9; John 16:33; 2 Cor 1:5; 2 Tim 3:12). This is why they considered the suffering, persecution and martyrdom of testimonial value. They experience the words of Paul in Colossians 1:24, "in my

flesh I am completing what is lacking in Christ's afflictions for the sake of his body, that is, the church."

Mennonites today also believe in the threefold baptism: Spirit, water, and blood. Baptism by Spirit refers to the transforming presence of the Holy Spirit. Water is a symbol of God washing the sin away and the believer being incorporated into the community. Baptism by blood refers to the individual's and the community's commitment to a new life; it brings the possibility of persecution, torture, and even death.

Mennonites refer to baptism as "an outward sign of an inward transformation." Baptism is a sign that a person has repented after hearing the good news of the gospel. The person has received God's forgiveness, renounced evil, and died to sin through God's grace in Jesus Christ. For Mennonites, baptism celebrates the gift of salvation, the gift of God's loving, forgiving and enabling grace.

For Mennonites, the believer's baptism is closely linked to the concept of salvation, church membership, discipleship and mission. Baptism is closely linked to salvation, not as a mere ritual or a moment of decision, but as a whole journey of faith characterized by a complete following of Christ in daily living and a commitment to the community of believers. Baptism is a public event where the believer's faith is expressed in the context of the faith community, where it will be nourished and receive discipleship, discipline and mission. Baptism and church membership are inseparable, since they incorporate the new believer into the community of citizens of the kingdom, which is the church. This is where one is accountable and responsible for others in matters of faith and life. By choosing to be baptized, people promise that they will be active and engaged members, not only in their congregations but in the global Mennonite church, in practicing "care, discipline, and fellowship."

The Lord's Supper

Only those who have been baptized can take part in communion. Participation in Communion is a remembrance of Christ's body and blood; the real body and blood of Christ is not present in the sacrament.

Communion, or the Lord's Supper, was and still is a central practice of faith in the church's life. In New Testament times, the Lord's Supper was in the middle of a meal shared around the table. Its meaning is not focused on the elements, as if they were sacred, but in the act of sharing. Although the Gospels and 1 Corinthians especially remember the Last Supper of Jesus with His disciples, and it was held during the Jewish Passover, all meals held in the Messianic community were communal. Apparently, not only the meals but the economy was shared. This was recorded about the early Christian communities (Luke 8:1-3; Acts 2:42-47; 4:32-34; 6:1-6; 1 Cor 11:17-34).

Furthermore, on many occasions Jesus was criticized for sharing the table with people who were considered undesirable and were seen as sinners by the Jewish community (Mark 2:16, Luke 15:2). Sharing a table meant solidarity with other people. Jesus' meals were a way of questioning the socio-religious Jewish system. Even Jesus taught His followers: "When you give a banquet, invite the poor, the maimed, the crippled, the lame, and the blind. And you will be blessed." For Jesus, eating together was a way of showing solidarity with the poor and vulnerable of society (Luke 14:13-14a). It was a concrete expression of restoration of the Kingdom of God: an eating and drinking in the Kingdom (Luke 22:16). Even the Jewish Passover bread was called "bread of the poor." So the symbolism of the Lord's Supper is the shared table, shared life, and shared solidarity. Sharing the Lord's Supper is an expression of solidarity in the life and mission assumed by Jesus.

Over time, food and the blessing of the bread and wine became separated. The Eucharistic celebration was incorporated into the main worship of the congregation (the Mass). The communal meals were continued in several congregations until the 8th century, when communal meals almost disappeared completely. However, many small Christian groups have discovered this practice and have incorporated it in their renewed community life, as the Anabaptists did in Switzerland and southern Germany.

Regarding the Lord's Supper, Anabaptists understood the blood and the body in a more symbolic than literal way. When Jesus shared the Passover meal, He asked His followers to follow His example and to do it in memory of His love, devotion, and suffering for them (Luke 22:19). The understanding is that the Bible says Christ ascended into heaven and is seated at the right hand of God (Luke 22:69; 24:51; Rom 8:34), and because of this Jesus can't be physically present at the mass in the elements of communion. Anabaptists believed that the mass promoted a magical understanding of the church's rituals and this took away any concern for the moral behavior of the person.

For Mennonites today, celebrating the Lord's Supper is an activity that is essentially communal and is multifaceted:

- It is a reminder of the events and teachings of service and sacrificial giving at the last meal that Jesus shared with His disciples. On that occasion Jesus washed the feet of His disciples as a sign of service, as well as preparing them for the suffering that He and His followers would experience (John 13:1-20; Luke 22:14-20; 1 Cor 11:23-25).

- It expresses the reality of the presence of Jesus in the believer's life and in the life of the body of Christ, which is the Church. Eating bread and drinking wine are not only an experience of private devotion, but it is where believers become aware of being part of a body. Believers are trained to abandon their individual identity to become part of the broader goal of God's presence in the world, which is the church, the community of believers (John 6: 55-56; Acts 2:42-47; 4:32; 1 Cor 10:16-17; 11:17-25).

- It is a new Easter and a new covenant (1 Cor 11:25). Historically, the Passover lamb strengthened the people for their departure from Egypt (Mark 14:12-26). John draws a parallel between Jesus and the Passover lamb. Thus, the Lord's Supper is a new Passover of Messianic liberation, parallel to the Passover with which Israel celebrated its liberation from Egypt. Eating the "flesh" of Jesus and "drinking His blood" leading to "eternal life" (John 6:4), enable the disciples to be militants in God's Kingdom (John 6:54; 1 Cor 5:7-8; 1 Peter 1:19; John 19:36). The texts of the Lord's Supper also refer to the new covenant and are characterized by conditions of coexisting among God's people that are well above those experienced in the old covenant (Jer 31:31-34).

- It's a collective act of evangelization where the sacrifice of Jesus, where He gave Himself to humanity with love, is remembered and announced (1 Cor 11: 26). The Lord's Supper is the celebration of the evangelistic proclamation of a community which gives itself to others as Christ gave Himself. In communion, we remember that the power of God is revealed in vulnerability and weakness, in loving surrender and dying. In the same way that the body and blood of Jesus were given as a ransom for many, the wheat and the grapes must be crushed to become bread and wine, and believers must be prepared to give their lives to become ground for the Kingdom of God. It means loving others just as Jesus loved, and surrendering to death for everyone (John 13:34-35; 15:13).

- It is an opportunity to foster healthy interpersonal relationships among members of the congregation. Given Paul's warning not to take supper unworthily (1 Cor 11:27), the call is to be at peace with God and our brothers and sisters. If anyone does not have good relations with a member of the congregation, they must refrain from partaking in the bread and wine until that relationship is restored.

- The Lord's Supper is eschatological in a prophetic sense. The Lord's Supper points to the culmination of history, the great feast of the Lamb (Revelation 19), when people of the whole earth will gather around the table, united by a common confession of the Lordship of Christ. Here, at the end of time, the unity of the whole creation that God intended for humanity will be completely restored. It will be the big celebration where people of all races, rich and poor, men and women, new believers and mature saints, will join as equals, without any discrimination, all as members of the extended family, to worship and praise the Lord. Meanwhile, our practice of the Lord's Supper will be an inclusive celebration that invites solidarity with the poor and marginalized and invites all to share life until the Lord's coming.

The Lord's Supper is therefore a multifaceted event. It is an update of the teaching and practice of Jesus, of the teaching and practice of the early church, and of the understanding and practice of the Anabaptists. The Lord's Supper reminds us that we are saved by Christ, through His teaching, example, death and resurrection. It reminds us that we have been saved in the context of a free community that has solidarity, and this is what the church is. It reminds us that we are saved by hope in the resurrection and in the culmination of history when the new creation of God may be fully realized "on earth as in heaven."

Foot Washing

This practice was given by Jesus during the Last Supper (John 13:1-17). This act of servanthood is a special time for church members to humble themselves before each other as they remember how Jesus humbled Himself going to the cross. This is usually connected with communion.

Dirk Philips, 16th century Anabaptist, comments regarding foot washing:

"The third ordinance is foot washing of the saints, which Jesus Christ commanded his disciples to observe for two reasons. First, because he wanted us to know that he must cleanse the inner man, and we have to allow him to wash the sins that so easily entangle (Heb 12:1) ... The second reason why Jesus instituted foot washing is for us to humble ourselves before others (Rom 12:10; Phil 2:3, 1 Peter 5:5; James 4:10-11) and for us to see our brothers in faith in the highest respect since they are the saints of God and members of the body of Jesus Christ and the indwelling of the Holy Spirit (Rom 12:10; Col 3:13; 1 Cor 5:16) ... Now that I, your Lord and Teacher, have washed your feet, you also should wash one another's feet. I have set you an example that you should do as I have done for you."

We can note that for Anabaptists of the 16th and later centuries foot washing was a symbol of humility and purification, a practice in preparation for attending the Lord's Supper and in imitation of Christ's actions. This practice disappeared in some Anabaptist congregations; in other churches the practice continued, though not frequently.

Currently in some cultures, foot washing may seem strange because it is not a common practice. Despite this, foot washing gives a concrete and deep sense of fellowship, understanding of mutual submission, service, love and devotion for the other. Also, to touch the feet of the other person, which is a very personal touch, reminds us that the family we have in the church is wider and is a priority to our biological family. The gesture of humility when kneeling as we wash the feet of our brother or sister, paves the path for the equality of all, despite social, economic, racial or cultural differences. It enacts the fellowship, love, service and mutual submission that we owe each other.

The gesture of kneeling while washing the feet of our brother or sister gives us a practical basis for the theory about mutual submission, love, and service, and frees us from spiritualizing these acts.

Bibliography
John Driver, *Counter Current: Essay on Radical Ecclesiology*, (Colombia, Guatemala: Clara-Seed), 1998.
Donald F Durnbaugh, *The Believers' Church*, (Scottdale, Pennsylvania: Herald Press, 1985).
John R Martin, *Ventures in Discipleship: A Handbook for Groups or Individuals*, (Scottdale, Pennsylvania: Herald Press), 1984.
John D Roth, *Beliefs: Mennonite Faith and Practice*, (Scottdale, Pennsylvania; Waterloo, Ontario: Herald Press), 2005.
John D Roth, *Practices: Mennonite Worship and Witness*, (Scottdale, Pennsylvania; Waterloo, Ontario: Herald Press), 2009.
John Rempel, Editor, *Minister's Manual*, (Newton, Kansas: Faith & Life Press; Scottdale, Pennsylvania: Herald Press), 1998.
The Mennonite Handbook, (Scottdale, Pennsylvania: Herald Press), 2007.
John Howard Yoder, *Body Politics: Five Practices of the Christian Community before the Watching World*, (Scottdale, Pennsylvania: Herald Press), 1992.

John Howard Yoder, editor, *Texts Chosen from the Radical Reformation*, Spanish translation by Nelida de Machain and Ernesto Suarez Vilela, (Buenos Aires: La Aurora, 1976).

John Christian Wenger, *Glimpses of Mennonite History and Doctrine*, (Scottdale, Pennsylvania: Herald Press), 1959.

Adventist Concepts of Discipleship and Nonconformity

Denis Fortin

A Biblical View of Discipleship[1]

Seventh-day Adventists believe that the person who accepts Christ as Savior is called to a Christ-like life of spiritual, mental, physical, and relational growth; like the child Jesus to grow "in wisdom and stature, and in favor with God and men" (Luke 2:52). The goal of our lives is to be transformed into the likeness of Jesus Christ within the fellowship of the church, His body.

Our Fundamental Belief #11, "Growing in Christ," states in part,

> "... Jesus' victory gives us victory over the evil forces that still seek to control us, as we walk with Him in peace, joy, and assurance of His love. Now the Holy Spirit dwells within us and empowers us. Continually committed to Jesus as our Saviour and Lord, we are set free from the burden of our past deeds. No longer do we live in the darkness, fear of evil powers, ignorance, and meaninglessness of our former way of life. In this new freedom in Jesus, we are called to grow

into the likeness of His character, communing with Him daily in prayer, feeding on His Word, meditating on it and on His providence, singing His praises, gathering together for worship, and participating in the mission of the Church. As we give ourselves in loving service to those around us and in witnessing to His salvation, His constant presence with us through the Spirit transforms every moment and every task into a spiritual experience. (Ps 1:1, 2; 23:4; 77:11, 12; Col 1:13, 14; 2:6, 14, 15; Luke 10:17-20; Eph 5:19, 20; 6:12-18; 1 Thess 5:23; 2 Peter 2:9; 3:18; 2 Cor. 3:17, 18; Phil 3:7-14; 1 Thess 5:16-18; Matt 20:25-28; John 20:21; Gal 5:22-25; Rom 8:38, 39; 1 John 4:4; Heb 10:25.)"

If we can be disciples of Jesus it is first because God is the embodiment of love (1 John 4:8). Even before Creation, God expressed love for humanity by working out the plan of salvation. Since the entrance of sin, however, humanity is separated from God and, on its own, cannot understand this kind of love (Isa 59:2). Therefore, God takes the initiative in self-revelation, wanting to restore the relationship with humanity and to save them from sin and its penalty. God's self-revelation is manifest through the life, death and resurrection of Jesus, His Word, nature, the work of the Holy Spirit in people's lives, and providential workings.

Humanity was created in the image of God, capable of love and fellowship with God and others, and with moral freedom to choose whether to obey and follow the Creator (Gen 1:26, 27). Adam and Eve were enjoying a daily relationship with God until sin separated them from God and one another (Gen 3:12). They exchanged their godly dignity and the truth about their Creator for the lies of a created being who has brought devastation and shame to all humanity (John 8:44). Through Christ, God reconciled Himself with humanity and provided the way by which humanity could be restored to relationship with Himself and their fellow human beings. Jesus revealed the deceptive, self-absorbed nature of Satan and all who follow him, while showing Himself to be a shepherd-Savior who died for His sheep to provide them with reconciliation and abundant life.

Like sheep following a trusted voice, believers know the voice of their Shepherd and are called to follow (John 10:27). They invite God's presence on a daily basis, and radical changes occur in the way they relate to the Creator and to others. Through Christ's transforming grace, believers are called to reflect God's character (Eph 5:1, 2) and through the influence of the Holy Spirit to come to a unique relationship with God through a steadfast relationship of obedience.

Jesus commands us to abide in Him to receive life and to maintain a living relationship with Him (John 15:4). Abiding in Jesus means believing in Him as the Son of God, obeying what He says, loving one another with the community of God's people, extending that love by obeying Christ's command to bring the gospel to the world, and following His example to make disciples of all nations (Matt 28:18-20).

Having spent three years teaching the Twelve, Jesus left them with the great gospel commission to follow His example in making disciples. To empower them to accomplish that commission, He gave them His greatest gift, the Holy Spirit (John 14:26; 16:13). They were to teach all things that Jesus taught. Disciples today still grow and mature through the Spirit. Only a Sprit-led disciple can make another disciple for Jesus Christ. Thus the life of a disciple extends the Master's love and ministry to the world.

God showed His love for the Church by sending His Son to die for her (1 John 4:9). He also designed that His love for the Church manifest itself through His disciples. He calls them to the task of loving one another and of edifying and building up the Church. The biblical teachings of the fruit and gifts of the Holy Spirit are the key to understanding how God loves and builds up the Church through His disciples. He provides every grace and ability that is needed to fulfill this commission.

The fruit of the Spirit provides the graces through which God's love is revealed in the relationships of disciples with one another. This fruit includes love, joy, peace, patience, kindness, goodness, faithfulness, gentleness, and self-control (Gal 5:22, 23). The gifts of the Spirit, such as teaching, evangelizing, faith, and service, provide disciples with the ministries that build up the body of Christ (1 Cor

12:28; Eph 4:11). God is responsible for the success of this work, only asking that His disciples serve as willing instruments in His hands.

Throughout history God has called men and women to testify of His goodness, share their faith, and invite those who did not know Him to follow. As the first disciples of Christ were invited to follow and then were commissioned to "go and make disciples," so each believer becomes part of a continuing line of witnesses who seek to expand the fellowship of believers. In simple form, Christian witness involves a passionate testimony of a personal encounter with Jesus and an invitation to follow Him.

Discipleship through the Life Span

Given this biblical understanding of discipleship, through the years Seventh-day Adventists have established numerous ministries and activities to facilitate what we now call discipleship through the life span. Although we have not articulated our vision of discipleship like this until recently, we have been attentive to the concept of discipleship since our early beginning. And like many other Protestant denominations, our concept of discipleship is founded on the understanding that education, both informal and formal, the knowledge of the Word of God, and service facilitate the formation of one's character and the transformation of one's life in preparation for God's kingdom and eternity. The Word of God is at the center of this concept of education and discipleship. In contrast to other denominations where the focus of the religious life is to partake of the proper sacraments in order to be saved, Adventists view discipleship as the acquisition of the knowledge and experience that will prepare one for heaven.

A devotion to Bible study is at the core of our efforts at discipleship and remains the focus of much of what we do. Early Adventists promoted the study of Scripture and through the years this commitment has remained an identifying mark of Adventism. To facilitate the study of Scripture we have offered public conferences and seminars on various biblical topics, particularly on the prophecies of the books of Daniel and Revelation. Much of our numerical growth of new converts has been achieved through these conferences and much of the practical focus of our pastoral and ministerial education is to equip our pastors to give these conferences.

Apart from these activities, the organization of a cross-generational Sabbath School program is certainly the predominant mechanism of discipleship and religious education the Adventist church has espoused since 1852. For about one hour each Sabbath morning in each congregation, various Sabbath school classes are offered for all age levels. Depending on the size of the congregation, this program includes Bible lesson studies for young children, for elementary and secondary age groups, for college students, and adults. To facilitate this program, an extensive array of weekly lesson guides are prepared by the Sabbath School department of the General Conference and are translated into a multitude of languages. On any given Sabbath, adult members in Canada will likely study the same topic as those in Rwanda, in Russia, in Mexico and in New Zealand.

Another crucial element of discipleship in the Adventist church is the extensive educational system we have created. From a small beginning in 1872 with the start of a one-room school in Battle Creek, Michigan, and the creation two years later of our first college (which is now Andrews University), Seventh-day Adventists now operate the largest protestant educational system in the world with 5,815 elementary schools (according to 2011 statistics), 1908 secondary schools, and 112 colleges and universities, and we employed 89,000 teachers and enrolled 1.750 million students. The Sabbath School program and the educational system have been at the heart of the process of discipleship and religious education in the church.

Through the years we have also created numerous other ministries and activities that have contributed to the discipleship of our church members and to the growth of the church. Various ministries have focused on teaching the faith to children. Among these we have the Adventurer Club and the Pathfinder Club which have provided co-educational scout-like programs to elementary and secondary age children and youth. On our college and university campuses we have had numerous types of activities, clubs and outreach programs. In our local congregations, other activities like youth, women's and men's ministries, small group ministries, and many more, have attempted to provide an environment in which members and visitors can grow in their faith and love for Christ and his Word. All these ministries and activities attempt to facilitate a spiritual development and growth through the lifespan, from birth to senior years, that at any moment of one's life one can be a committed disciple of Jesus Christ.

Relationship to the World

How Adventists have related to the world is a matter that deserves much more study than we've done so far. In 1989, Malcolm Bull and Keith Lockhart published such a study, *Seeking a Sanctuary: Seventh-day Adventism and the American Dream*. Their main conclusion is that Adventists have sought to provide an alternative to the American dream, as they replicated the institutions and functions of American society. And in doing this the Adventist relationship with the world has been ambiguous. This relationship with the world has also been characterized by both a personal and a denominational response, and both have changed over time.

Like many other Protestant denominations, membership in the Seventh-day Adventist church is voluntary and for those who are born in the church, a decision to join the church is made at the time of baptism. Being a Christian requires obedience to clear ethical demands and a religious experience of piety and faithfulness is expected. One leaves the world, so to speak, in order to join the Seventh-day Adventist movement. Along the lines of H Richard Niebuhr's typology of the relationship of the church to culture, Seventh-day Adventism started out as a movement against culture in some sense, but has settled as a denomination in tension with culture, with more and more attempts at transforming culture.

The theological roots of the Adventist relationship with the world are to be found in their doctrine of the Sabbath, their eschatology, and their ecclesiological self-understanding and mission. At the heart of Seventh-day Adventism is also a restorationist view of church history and an attempt at recapturing New Testament Christianity. Yet we have not always been successful at reaching this goal. Like Judaism in relation to other world religions, Adventists are easily distinguished from other Christians by their observance of the Sabbath. The careful observance of a day that runs counter to mainstream Christianity has caused Adventists to not only be different but also to feel different. A desire to observe Sabbath in a society that does not value this day has made Adventists feel ostracized from their communities, sometimes lose employment, and at times even caused them to be persecuted for their faith. In response to this faith need, Adventists have tended to congregate together in some communities where their own institutions (schools, hospitals, publishing houses, etc) generated employment opportunities, avoiding a Sabbath-keeping conflict. Adventists have also tended to take up professions that minimize this conflict or to choose self-employment. It is in this context and out of this experience that Adventists have been such strong supporters of religious liberty for all people.

The Adventist teaching on the second coming of Christ has also affected their relationship with the world. Adventists see themselves as having a prophetic mission and destiny. In the book of Revelation an end-time message is proclaimed by three angels to all the world (14:6-12) to prepare the world for Christ's coming (14:14-20). Two key passages of Revelation (14:12; 12:17) are interpreted as referring to a special group of people at the end of time which will keep the commandments of God and have the faith of Jesus. Thus obedience to God's will as revealed in the Ten Commandments and adherence to a simple New Testament faith as taught by Jesus are believed to be the identifying marks of those who will see Jesus coming on the clouds of heaven at His coming. Adventists understand themselves as the fulfillment of this prophecy and sharing this message with the world is their mission.

In response to Jesus' call for His disciples to be in the world but not of this world (John 17:15, 16), Adventists have taken seriously their commitment to a lifestyle that will reflect God's character and will prepare them for heaven. To enhance this preparation for eternity, Adventists have shunned the world and its ways by emphasizing proper behavior and healthy lifestyle choices. In counterpart, some behaviors have been reprimanded, such as drinking, smoking, dancing, and some public entertainment activities (theatre, cinema, etc). Instead, simplicity of lifestyle has been promoted with the shunning of expensive clothing and possessions, and the avoidance of jewelry. Even vegetarianism is seen as a part of this preparation for eternity—what we won't eat in heaven, we might as well get along without on earth.

These biblical concepts have undergirded the Adventist attitude and response to the world. However, the traditional relationship of uneasiness with the world has morphed in the last generation or so. What used to be clearly marked or considered as "the world" is now not perceived to be as offensive. Much has happened in society that has led many Adventists to reconsider some of their earlier positions. Like Niebuhr explains in his works, a process of ecclesiastical institutionalization and adaptation to the world has been evident in Adventism.

Our approach to lifestyle issues (the dos and don'ts of the Christian life) became a serious point of conversation a couple generations ago. There is little doubt that Adventists used to be fairly legalistic about life and our religious practices. Although we have always believed in salvation by grace through faith in Christ's death on the cross, our teaching about salvation emphasized the good works a believer saved in Christ should do. Then the proverbial pendulum swung from a legalist approach to life to almost an antinomian perspective. And consequently the result has been much less agreement on what an Adventist now "looks" like. Although we are still in strong agreement regarding Sabbath observance, healthy lifestyle choices and avoidance of harmful substances, there is some diversity of opinion and practice regarding the wearing of jewelry and personal entertainment choices. Even how to keep the Sabbath is no longer an opinion we all agree on. Perhaps some would say that the distinction between the church and the world has become blurry and we are in need of revival and reformation again.

But changes in the Adventist relationship with the world have not happened only at the personal level. The denomination's response to the world has also morphed. It is a paradox that for a denomination that is so committed to emphasizing the soon return of Christ and the need to prepare people for this event, Adventists have built themselves a comfortable "kingdom" on earth. Given our emphasis on pre-millennialism and the utter destruction of this earth and its treasures at the second advent of Christ, it is somewhat puzzling that we have encouraged the development of vast and extensive educational and medical systems, we promote local welfare activities and reforms, and we have developed a fairly large and well-structured church organization. Many of our other ministries, such as publishing and media, have substantial assets.

If, as we say, we believe in the cataclysmic soon coming of Christ, we have certainly established a significant Adventist "kingdom" on earth. These ministries and social activities, however, should be understood within the context of our missiological thought. Adventists believe that the mission of the church is an extension of the work of Christ who went about teaching and healing. This mission to spread the gospel and the three angels' messages to all the world is more effective and successful if all aspects of human life are touched. Hence, health and temperance reforms, education, and social welfare are integral aspects and functions of the mission of the church to proclaim a loving and saving message to a dying world in dire need of hope. Adventist eschatology influences its missiological views which in turn drive its social thought. In this sense, our approach to culture has become one that seeks to transform it, within our circle of influence, while at the same time we believe this world is bound for destruction as it is intrinsically evil and beyond redemption. This is also reflected in the ambiguous nature of our relationship with the world.

Perhaps the transformation of the Adventist relationship with the world, from being against culture and in tension with it to attempting to transform it, within the limitations explained above, becomes more obvious when we consider the fact that in some countries Adventists have become a large segment of the general population (for example, Jamaica, Peru, Bolivia, and some places in Africa). The current Governor General of Jamaica, Sir Patrick Allen, is an ordained Seventh-day Adventist minister. In many places, Adventists now have elected and appointed government officials.

Hence, they are less and less against the local culture, but more and more attempting to transform it.

This shift in the relationship with the world is also evident when it comes to military service and bearing of arms. Although our official church position remains that we are not supporting voluntary service in the armed forces nor the bearing of arms, we now have thousands of young men and women in the United States armed forces and all of them bear arms and have some conflicts with Sabbath keeping. Anecdotally, we know that many Adventists in the United States own personal weapons and guns (and not for the purpose of providing food for their families). I personally believe the Adventist position on non-combatancy was adopted more as a pragmatic teaching during times of conflicts and warfare than as a solid biblical and theological position at the core of the church's teaching. We seldom discuss it now. Hence, our *de facto* position has become one of freedom of choice. In this case, it is not a question of the church against culture or even attempting to transform it; it is the church working with culture, a culture of violence.

The Adventist relationship with the world is thus an ambiguous one. As disciples of Christ we are committed to living a life of faith in obedience to the Word of God. But the larger our church becomes and the more diverse we are, the more we will be required to wrestle with what it means to be in this world and yet not of it. Still, it is our hope that Jesus will soon return and this process of wrestling with these issues won't be necessary. It is a paradox that this blessed hope may also prevent us in the meantime from having a stronger witness in this world of sin.

ENDNOTES

[1] This section is adapted from the brochure, *Growing Disciples*, published by the Ministries Committee of the General Conference of Seventh-day Adventists for the 2007 Annual Council.

Seventh-day Adventists and Military-Related Service

Gary R Councell

Christians hold citizenship in this world by accident of birth and in the "kingdom of heaven" by choice of "new birth." This dual citizenship often creates spiritual dilemmas of allegiance and priorities, further intensified by cultural, ethnic, linguistic and national differences. Seventh-day Adventist Christians belong to a religious "United Nations" of members who live in more than 200 countries around the world.

Most Adventists readily agree in theory that matters of faith take precedence over temporal concerns, yet they probably would admit their actual practice is often incongruent with beliefs. So how can spiritual priorities be more consistently applied in daily living? Is service in government agencies yielding allegiance to modern Caesars and this world? When governments require citizens to serve in ways that conflict with conscience, how should an Adventist Christian respond?

Adventism organized into a religious denomination during the "Uncivil War between the States" (1861-1865). As a prophetic church, Seventh-day Adventists believe the last days will bring "wars and rumors of wars" and "nation rising against nation" (Matt 24:6, 7). There will be no peace. These conflicts will culminate ultimately in the battle at Armageddon[1] (Rev 16:1-16). Adventist psyche rests in part on the concept of warfare—the Great Controversy between Christ and Satan (good and evil). Aside from their understanding about the "Theater of the Universe," Adventists keenly engage in other battles against social evils and political wrongs. Our history is replete with aggressive and defensive postures over issues such as temperance, slavery and Sunday laws. The Seventh-day Adventist Church is a highly organized, militant organization with a global mission.

Ellen G White Comments on Military Service

Ellen G White lived in the 19th century during a time when there were many wars: Mexican War, Civil War, Indian Wars, Spanish-American War, wars in Europe and the beginning of World War I. Yet, she wrote very little about those events and had even less to say about military service and soldiering. Obviously, she opposed war. Typical of her views is the statement, "Satan delights in war, for it excites the worst passions of the soul and then sweeps into eternity its victims steeped in vice and blood. It is his object to incite the nations to war against one another, for he can thus divert the minds of people from the work of preparation to stand in the day of God."[2] Wars of conquest violate the Eighth Commandment.[3] "Satanic agencies have made the earth a stage for horrors, which no language can describe. War and bloodshed are carried on by nations claiming to be Christian. A disregard for the law of God has brought its sure result."[4]

On the other hand, her comments about soldiers and the military are quite favorable. She compares the Church of Christ to an army and Christians to soldiers.[5] Two statements are quite surprising: "Freedom of choice is given to every soul, but after a man has enlisted, he is required to be as true as steel, come life or come death;"[6] and speaking about angels, "Time and again have they been the leaders of armies."[7]

Being Northerners, early Adventists were Abolitionists—against slavery, even before the Civil War over slavery. When war came, some Adventists in Battle Creek proposed an armed regiment of Sabbath-keepers that would "strike this rebellion a staggering blow." Pioneer leaders studied the issues and concluded that the position most consistent with biblical principles was noncombatancy. Ellen White received visions about the conflict,[8] and wrote this admonition: "I was shown that God's people... cannot engage in this perplexing war, for it is opposed to every principle of their faith. In the army they cannot obey the truth and at the same time obey the requirements of their officers."[9] Yet, she does not condemn those Adventists who served in the military, including a conference president who enlisted to fight. Generally, Adventists attempted exemption from conscription by paying a commutation fee of $300, or by accepting assignment to hospital duty, or by caring for freedmen.

Later in her ministry, Ellen White intimates disapproval towards those who tried to escape the draft by inducing disease or maiming themselves "that they might be rendered unfit for service."[10] While working in Europe, she observed military drills, including training with cannon and rifles. When three workers in the Church press were summoned for three weeks of military drill, Mrs. White commends the men on their regimental ribbons and uniforms, but makes no remarks about their using weapons.

"Government calls do not accommodate themselves to our convenience. They demand that young men whom they have accepted as soldiers shall not neglect the exercise and drill essential for soldier service. We were glad to see that these men with their regimentals had tokens of honor for faithfulness in their work. They are trustworthy young men. They did not go from choice, but because the laws of their nation required this."[11]

While living at St Helena, California, Mrs White visited the Soldier's Home in Yountville and ministered to the residents there. She mentions Elder G A Irwin, General Conference President, also visiting and meeting "a soldier with whom he had many times stood side by side in battle."[12] In four letters about her visits she mentions the soldiers' service with admiration and gratitude. She does not condemn them or raise the issue of combatancy.

The Official Position

The Seventh-day Adventist Church officially organized during a tragic civil war that divided the United States of America (1861-1865). Early in their denominational formation Adventists were confronted with the dilemma of how to fulfill civic and faith relationships responsibly, especially when temporal and religious obligations were in apparent conflict. After much prayerful and thorough study, early Church leaders concluded that the best position to adopt was the principle of noncombatancy. This stance was officially registered with the United States federal government in 1864 and has remained the position of Seventh-day Adventists ever since.

Noncombatant service and training is defined as follows:

1. The term "noncombatant service" shall mean (a) service in any unit of the armed forces which is unarmed at all times; (b) service in the medical department of any of the armed forces, wherever performed; or (c) any other assignment of the primary function of which does not require the use of arms in combat; provided that such other assignment is acceptable to the individual concerned and does not require them to bear arms or to be trained in their use.

2. The term "noncombatant training" shall mean any training which is not concerned with the study, use, or handling of arms or weapons.

The official stand of the Church was reaffirmed by action taken at the 1972 Annual Council of the General Conference of Seventh-day Adventists held October 14–29 in Mexico City, Mexico:

"Genuine Christianity manifests itself in good citizenship and loyalty to civil government. The breaking out of war among men in no way alters the Christian's supreme allegiance and responsibility to God or modifies their obligation to practice their beliefs and put God first.

"This partnership with God through Jesus Christ who came into this world not to destroy men's lives but to save them causes Seventh-day Adventists to advocate a noncombatant position, following their divine Master in not taking human life, but rendering all possible service to save it. As they accept the obligation of citizenship as well as its benefits, their loyalty to government requires them willingly . to serve the state in any noncombatant capacity, civil or military, in war or peace, in uniform or out of it, which will contribute to saving life, asking only that they may serve in those capacities which do not violate their conscientious convictions."

This statement is not a rigid position binding Church members, but gives guidance leaving the individual member free to assess the situation for her or himself.

When national laws permit options, Church members, in making a personal decision on how to fulfill obligated terms of service to their country, should first consider the historic teaching of the Church on noncombatancy. If because of personal convictions they choose otherwise, pastors, chaplains, teachers or other church workers should aid the member in satisfying any legal requirements for securing their choice and should minister to the member's spiritual needs as follows:

a. For those choosing civilian alternative service in lieu of military service, pastoral counsel and guidance should be provided when it is established that such a request is based on consistent religious experience. Pastors, chaplains, teachers, or other church workers should provide statements of their personal knowledge of the member's position on the following: (1) church membership, (2) attendance and participation in services of the church, (3) personal standards of conduct, (4) previous expressions of belief supporting the request for exemption. Those providing such statements should request government officials to respect and honor the individual's personal convictions.

b. For those who conscientiously choose military service as a combatant, pastoral counsel and guidance should be provided in ministering to their needs since the Church refrains from passing judgment on them.

Notice that the Seventh-day Adventist Church advocates a noncombatant position, but does not require it. Thus, some church members are willing to train with and use weapons; while others cannot, because of their own individual conscience, have anything to do with weapons or military service. Historically, most Seventh-day Adventists have served as noncombatant medics for several reasons: (1) Such service minimizes Sabbath conflicts (saving and maintaining life is honorable on Sabbath), and (2) Such service is more in harmony with the Church's stated recommendation.

The Seventh-day Adventist Church does not seek to be the conscience for any member or commander. But we do seek to inform the conscience and behavior of both, so decisions can be made with maximum understanding and thought.

A Timeline of Conscientious Objection and Noncombatancy within the Seventh-day Adventist Church

Since the beginnings of the Seventh-day Adventist Church, the denomination has been challenged with the issues of what members should do in time of war. Each member is admonished by Jesus to be a loyal citizen of their country ("Render therefore unto Caesar what is Caesar's...") and at the same time remain loyal to God ("and unto God what is God's"—Matt 22:21). Obviously, this can create tension for someone who also reads in the Ten Commandments, "Thou shalt not kill [murder]," and then faces a military requirement to train with a weapon.

The Adventist position has developed historically along these lines:

1843-1860 Beginnings of the movement. The early Adventists were New Englanders. From there they migrated to northern Midwest states. There were no members south of the Mason-Dixon Line. Most Adventists viewed slavery as morally wrong; some assisted in the Underground Railroad. The *Review and Herald* printed an article that advocated disobeying the fugitive slave law.

1860-63 The Adventist Church formally and legally organized in

North America.

1861-65 The Civil War: Some Adventists advocated fighting for the Union and freeing slaves; for example, forming a battalion of soldiers from Battle Creek. Adventists were not a "peace church." Conscription forced a response to the war: believers sought substitution or paid the commutation fee of $300.

1862 James White's editorial in the *Review*, "The Nation," says, "The fourth precept of that law says 'Remember the Sabbath to keep it holy;' the sixth says 'Thou shalt not kill.' But in the case of drafting the government assumes the responsibility of the violation of law of God, and it would be madness to resist."[13]

1864 Adventist leaders appealed successfully to the Governor of Michigan and received recognition as being conscientiously opposed to the bearing of arms. Similar letters to the governors of Wisconsin, Illinois and Pennsylvania were sent and received with approval.

1886 Ellen G White, while visiting Switzerland, commended several men who must do their military time in the Swiss Army. While she commented on their regimental ribbons and uniforms, she made no remarks about use of weapons.[14]

1914-18 World War I split the denomination in Europe. German church leaders advocated cooperation with the government in military service, leading to the formation of the Reform Seventh-day Adventist Church.

1918 President Woodrow Wilson issued an executive order allowing for religious conscientious objectors to serve in the U S military.

1934 Dr Everett Dick began medical military training for young men at Union College in Lincoln, Nebraska. The unit was called the Union College Medical Corps.

1936 Dr Cyril B Courville organized a similar unit known as the Medical Cadet Corps at the College of Medical Evangelists (now named Loma Linda University).

1939 The General Conference adopted a plan for training young men for military service. A Medical Cadet Corps Council was formed. The various college programs were united under the name, Seventh-day Adventist Medical Cadet Corps.

1941-45 World War II brought difficult conditions for Adventist draftees. Many served as non-combatant medics. One, Cpl Desmond T Doss, was awarded the Congressional Medal of Honor for bravery in saving the lives of more than 70 soldiers in Okinawa.

1950 Dr Everett Dick reactivated Medical Cadet Corps training at Union College one month before the North Korean invasion of South Korea.

1953 U S Army began Operation Whitecoat (1953-1973) in which nearly 2,500 Adventist young men volunteered as human subjects in preventive medicine studies.

1954 The Annual Council stated that the official position of the Church is noncombatant. The National Service Organization was implemented to work with Adventist military personnel.

1969 Annual Council (October 12) reaffirmed the statements of 1954, then went on to change the wording to "the Church advocates noncombatancy, but allows members to elect to be pacifists as well."

1972 Annual Council affirmed the statements of 1954 and 1969, but decided the question is a personal matter of conscience for each member. The denomination continued to encourage church members to consider the historical position of noncombatancy. It also recognized that some members may conscientiously choose to be combatants. The Church committed to providing pastoral care and religious support to members, regardless of their personal position.

1974 Conscription ended and manning of U S Armed Forces was solely from voluntary enlistments. Medical Cadet Corps programs quickly faded and ended. Appointment of National Service Organization secretaries from division down to local church level also rapidly stopped. For the next three decades military-related issues were seldom mentioned in school curriculums, Church literature or by youth departments.

1990 An estimated 15,000 Adventists served in the militaries engaged in the Persian Gulf Conflict. The "war" was over quickly and the denomination took little note of it.

2001 On September 11 terrorists attacked the United States killing nearly 3,000 persons and destroying the World Trade Center in New York City. The Global War on Terror followed, again with minimum response from the Church.

2006 Adventist Chaplaincy Ministries held a National Service Organization meeting to review Church response to military service and develop a strategy to raise awareness about military-related issues.

2007 Implementation of the ACM strategy for NSO began and continued during subsequent years.

Thus, it is seen that the first statements were modified from a pure combatant stance, when drafted into service, to a noncombatant position to a noncombatant recommendation without a Church requirement to be a noncombatant. Careful examination of the dates helps explain the changes. Initially, during the Civil War, the Adventist Church was struggling with many issues of identity and theology. There was some confusion and much discussion. The refined decision was to serve honorably in the military, but to do so as noncombatants.

That remained in place until 1969. What happened then? The United States was involved in Vietnam, and only those individuals who could show religious backing for their pacifism could be released to alternate duty. Since the Adventist Church's stance was noncombatancy (serving without weapons), any Adventist drafted who claimed to be a pacifist was denied that status because the stance was at variance with the Church's stated policy. Hence, the 1969 change recognized the choice of pacifism, while still encouraging members to serve as noncombatants. When members are allowed to select how they will serve, they may also elect to serve as combatants, although that is not the recommended type of service.

This remains the Church's stance today. The Seventh-day Adventist Church advocates noncombatancy for members who serve in the military, but accepts those who elect to serve in other capacities or not to serve at all—according to the conscience of the individual member. The Church ceased being the conscience of the individual and began a process of informing the individual in order for him/her to make individual decisions for which they are personally responsible.

During the initial stages of Church organization most Adventists lived in the Northern part of the United States. Today, nearly 20 million members live in 200 countries around the globe. Some nations do not provide options for military service or noncombatancy; hence, it would be impossible for the Church to mandate that members in those countries serve in that capacity. Thus, the current recommendation (not requirement) for noncombatant service is the most viable.

U S public law, the Geneva Convention, and military regulations designate chaplains and physicians as noncombatants. Military chaplains are prohibited from carrying or using weapons. If they elect to do so, medical personnel may carry weapons to protect their patients. Many medics have served without bearing or using weapons. Corporal Desmond T Doss, a noncombatant medic in the U S Army, was awarded the Congressional Medal of Honor (the highest USA military medal of valor) for saving more than 70 lives under enemy fire in the battle for the Maeda Escarpment on the Pacific island of Okinawa in 1945. Since World War II, several other noncombatant medics have been awarded high medals for valorous acts of bravery to save life during conflicts.

Adventist Chaplaincy Ministries

Membership in the Seventh-day Adventist Church is growing rapidly, but success brings its own challenges. The vast majority of members are converts, or "first generation" Church members. They may have sufficient doctrinal understanding to join the faith, but many lack any appreciation for the Adventist heritage, lifestyle and practical nuances of membership. Even in North America, the majority of new believers have never heard of Corporal Desmond T Doss or been told the official Church position on military service. A small group of second and third generation military families also exists within Adventist circles. They are a subset of the greater military subculture in the United States. To further complicate matters, since the cessation of the Vietnam Conflict and termination of conscription in the United States (1973), the Adventist Church benignly neglected to address the issues of military service or instruct young adult members about noncombatancy in our Church journals, educational curriculums or Sabbath Schools. Medical Cadet Corps training disappeared, mostly from lack of interest. Conference leaders and Church educators wrongfully assumed Adventists would not voluntarily enlist in the military services.

The General Conference Adventist Chaplaincy Ministries Department launched a thorough review of their programs in 2006 that led to transformation of strategic direction, emphasis and policies. The assessment revealed several startling discoveries:

1. For a variety of valid reasons, Adventists voluntarily enlist in military service. Perhaps Pathfinders with uniforms, badges, ribbons, marching, drills, flags, etc, instill an appreciation for discipline and militaristic organization. Could Church youth programs actually influence joining and feeling comfortable in the military? This trend of voluntary enlistment is not limited to North America or the USA as is commonly supposed. (Best estimates of the numbers of Adventists serving in U S Armed Forces hover around three-tenths of one percent of the total military strength, or between 6,000 to 7,500 men and women.) Adventists proudly serve in the militaries of their homelands around the world, even if some church leaders refuse to acknowledge their presence and provide pastoral care.

2. Virtually all Adventists in military service of all nations, except for chaplains, are combatants. (As of 2011, the Department of Defense affirmed that enlisting as a noncombatant (1-A-O) was no longer permitted. The U S Government Accountability Office reported 425 applications for conscientious objector status (21 for 1-A-O noncombatant classification) out of a total force of 2.3 million service members in the U S Armed Forces during the years 2002 thru 2006. None of the 1-A-O applicants were known to be Adventists. Slightly over half of the applications (224) were approved; only 10 of 21 applications for 1-A-O classification were approved. Processing time averaged 200 days. (The GAO report cited is dated November 2007; later statistics have not been readily available).

3. During initial basic entry training, accommodation for Sabbath observance is highly improbable and rarely granted. Once

personnel settle into military duties, obtaining accommodation for religious practices is less difficult—depending on the laws of the nation and regulations of the military force. The U S Congress passed a public law in 1984 mandating the Department of Defense to develop directives for accommodating religious practices (including diet and Sabbath observance).[15]

4. The composition of military forces changed. Most nations rely on conscripts. Only 55 nations have ended involuntary conscription. Over half of volunteers are married or marry while serving in the military. Two-thirds of U S Armed Forces personnel are married. Females make up 14 percent of U S active duty military forces. Nearly 30 nations permit females to serve in their militaries.

5. On March 8, 2011, the Military Leadership Diversity Commission released a report on the inclusion of women in combat-arms units. As the country continues moving towards permitting females to enlist and serve in the armor, artillery and infantry, more than likely pressure for drafting females would also increase if conscription were reinstated. What kind of impact would drafting young women have on the national psyche, on any denominational response, and upon young women who would be facing potential conscription and placement in a combat unit?

Adventist Chaplaincy Ministries and the National Service Organization

These trends changed how the official military liaison office of the Seventh-day Adventist Church, the National Service Organization (NSO), serves Church members in military service. The North American Division once sponsored NSO Centers for military members as places of "refuge" and fellowship over Sabbath. When the Cold War ended, the U S Armed Forces reduced personnel nearly 40 percent, and Congress mandated Base Realignment and Closures in 1988 and 2002. As a result, the NSO Centers were underutilized and increasingly costly to maintain. In 2008 the last one was closed and the property sold. Funds were redirected to support twenty-five[16] overseas Adventist Military Chapel Worship Groups with Sabbath School supplies, worship items and outreach materials. In accordance with the official position of the Church on military service, Adventist Chaplaincy Ministries continues to provide pastoral care and religious support to all known military-related Church members.

It is estimated that about 1,200 Adventists serve in chaplaincy roles in various countries. Most are in educational and healthcare settings, while some serve in military and prison situations.

In North America 25 chaplains serve in campus ministry, more than 40 in community ministry, 30 in corrections, nearly 300 in healthcare, and 115 in military. Currently more than 125 applications are in process.

Adventist Chaplaincy Ministry (ACM) is the official ecclesiastical endorsing agency of the Seventh-day Adventist Church in each division for clergy called to serve as chaplains. ACM serves each division as the official military relations office and coordinates the work of the National Service Organization. It raises awareness of military-related issues, provides for the spiritual wellbeing of church members who serve in military-related situations, and cares for Adventist veterans.

Conclusion

Although SDAs officially advocate a non-combatant role in military service, this has never been a requirement for membership. From the earliest days of the movement, when the Civil War forced Adventists to face the issue, the decision has been left with the individual. Many Adventists have served their country without carrying a weapon, but some have felt clear in conscience to bear arms. Still others have adopted a pacifist position. The Church today, spread over more than 200 countries, embraces members in all three types of response and provides spiritual support through its network of chaplains.

ENDNOTES

[1] Armageddon means "the mountain of Megiddo." Most scholars believe this battle is the final spiritual conflict, but that does not exclude an actual physical battle.

[2] Ellen G White, *The Great Controversy*, 589.

[3] White, *Patriarchs and Prophets*, 309.

[4] White, *SDA Bible Commentary*, vol 7, 974.

[5] White, *Testimonies for the Church*, vol 5, 394; vol 9, 116.

[6] White, *Evangelism*, 647.

[7] White, *Sons and Daughters of God*, 37.

[8] See White, *Testimonies*, vol 1, chapters 53-55, 69.

[9] White, *Testimonies*, vol 1, 361.

[10] White, *Testimonies*, vol 5, 458.

[11] White, *Selected Messages*, vol 2, 335.

[12] White, Letter 1903.

[13] *Review and Herald*, August 2, 1862, vol 20, 84.

[14] White, Letter 23, 1886.

[15] See Department of Defense Instructions 1300.17, dated February 10, 2009.

[16] The number varies with the military mission and numbers of Adventists assigned overseas.

Anabaptist Understandings of Peace, Non-violence, and Separation of Church and State

Thomas R Yoder Neufeld

Introduction

L ike Adventists, Mennonites emerged out of a movement that began in a serious attempt to recover the integrity of life of the New Testament churches.[1] Central to that was the insight that to be "Christian" is to follow Jesus, not least with respect to non-retaliation and peacemaking. Both practice and understandings have shifted in the years since those beginnings. This is to be expected, given that what was once a highly diverse European renewal movement in the 16[2] century[2] has become an even more diverse global communion of churches facing a wide variety of challenges and opportunities in the 21st century. It is important to identify the roots of Anabaptist understandings of peace before identifying characteristics of our present understanding(s). The best way to do this is for me to tell our story with respect to peace and non-violence, acknowledging that others might well tell it somewhat differently. I will rehearse the main features by identifying a number of "chapters," concluding with a brief discussion of present challenges.

Chapter 1

Historical, Theological, Ethical, and Biblical Foundations

While scholars will differ on the full complexity of factors that led to the emergence of what came to be called Anabaptism in the 16th century, several factors stand out:

1. Biblical authority (*sola scriptura* radically understood) was a conviction learned from the leaders of the Reformation, but taken in a more radical direction as it pertained to both the understanding of church as made up of those who have been baptized on confession of faith, and who have committed themselves to follow Jesus in life, not least with respect to willingness to suffer at the hand of enemies.

2. Biblical authority was thus wedded to a resolute insistence not only on confessing and believing, but on doing. Today Mennonites sometimes talk about this as "orthopraxy" over "orthodoxy." For Anabaptists this meant that scriptural authority was seen to require "*Nachfolge*" ("following after"), which English-speaking Mennonites today typically call "discipleship."[3] For example, Jesus prohibited retaliation and defense, therefore His followers are to refuse to retaliate or defend themselves. Jesus commanded the love of enemies, and intended His followers to do so.

3. Whereas Anabaptists were accused of breaking apart the unity of Christendom with their stance on baptism and their refusal to take the oath, this stance was not a rejection of community but

rather a clear commitment to live discipleship *in community*, with the community of consequence being not the whole of society but the body of Christ. This community is constituted of believers who have experienced regeneration and have been baptized on the basis of that faith, with full knowledge of the costliness of that decision. The church is to be a fitting bride for her husband, Christ, and that means making sure the church is faithful.

It is clear that this is an ideal rather than a full and fair description of early Anabaptists. Anabaptists held to this set of ideals in diverse ways, with diverse theologies, eschatologies, and hermeneutics—and with varying success. But it was this insight and vision that brought the tradition into being, one that was to prove enormously costly in the early decades.

While historians are careful not to oversimplify or to homogenize the views of early Anabaptists,[4] one very influential stream of thought and discipline on what "Anabaptist" has come to mean is represented by the so-called *Schleitheim Confession*. This was less a creed than an agreed-upon statement of the South German and Swiss "Brethren," gathered in the town of Schleitheim in 1527, led by the former Benedictine prior, Michael Sattler. It is called the *Brotherly Union (or Agreement) of a number of children of God concerning Seven Articles*. Relevant to our topic are Articles 4 and 6, the first concerning "separation," the second "the sword."[5]

Article IV. Regarding Separation

"To us then, the commandment of the Lord is also obvious, whereby He orders us to be and to become separated from the evil one, and thus He will be our God and we shall be His sons and daughters" [2 Cor 6:17].

"Further, He admonishes us therefore to go out from Babylon and from the earthly Egypt, that we may not be partakers in their torment and suffering, which the Lord will bring upon them" [Rev 18:4]....

"Thereby shall also fall away from us the diabolical weapons of violence—such as sword, armor, and the like, and all of their use to protect friends or against enemies—by virtue of the word of Christ: 'you shall not resist evil'" [Matt 5:38].

Article VI. Concerning the Sword
"The sword is an ordering of God *outside the perfection of Christ*. It punishes and kills the wicked and guards and protects the good. In the law the sword is established over the wicked for punishment and for death and the secular rulers are established to wield the same" [Rom 13:1-7].

"But *within the perfection of Christ* only the ban is used for the admonition and exclusion of the one who has sinned, without the death of the flesh, simply the warning and the command to sin no more" [John 8:11; *emphasis added*].

We note several features:

1.   There is a clear church/world distinction (often referred to as "two kingdoms"). Separation from the world means "going out from Babylon and the earthly Egypt" which are under the judgment of God, not least because of the use of "diabolical weapons of violence."

2.   Fundamental is recognition of the authority of Scripture, including Romans 13, with respect to the role of the state within God's "ordering" of the fallen world.

3.   What must be expected of the church ("within the perfection of Christ") cannot be expected of the state ("outside the perfection of Christ"), which is part of the unregenerate world, albeit under the lordship of God.

4.   Rejection of the sword thus means rejection of church participation in the affairs of an evil world in which magistrates must act in ways not fitting for those who are "in Christ."

5.   Faithfulness to Christ is inevitably tied to suffering, given the unregenerate nature of the world and Jesus' own fate at its hands.

Jesus' teaching, in particular as gathered by Matthew in the Sermon on the Mount, played a significant role for Anabaptists. But they did not see this ethic simply as obedience to commands, but understood it to emerge from regeneration, from the work and fruit of the Spirit. Pauline texts figure prominently, notably Romans 12 and 13.

What then of the state? Romans 13:1-7 is key in the Schleitheim statement, as it is in other Anabaptist writings. Anabaptists were not particularly positive in their anthropology. They believed that no one can take up the cross without being drawn by the Spirit and divinely given the wherewithal to do so. The refusal to take up arms was thus not a philosophical stance so much as a clear implication of being part of a regenerate, vulnerable, and suffering body of the risen Christ. The world, in contrast, those (still) "outside the perfection of Christ" are under the sway of the devil. God is sovereign over the whole world, including the nations. God sees to it that there are authorities that reward good and punish evil. But such work remains "outside the *perfection* of Christ," and thus not part of the "order" which the church inhabits. The church's calling as the body of Christ is to participate in the suffering of Christ, and only in that way to participate in Christ's sovereignty. In short, Christians are called to be a faithful and suffering remnant. "Defenselessness" (*Wehrlosigkeit*) rather than "nonresistance" best captures the stance of these early Anabaptists.

Schleitheim reflects one important statement of Anabaptist belief and practice. But it was not the only one. It has been criticized as tending toward an obedience ethic, vulnerable to legalism. As Arnold Snyder has shown, other Anabaptists, rooted in more mystical traditions of identification with Christ (e.g., Hans Denck, Pilgram Marpeck) stressed participating in the love, patience, and suffering of Christ as a witness in the world, and thus "overcoming" evil, à la Romans 12. "Loving resistance" might better capture their approach than "nonresistance."[6]

Further, scholars such as James Stayer[7] have raised questions as to how consistent and widespread the anti-sword stance was for early Anabaptists. In the early years, especially among those heavily influenced by the Peasants' Revolt or by a very high degree of eschatological expectancy, some Anabaptists were quite open to the violence of the sword. Eschatological, even apocalyptic, expectancy did not set them apart from others, including reformers like Luther.[8] But some took it in a direction that led to calamitous violence, as, famously, in the city of Münster. Bernhard Rothman, influenced by Melchior Hoffman and Jan Matthijs, identified Jan van Leiden as the "second David" whose task it was to wield the sword in preparation for the coming Prince of Peace in a war of vengeance against Babylon, an enterprise Rothman called the "restitution." This Anabaptist "kingdom" was brutally crushed. In response to this catastrophe, Menno Simons, a former parish priest, organized the Anabaptist groups and reoriented them to a reading of the Bible in which nonresistance was to mark the life of the faithful. Their sole "weapon" was to be the Word of God. At the same time, Menno had a sense that Romans 13 seemed to allow for the possibility of rulers being true Christians, even if only in rare circumstances, given the nature of the two kingdoms. He certainly criticized rulers heavily for going against their God-given responsibility to reward good and punish evil, not the other way around. We must keep in mind that Menno's world was not one marked by democratic participation of the citizenry, and he and his fellow Anabaptists did not face the kinds of questions a democratic context raises for Christian citizens today.

By the middle of the 16th century the refusal to bear the sword, whether in state-sanctioned violence or in self-defense, won the day among Anabaptists. This ethos prevailed for centuries, and remains alive to this day wherever the church is experiencing great stress and suffering, perhaps nowhere more powerfully than in those Anabaptist communities sometimes suffering persecution (Zimbabwe, Ethiopia, India). It was on full display in the murder of Amish school children on October 3, 2006, in Nickel Mines, PA.[9] The Amish (close cousins of the Mennonites) response of forgiveness baffled a worldwide audience. Their explanation was simple: "Jesus tells us to forgive." The Amish recite the Lord's Prayer daily ("Forgive us as we have forgiven those who trespass against us"), and rehearse Jesus' teaching on forgiveness in Matthew 18 at communion time. Forgiveness and non-retaliation are for the Amish nothing other than a communal reflex inculcated by prayer and worship. In a telling evocation of the theme of suffering as witness, Amos Ibersol, the father of one of the children, stated: "This is how God puts His word into the world."

Chapter 2

Migration, Marginalization, and Adaptation

This chapter deals with developments in the following centuries. I will only briefly identify a few features relevant to our topic.

Hostility toward Anabaptists, including persecution and outright martyrdom, had its effect on the movement. As is typical of movements generally, there was a certain sifting of beliefs and practices, and a variety of survival strategies. Refusal to bear the sword came to characterize the movement as a whole, as stated earlier. "Defenselessness" (*Wehrlosigkeit*) of a suffering marginal remnant under often intense persecution came to characterize the experience and the self-perception of many Anabaptists. This is illustrated by Thieleman J van Braght's famous *Martyr's Mirror*, published in 1660 in Dutch. The full title of this martyrology is *The Bloody Theater or Martyrs Mirror of the Defenseless Christians*.[10] For many Mennonites and Amish it was for centuries second only to the Bible in importance.

Sometimes explicit arrangements were sought with governments to permit exemption from participation in the military. When such permission was not given or it was rescinded, Mennonites often migrated (e.g., from Switzerland and the Palatinate to Pennsylvania and to Canada, and from the Netherlands to Prussia and then South Russia [Ukraine], and from there to the US and Canada). While success in agriculture, engineering, and trade led many Mennonites to accommodate to prevailing culture, the ethos of non-participation in the world continued to leave its mark, most especially on efforts to find ways of not being drawn into military service. Sometimes this was accomplished through repeated migration, other times through payment of fees, alternative noncombatant service, and very occasionally imprisonment for refusal to participate in the military.

What does not characterize this chapter is a strong sense of a call to *active* peacemaking. More typical was *Absonderung*, or separation as an attempt to remain unstained by the world (however unsuccessful that has repeatedly proven to be). The well-known phrase, *die Stillen im Lande*, (the quiet in the land) captures this stance well.

We should add here that the clear distinction between "us" and "them," between Mennonites and an evil and sinful world, has lead at times to a view in which "for them" a harsh and heavy hand is needed. Mennonites have thus often supported strong policing and often a strong military, invoking Romans 13:1-7 as biblical and theological cover. Anticipating later "chapters," this has carried over into the present era as many Mennonites have voted on the conservative end of the political spectrum. What must be expected of the church not only cannot but *must not* be expected of the world.

Chapter 3

Missionary Movement and Global Expansion

The Mennonite community today is not what it was a century ago. Despite having developed a strong ethnic identity as a consequence of migration, non-conformity, and isolation, Mennonites began to be engaged in missionary work roughly at the beginning of the 20th century. As a consequence, today the majority of the worldwide Mennonite community, including the Brethren in Christ, is no longer of European descent. To illustrate, in 1900 there were an estimated 250,000 Mennonites, 98% of them in Europe and North America. Today the number was estimated at 1.6 million, with 60% of Mennonites and Brethren in Christ living in the Global South.[11]

The relevant point related to this chapter of the peace story is that in the interests of evangelism and church planting, the "peace position," as the refusal to bear arms was often called, was typically toned down as one of those distinctives (along with cultural peculiarities) that should not be allowed to stand in the way of the gospel. Within the contexts of missionary work, nonresistance and refusal to bear arms were often not identified as being at the very core of true faithfulness, but rather as of secondary importance, or as a hoped-for but not explicitly demanded consequence of true conversion. This was aided by the fact that Mennonites worked alongside missionaries from main-line and evangelical traditions who did not share the "peace position." Moreover, in many or most places of Mennonite missionary work governments made no provision for conscientious objection; and any highlighting of such an ethic would in many contexts have led to a severe response on the part of both society and government. This muting of the peace dimension of the gospel would in the present era come under considerable criticism from Mennonites in the Global South who have felt they were not given the whole gospel.

Meanwhile, in Europe the Anabaptist communities either withdrew as much as possible or did not resist the demands of the state, most particularly in the World Wars of the 20th century. While some sense of historical tradition regarding the bearing of arms remained (*"Wir haben immer nur in die Luft geschossen"* [we always only shot into the air], one German Mennonite church elder told the youth at a gathering at which I was present), for the most part this sometimes dim memory did not lead to resistance, let alone suffering because of such refusal. Few European Mennonites went to jail for principled refusal to bear arms. Noncooperation was not a major part of European Mennonite culture.[12]

In South Russia (now Ukraine), where Mennonites had migrated because of increased militarization in Prussia (now Poland), Mennonites became medics during World War I, or were given permission to work in the forests. During the worst years of the Revolution and immediately after, some desperate Mennonites organized themselves into what was called *"Selbstschutz"* (self-defense militias)[13], an initiative that was and remains highly controversial, both because it contravened the long tradition of not bearing arms, but also because it likely provoked greater violence against the communities.

In North America, during World War I there was no provision for conscientious objectors, and some Mennonites, Hutterites, and Amish went to prison. In World War II provision was made by the governments of Canada and the United States for work in camps, mental institutions, etc (about 150 camps in US, and 12,000 COs). In Canada there were fewer conscientious objectors, given the smaller size of the population. Following are some Canadian statistics gathered by John A Toews for four Mobilization Districts (Toronto, Winnipeg, Regina, and Edmonton) that serve to illustrate the numerical distribution of conscientious objectors in the various confessional communities.[14]

Mennonites	4425	Hutterites	482
Doukhobors	406	Jehovah's Witnesses	172
Tunkers	79	Christadelphians	72
Seventh-day Adventists	58	United Church	47
Brethren	34	Plymouth Brethren	28
Pentecostal	18	Evangelical	11
Society of Friends	8	Church of Christ	7
Anglican	4	Baptist	3
Roman Catholic	1	Salvation Army	1
Christ Disciples	1	Presbyterian	1
Christian Science	1	Megiddo mission	1
Pacifist	1	No religion specified	297
Total 6158			

Overall, however, roughly half of eligible young Mennonite men went into the services of the United States and Canada.[15]

Chapter 4

Rediscovery of the Anabaptist Vision

Emerging out of this experience of the World Wars was a growing sense among Mennonite leaders of a need to reawaken an awareness of Anabaptist roots, in particular of what it means to be faithful to Christ with respect to nonconformity to the world, peacemaking, and the bearing of arms. I mention here only a few of the persons who played a pivotal role.

Harold S Bender

The historian and church leader Harold Bender looms large in recent Mennonite history and institutional life. Apart from serving for many years as president of Goshen College and Seminary, he was president of Mennonite World Conference from 1952-62. In 1943 he gave the presidential address to the American Society of Church History, entitled "The Anabaptist Vision."[16] It proved to be a watershed event, not only in the way non-Mennonite historians would come to view Anabaptists, but for Mennonites as well. Bender identified three characteristics of the Anabaptist vision: (1) discipleship, (2) newness of life within the context of the church, (3) love and nonresistance. I quote from the last paragraph of his influential statement which echoes some of what we saw in the Schleitheim statement:

"The Anabaptist vision was not a detailed blueprint for the reconstruction of human society, but the Brethren did believe that Jesus intended that the kingdom of God should be set up in the midst of earth, here and now, and this they proposed to do forthwith. We shall not believe, they said, that the Sermon on the Mount or any other vision that He had is only a heavenly vision meant but to keep His followers in tension until the last great day, but we shall practice what He taught, believing that where He walked we can by His grace follow in His steps."

Bender argued thus for difference and at the same time for renewed engagement, but *as church*. More, he argued that full living out of the teachings of Jesus should not be deferred to the future, but to the here and now. Eschatology should not be allowed to undermine the present mission of the church.

At the same time, while placing love and nonresistance at the center of an Anabaptist understanding of faithful Christian living, there was real squeamishness about identifying the Mennonite "peace position" as "pacifism." Pacifism was deemed to be premised on too optimistic an anthropology, and at the same time prone to being drawn into what were perceived to be the force-filled and violence-inviting civil rights efforts of Gandhi and King, for example. This was addressed directly by Bender's influential colleague at Goshen College, Guy F Hershberger, in his *War, Peace, and Nonresistance* [1944].

As important as Bender and Hershberger were, it was the young scholars Bender directed into graduate studies who would continue to play a formative role in shaping what Anabaptism has come to mean with respect to the prominence given to peace and peacemaking. Most notable among Bender's protégés was John Howard Yoder.

John Howard Yoder

Simultaneously a church historian, biblical scholar, and ethicist, Yoder's writings have dominated the discourse among Anabaptists for decades, most especially in relation to the whole set of issues surrounding peace, though by no means exclusively so. His work is a mix of historical retrieval of roots in the Anabaptist origins of the 16th century, with focus on ecclesiology, discipleship, and the refusal to bear arms, and, because of the ongoing role of the Bible, a new look in particular at Jesus' teachings and its impact on the apostolic writings of the New Testament.

Yoder's most widely read book is the *Politics of Jesus* (first published by Eerdmans in 1972), which turns out to be less a study of any particular teaching of Jesus than a reading of the New Testament as a whole (including the letters of Paul and Revelation) as demanding of the church a "politics" informed by and conformed to the teaching and work of Christ.

Non-retaliation and love of enemies of course inform such a politics. In an influential take on Romans 13 Yoder attempted to make a distinction between subordination and obedience. God is Lord of the whole world, "ordering" the nations even when they are in rebellion to God's will as shown in Christ. Like Jesus, the body of Christ is subordinate to these powers, but obedient only when it does not contravene the will of God in Christ. "Subordination" means willingness to bear the consequences when disobedience to the powers is called for, in the confidence that the way of the cross is the form of Christ's lordship within an as yet unredeemed world.[17]

Yoder was always committed to taking the discussion into the wider church, engaging both Evangelicals and the wider ecumenical traditions, and from there his own Mennonite community. He did more than any one individual to provide a sense of identity for Anabaptists, as well as foster the discourse around peace and peacemaking in the wider church, and indeed in the wider society.

From 1955 to 1962 Yoder and other Anabaptists and members of the Historic Peace Churches participated in an ongoing dialogue with representatives of Lutheran and Reformed churches in Europe in the Swiss village of Puidoux, Switzerland. These dialogues were devoted to the theme "The Lordship of Christ over Church and State." From this came a small but important booklet by Yoder, entitled, *The Christian Witness to the State*, published in 1964. Yoder argued that the life of the church is in the world, pushing the world and its institutions in the direction of the kingdom of God. He employed the notion of "middle axioms," intending thereby to point to values present in persons and institutions in "the world" that the church can appeal to in order to nudge it in the direction of God's intentions for humanity as incarnated and taught by Jesus. But in order to be "out there" and engaged in such a task, the church needs to know who it is, and especially who its Lord is. The church needs to be a discipling, disciplined, and disciplining community of disciples, so as to aid those who are engaged in the various contexts of life to remember and to discern what it means to be faithful to Christ's call. In effect, Yoder challenged main line traditions, churches very much at home "in the world," to learn to be "not of it." As importantly, he challenged Mennonites who had often tried to get out of the world in order to be "not of it," to be "in it" even as they persist in doing their best to be not "of it."

In the last years of Yoder's life, which ended suddenly in 1997, Jeremiah's letter to the exiles in Babylon in Jeremiah 29 played an increasingly determinative role in Yoder's thought and writing. In that letter God promises the exiles a "future with hope" (Jer 29:11), and enjoins them in the meantime to seek the *shalom* (usually translated too restrictively as "welfare") of the city to which they have been exiled, for "in its *shalom* will be your *shalom*" (29:7). Yoder took from this a model for the church and its calling. The church is not at home in the world, but in exile. Its normal state is *diasporic*. But while in exile the church is to seek that city's *shalom*—its peace, its welfare.[18]

Such work and witness will meet resistance, and calls for resistance from the church in turn. Yoder made the "powers" an important aspect of his view of the context of the church's life and mission. Rather than seeing these as personal demonic realities, Yoder saw them as the structures and institutions ("-isms" and "-ologies"[19]). They have been divinely created (Col 1:15-20), but they are in rebellion to God (Eph 6:12), and thus now part of a fallen creation. They thus call forth the critical and hopeful witness of the church. Relevant here is that one of these "-isms" is militarism, and one of the "-ologies" is the ideology that military might brings security.

This perspective has had an enormous impact on Mennonites and Anabaptists generally, signifying nothing less than a sea change in disposition: peace*making*, and more recently peace-*building*, not only staying away from conflict; fusing peace with justice, understood as active engagement to make things right, even if that brings conflict (resistance rather than nonresistance); witnessing *in* the world rather than fleeing it. Work not only *in* but *for* the "city" (of exile) is cast in a positive light. Peacemaking has become central to the mission of the church.

To summarize characteristic emphases in Yoder's thought in relation to our topic:

1.   Peacemaking is rooted in discipleship and is core to the church's mission.

2.   The church is a community of disciples, and discipleship means following Jesus (something Yoder read not only in the gospels, but in the whole of the New Testament, as his *Politics* illustrates, a point many of his followers have forgotten, but one entirely in keeping with the wellsprings of Anabaptism).

3.   The church is engaged in a struggle with the "powers," which are to be taken as both fallen and at the same time as part of God's good creation in Christ. The church's mission is thus both confrontative and transformative.

4.   The church must be true to itself as the "body of Christ" while pushing the world as far as it allows itself to be pushed in the direction of the "kingdom." Yoder did not wish to minimize the distinction between church and world, but, in keeping with "seeking the *shalom* of the city" the church is to seek opportunities to nudge the world in the direction of God's will.

5.   The church is not hostile to the world, even as it resists the "powers," nor does it write off the world as evil, but sees Jesus as the incarnation of the will of God for the whole world he loves and

wishes to save.

It is impossible to discuss present day Anabaptist practice and thought with respect to peacemaking, nonviolence, and the church's calling, without taking Yoder's formative influence into account. He thus represents an important bridge figure to the last chapter of this story, bringing us to the present day.

Chapter 5

Activist Peacemaking

Yoder and others like him awakened Mennonites, and indeed the wider church, to the importance of peace and peacemaking. By linking "peace with God" to the practicalities of peacemaking in the world, peacemaking moves to the center of the gospel and the mission of the church. When we place this shift of emphasis within a wider cultural and sociological context, we note shifts from homogeneous rural life to a context of urbanization, education, ethnic diversification, acculturation, and openness to both Evangelical and ecumenical church influences, whether in North America, Europe, or globally. In short, Yoder's biblical and theological stress came at the same time that Mennonites were opening the windows to the world.

All this might suggest that Mennonites, even within the North American context, are all in agreement on this shift from nonresistance to activist peacemaking. That is far from the case. Many Mennonites are dubious about how realistic pacifism is and prefer to hold to a nonresistant position for themselves, while supporting a strong police and military stance of their governments, as stated earlier. Others have abandoned any kind of a peace position, even if rather quietly, since their views do not enjoy official space within Mennonite institutional life.[20] That said, among those who publically carry the discourse around peace issues, Anabaptists have come to a shared understanding that Jesus' call to love is more than saying no to participation in the military or to self-defense and yes to relief for those in need. Peacemaking means positive engagement, active reaching out, and working to overcome hostilities and to address the roots of hostility, injustice, and hatred. In recent decades there have thus been concerted efforts to develop strategies to overcome conflict, to transform situations of hostility. Mennonite Central Committee, for example, which began as a relief effort in the 1920's for fellow Mennonites starving in the Soviet Union, has widened its mandate to active work for justice and peace. Within North America, Mennonites have peace study programs at both undergraduate and graduate levels.[21] "Peace" has become a major teaching emphasis in Anabaptist settings globally.

By placing the life of the church in the world, with the mission to seek its *shalom* (Jeremiah 29), the ground has been prepared for a new way of seeing the work of peacemaking. Yoder spoke of "experimental plots,"[22] the fruits of which can then be shared with the wider society, as has happened in areas of peacemaking, justice, and ecology. Mennonites have thus developed prison and justice ministries around a paradigm called "restorative justice." Here I note especially the widely read work of restorative justice pioneer Howard Zehr, *Changing Lenses: A New Focus for Crime and Justice* (Christian Peace Shelf; Herald Press, 1990), and the scholarly and practical contributions of John Paul Lederach, now teaching at Notre Dame University.

Anabaptist communities in the global South have been waking up to this emphasis, first asking why it was that Mennonite missionaries did not make peace a more critical part of their evangelism and teaching; and second, embracing practical peacemaking with a passion that is often lacking in Europe and North America. Let me list just a few of the specific efforts among the many beyond those initiated and supported by Mennonite Central Committee:

- Christian Peacemaker Teams active in, e.g., United States, Canada, West Bank, Colombia, Iraq
- JustaPaz in Colombia, notably through the pioneering work of Mennonite human rights lawyer Ricardo Esquivia
- Korea Anabaptist Center in Korea
- Mennonite Creation Care Network
- Mennonite impetus to the World Council of Churches' *Decade to Overcome Violence*[23]

Concluding Assessment: Promise and Peril

Today the word *Anabaptist* likely refers less to believers' baptism, a radical take on *sola scriptura*, a strong ecclesiology with an emphasis on church discipline, or to a strong sense of church/world dichotomy, than it does to placing ethics at the center of Christian life, with a particular emphasis on nonviolence and peacemaking. Adherence to "the way of Jesus," with a special (sometimes exclusive) focus on his teachings on forgiveness, non-retaliation, and love of enemies, is central to such an ethic. To illustrate, in places like the United Kingdom, deliberate efforts have been made not to establish Mennonite or Anabaptist churches so much as to insinuate Anabaptist understandings of discipleship and peacemaking leaven-like into the life of existing churches, whether Evangelical or mainstream.[24] In North America, radical Evangelical church leaders like Shane Claiborne and Gregory Boyd quite explicitly testify to their affinity with "Anabaptist" perspectives, in particular with an ethic opposed to militarism and nationalism.

That does not mean, of course, that peace is the only issue Mennonites care about. Admittedly, the stress on practical peacemaking has come for some to represent the core and the circumference of what the church is about, running the serious risk of reducing the gospel to pacifism. But much more importantly, great strides have been and are being made to forge a holistic understanding of the gospel, in which peace encompasses the relationship with God (Rom 5:1; 2 Cor 5:18) and that between people and peoples (Eph 2:11-22). For the church not to be a "peace church" is increasingly viewed as a contradiction in terms.

Peacemaking is thus a "shared conviction," as we say in the Mennonite World Conference. The fifth in the list of Shared Convictions reads: "The Spirit of Jesus empowers us to trust God in all areas of life so we become peacemakers who renounce violence, love our enemies, seek justice, and share our possessions with those in need."[25] This conviction is shared among the many churches gathered in the communion of the Mennonite World Conference, even if we differ among ourselves regarding implications with respect to the state, criminal justice, even central issues of theology such as atonement. Romans 13:1-7, and its various points of relevance, continues to vie with the Sermon on the Mount.

Transitions

The Anabaptists of the 16th century are not the Anabaptists of the 21st century. Let me briefly identify a few of the transitions that have impacted how we are addressing the call to be peacemakers today. Some are positive, representing a movement toward greater faithfulness to the call of Christ; others carry within them serious challenges to faithfulness.

rural	→	urban
Euro-centric	→	Global
separation	→	engagement
nonconformity	→	conformity
church vs world	→	church in world
nonresistance	→	resistance
defenselessness	→	nonviolence
quietism	→	activism
passivism	→	pacifism

Promise and Peril

Given the shifts and transitions identified above, we should not be surprised that today Anabaptists see the church very much "in" the world, rather than separate from it. Many if not most of us are impatient with sectarianism, with turning our back to the world. We no longer wish to be the *Stillen im Lande* (quiet in the land), even if we do not agree on what we should be noisy about. Mennonites and Anabaptists generally are succeeding in often wholly unexpected ways in finding a hearing in wider society on matters of peace, non-violence, etc. There is much to be celebrated in this turning of our face toward the world. There is a great deal of room for witness, for experimenting, for modeling (recall Yoder's "experimental plots"). Without doubt this is a rich "harvest of justice" promised to those who "make peace" (James 3:18).

Such a disposition of openness and engagement, however, also carries great risks. First, when creative and risky initiatives are ac-companied by a loss of a sense of the difference between church and world, between what must be expected of the church and what cannot be demanded of a world that does not confess Christ, then such risk becomes perilous for us *as church.*

Second and relatedly, by placing peacemaking into a largely social and activist framework, and finding a hearing for such engagement among sectors that are not particularly Christian, or not particularly concerned to ground such a stance christologically and ecclesiologically, there is great danger of forgetting the biblical, christological, and soteriological tap root of peace, or to have already succumbed to such a loss of memory. Indeed, nonresistance, suffering, and being separate, are increasingly not only incomprehensible to contemporary Mennonites committed to peacemaking, but are seen as a betrayal of peace itself (e.g., the ongoing debate within Christian Peacemaker Teams as to whether the name "Christian" is too exclusive and thus discriminatory). The Anabaptist churches of the global south have rightly complained that they were not given the whole gospel when peace was downplayed. Are they again receiving a newly truncated gospel?

Third, those who tie their pacifism to a very optimistic anthropology find themselves speaking "kingdom" language as shorthand for a quite predictable political agenda. The big danger here is whether it will have the resilience to outlast the present moment. I might offer a cautionary example: liberal pacifism failed miserably against the realities of Hitler. Abandoning of commitment to pacifism was highest among those informed by an optimistic anthropology. Those who stuck with it had a rather simple commitment to obeying Jesus, a resolve honed by communal discipline and tradition.

Fourth, those in the Mennonite community with an orientation to outreach, mission, and evangelism are often alienated from the discourse surrounding peace, suspecting it of reflecting a social gospel premised on social betterment rather than conversion and regeneration in Christ. That said, many such Mennonites are often blind, as are Evangelicals generally, to their own captivity to a fusion of evangelical theology and practice with nationalism and militarism. Such a fusion is often not seen or acknowledged as political and as its own form of a social gospel, and thus not scrutinized as potentially a deep betrayal of the gospel.

In my view, our challenges today as Mennonites and Brethren in Christ with respect to the whole web of issues surrounding peace are two-fold: one lies in recovering why and how the Bible should matter in grounding our peacemaking. The Bible needs to do more than provide some illustrative proof-texts for those who still need that kind of thing. The second is much more important yet, namely, the need to draw from the center of the gospel the content and the practice of peace. The elements of such a biblically grounded gospel are:

- an enemy-loving God whose creative and inventive love was shown throughout the Bible, and most especially in the self-giving of Jesus to the point of his death on the cross (Rom 5);
- trust in God as Lord of history who calls the church to be the body of that most vulnerable and most victorious of Lords, who chose suffering as the means of reconciliation, all the while assuring the faithful that God is sovereign, that the right will prevail, that evil will be judged, even if in shockingly inventive ways (cross, suffering and deliberately vulnerable community; 1 Thessalonians 5[26]);
- nonresistance, but never as disengagement from the world, but rather as individual and communal participation in the often maddening, loving, and stubbornly persistent patience of God (2 Peter 3; Matt 5:43-48), one that looks scandalously like divine absence or moral irresponsibility;
- alongside such nonresistant patience also true resistance, the overcoming of (being victorious over) evil with good (Romans 12);[27]
- confidence in the certainty of the full coming of God's reign, the full manifestation of Christ, and that our efforts at vulnerable perhaps even suffering peacemaking are both the exercise of that hope and confidence, and in a mysterious way participate in that coming (1 Thess 5:1-11).

I can summarize the challenges Mennonites face with respect to peace as follows:

- Maintain (or recover?) deep biblical roots for peacemaking, rooted in "following Jesus."
- Maintain (or recover?) a spirituality that recognizes the need for "regeneration" for sacrificial peacemaking.[28]
- Maintain (or recover?) what it means to be church as the body of the peacemaking Christ in a world not yet at peace with God.
- Develop ever deeper wisdom on how to be "in" the world, participating in it, seeking its shalom, while remaining (or becoming?) not "of it," so as to bring about its transformation.

In short, the core issues of peace for Anabaptists as for all Christians have to do not in the first instance with a philosophy and practice of nonviolence, nor with a political and sociological critique of violence in its manifold manifestations, but first and foremost with:

- Christology: Who is Jesus Christ as Saviour, Lord, and thus model?
- Soteriology: What are we "saved" from and for?
- Eschatology: What is the nature of our hope? What role does peacemaking have in relation to the coming of God's reign?
- Ecclesiology: What is the identity and task of the church and its members as the Messiah's body resident in the world?
- Pneumatology: What does the Spirit wish to enliven and empower as the body of the Messiah lives out Jesus' own deliberate vulnerability as love for enemies?

To attempt to answer those questions will get us close to the Anabaptist core convictions that brought about the movement to begin with. It is also my contention that that is in the end the surest way we will both arrive at a solid peace stance, one that can withstand the passing of its present popularity and the potential for inviting suffering rather than (apparent) success. It is the way of Jesus as witnessed to in the New Testament.

ENDNOTES

[1] Endnotes will serve solely to point the reader to important, and in most cases, easily accessible resources, many now on the web. Of particular use is the *Global Anabaptist Mennonite Encyclopedia Online* (www.gameo.org), which contains articles, many recently updated, with further bibliography.

[2] For a good, brief, survey of Anabaptist beginnings, and articles on other issues raised in this presentation, see the article in the online version of the *Mennonite Encyclopedia* by, Harold S Bender, Robert Friedmann and Walter Klaassen, "Anabaptism," *Global Anabaptist Mennonite Encyclopedia Online*, 1990, Web, September 5, 2011. http://www.gameo.org/encyclopedia/contents/A533ME.html.

[3] In many Evangelical communities "discipleship" refers to teaching and mentoring new believers into Christian faith and practice. In Mennonite Anabaptist circles it connotes ethics more than teaching.

[4] C Arnold Snyder has shown the theological coherence despite the evident diversities among Anabaptists in his *Anabaptist History and Theology: an Introduction* (Kitchener, Ontario: Pandora Press, 1995). See also his succinct booklet prepared for the Mennonite World Conference, translated into many languages, entitled *From Anabaptist Seed* (Intercourse, Pennsylvania: Good Books, 2007), and *Following in the Footsteps of Christ: the Anabaptist Tradition*, Traditions in Christian Spirituality Series, (Maryknoll, New York: Orbis, 2004).

[5] Translated and edited by John Howard Yoder, in *The Legacy of Michael Sattler* (Scottdale, PA: Herald Press, 1973). Scripture references in the text are Yoder's. Yoder's translation of the Schleitheim Confession can be accessed at http://www.mcusa-archives.org/library/resolutions/schleithiem/ [sic]. See also the translation at http://www.anabaptistwiki.org/mediawiki/index.php/Schleitheim_Confession_(source), and the article "Schleitheim Confession (Anabaptist, 1527)," *Global Anabaptist Mennonite Encyclopedia Online*. http://gameo.org/index.php?title=Schleitheim_Confession.

[6] *Anabaptist History and Theology* 190.

[7] James M Stayer, *Anabaptists and the Sword* (Lawrence, Kansas: Coronado Press, 1972).

[8] See Walter Klaassen, *Living at the End of the Ages: Apocalyptic Expectation in the Radical Reformation* (Lanham, Maryland: University Press of America, 1992).

[9] See Donald B Kraybill, Steven M Nolt, David L Weaver-Zercher, *Amish Grace: How Forgiveness Transcended Tragedy* (San Francisco: Jossey-Bass, 2007).

[10] Nanne van der Zijpp, Harold S Bender and Richard D Thiessen, "Martyrs' Mirror," *Global Anabaptist Mennonite Encyclopedia Online*, March 2009, Web, September 18, 2011. http://www.gameo.org/encyclopedia/contents/M37858ME.html.

[11] MWC represents 100 Mennonite and Brethren in Christ national churches from 57 countries on six continents. Source: http://www.mwc-cmm.org/index.php/about-mwc.

[12] Lapp and van Straten report that the issue of participation in the military did

emerge as a contentious issue at the third MWC assembly in Amsterdam in 1936, most particularly between the North Americans and the Dutch on one side, and the Germans on the other. Representatives of European and North American Mennonite Peace Committees met following the assembly to discuss ways to support Mennonites who suffered for refusing to do military service. So evidently some did refuse military service in the lead up to World War II. John A Lapp and Ed van Straten, "Mennonite World Conference 1925-2000: From Euro-American Conference to Worldwide Communion," *MQR* 77/1 (2003), 17.

[13] Cornelius Krahn and Al Reimer, "Selbstschutz," *Global Anabaptist Mennonite Encyclopedia Online*, 1989. Web. September 18, 2011. http://www.gameo.org/encyclopedia/contents/S444ME.html.

[14] An excellent Canadian website, geared particularly to newcomers to the issues, has been set up by the archivist for Mennonite Church Canada, Conrad Stoesz, exploring conscientious objection in Canada during World War II: http://www.alternativeservice.ca/.

[15] For an excellent article on conscientious objection among Mennonites, see especially Guy F Hershberger, Albert N Keim and Hanspeter Jecker, "Conscientious Objection," *Global Anabaptist Mennonite Encyclopedia Online*, 1989, Web. September 18, 2011. http://www.gameo.org/encyclopedia/contents/C6664.html.

[16] Harold S Bender, "The Anabaptist Vision," *Church History* (March 1944) XIII, 3-24, with slight revisions. Available at *Global Anabaptist Mennonite Encyclopedia Online*. http://www.gameo.org/encyclopedia/contents/A534.html.

[17] Other writings relevant to our present topic are *Christian Attitudes to War, Peace, and Revolution*, lecture notes originally published by the Mennonite seminary, now by Brazos, 2009), *Karl Barth and the Problem of War* (1970), *Nevertheless: Varieties and Shortcomings of Religious Pacifism* (1971/1976), *What Would You Do? A Serious Answer to a Standard Question* (1983), *When War is Unjust: Being Honest in Just War Thinking* (notably first published by the Lutheran Augsburg Press, 1984), *The Original Revolution: Essays on Christian Pacifism* (1971). An excellent survey of Yoder's plenteous writings and thought, as well as a rich bibliographical resource of his writings can be found in Mark Thiessen Nation, *John Howard Yoder: Mennonite Patience, Evangelical Witness, Catholic Convictions*, (Grand Rapids, Michigan: Wm B Eerdmans, 2006).

[18] The last collection of essays Yoder prepared for publication before his death is, significantly, titled *For the Nations: Essays Public and Evangelical* (Grand Rapids, Michigan: Eerdmans, 1997), in which Jeremiah 29 provides the *Leitmotif*, 6.

[19] Yoder, *Politics of Jesus*, 1994, 142-43.

[20] I have outlined various Mennonite peace positions in "Varieties of Contemporary Mennonite Peace Witness: from Passivism to Pacifism, from Nonresistance to Resistance," *Conrad Grebel Review* 10, no 3, September 1, 1992, 243-257.

[21] For example, Associated Mennonite Biblical Seminary, Eastern Mennonite Seminary, Fresno Pacific University, Canadian Mennonite University, and at Conrad Grebel University College at University of Waterloo.

[22] Yoder, *Christian Witness to the State*, 17.

[23] Notably through the efforts of German Mennonite theologian Fernando Enns, now teaching in Amsterdam, and the staff person responsible for the "Decade," Hans Uli Gerber of Switzerland.

[24] Emerging from the "Anabaptist Network" in the United Kingdom has been the writing of Stuart Murray, most recently his *The Naked Anabaptist: the Bare Essentials of a Radical Faith* (Scottdale, Pennsylvania/Waterloo, Ontario: Herald Press, 2010).

[25] http://gameo.org/encyclopedia/contents/shared_convictions_mennonite_world_conference_2006. See also the commentary on the shared convictions by Alfred Neufeld, *What We Believe Together: Exploring the "Shared Convictions" of Anabaptist Related Churches* (Intercourse, Pennsylvania: Good Books, 2007).

[26] Thomas R Yoder Neufeld, *Killing Enmity: Violence and the New Testament* (Grand Rapids, Michigan: Baker Academic, 2011), 135-143. In the UK it is published by SPCK as *Jesus and the Subversion of Violence: Wrestling with the New Testament Evidence*.

[27] Thomas R Yoder Neufeld, "Resistance and Nonresistance: the Two Legs of a Biblical Peace Stance;" Schrag Lectures, Messiah College, April 9, 2002, in *Brethren in Christ History and Life* 25/2 (2002), 257-86, and in *Conrad Grebel Review*, Winter, 2003, 56-81.

[28] Of particular importance in Mennonite circles for raising this issue was the brief article by Stephen F Dintaman, "The Spiritual Poverty of the Anabaptist Vision," *Conrad Grebel Review*, 10/2 (Spring 1992), 205-8. It was widely published in various venues, even precipitating a conference dedicated to wrestling with its implications.

From Symposiums to Stadiums: Promoting Religious Freedom

John Graz

Religious Freedom Is in Our DNA

During his speech at the 8th annual Religious Liberty Dinner in Washington DC in 2010, Dr Ted Wilson, President of the General Conference of Seventh-day Adventists, said: "Religious Liberty is in the DNA of the Adventist Church."[1] In 2012, he reaffirmed this position at the 7th IRLA World Congress on Religious Liberty in Punta Cana, Dominican Republic. He concluded with a call to all participants "to instill in young people the love for preserving religious liberty and freedom of conscience." "Let us encourage them" he said, "to join in this vitally important pursuit of freedom of conscience for all."[2]

In many ways he was right. Since the beginning of its history, the Seventh-day Adventist Church has given great importance to religious liberty for several reasons.[3] Adventists see the history of the world as a great conflict between God and Satan.[4] Freedom of choice is an expression of God's character of love. It also explains the fall of the angels and the fall of our first parents. All were created with the freedom to love and serve God, or to reject Him. There is no love without the freedom to love. On the contrary, the father of lies, Satan, does not respect free choice. He persecutes people who are faithful to God.[5]

Persecution is his trademark and he has practiced it during the history of our world. He changed his name and he dressed differently, based on the context and culture; but he always used the same methods—coercion and persecution. He has done it from the beginning, and he will do it until the end of the world. Jesus told His disciples that they would be persecuted before His return. He said, *"You will be persecuted and put to death; you will be hated by all nations because of me."*[6]

For Adventists, religious freedom has a strong biblical, historical, and theological foundation. They recognize their Anabaptist heritage and share the Mennonite and Baptist position on church-state separation. At the General Conference Session in February 1893, they unanimously passed the following preamble: "In view of the separation which we believe should exist between the Church and the State, it is inconsistent for the Church to receive from the State pecuniary gifts, favors, or exemptions."[7]

It also has an important eschatological dimension. The first article on this topic was written by John N Andrews in 1851. He understood the importance of religious freedom mainly in the context of the end time.[8] In 1864, facing the problem of Adventists in the armies during the Civil War, and their position as noncombatants, Andrews made the link between religious freedom and what we would call today a "human rights case." A few years later, when Adventists opposed the program of the National Reform Association to pass religious legislation, including Sunday Laws, freedom of conscience was mentioned.[9]

Ellen G White, who had a great influence on the organization and on the working methods adopted by the Church, stated that: "*We are not doing the will of God if we sit in quietude, doing nothing to preserve liberty of conscience... Let there be more earnest prayer; and then let us work in harmony with our prayers.*"[10]

Adventists know that, as disciples of Christ, they will be persecuted as Jesus predicted. But at the same time they are committed to defending religious freedom. There is a tension here.[11] People often ask me, "Why do you defend religious freedom if you believe at the end believers will be persecuted?" A similar question could be asked about health, peace, justice and poverty. Why do we build hospitals around the world when we know that, at the end, everyone will die?

The answer is: We defend and promote religious freedom for all people everywhere because *the freedom to choose* is a precious gift from God for all human beings. It has to do with His character of love, with the principles of His kingdom and with Jesus' example. Jesus never forced anyone to follow Him or to believe in Him. Freedom to choose is one of the essential signs of our human dignity.[12]

For Adventists, promoting and defending religious freedom is also a prophetic mission. They see themselves as called to fulfill the mission until Jesus returns. Ellen White wrote: "The banner of the truth and religious liberty held aloft by the founders of the gospel church and by God's witnesses during the centuries that have passed since then, has, in this last conflict, been committed to our hands."[13]

Among Christian churches, the Seventh-day Adventist Church sees itself as the recipient of a special mission which is embedded in its vision of the end. It is a rather unique characteristic. In denouncing the period of persecution during the Dark Ages, and the future coalition of churches against the faithful people of God, the popular evangelists keep religious freedom in the loop. They portray persecution as the irrevocable sign of apostasy. The Apostate Christians are persecuting the faithful with the support of the State. It is not theological error which puts them on the side of the enemy of the truth, but the fact that they persecute those "...who obey God's Commandments and remain faithful to Jesus."[14]

All Adventists believe in religious freedom. Because they believe in prophecy, conservative Adventists believe also in the ministry of religious freedom. Because they believe in human rights, liberals should also support religious freedom. But unfortunately, it happens often that conservatives and liberals, for different reasons, don't see the importance of the human rights aspect of religious freedom.[15]

A History of Passion

A former US Ambassador for International Religious Freedom said in a conversation with me that Adventists have been the most consistent among the Christians in their defense of religious freedom for all.

In the late 1880s, the small Adventist Church made a difference in the United States by opposing Sunday laws. As people who observe the Sabbath on Saturday, they see any action from the State to impose a day of rest as a strong violation of religious freedom and a betrayal of the First Amendment of the United States Constitution. The State should not impose a day for religious observance. It is a matter of conscience. In this battle, Adventists saw themselves as defending the biblical truth that the seventh day of the week is the Sabbath day of rest. They also saw themselves as defenders of the heritage of the American founding fathers like Jefferson[16] and Madison: The State should not interfere in the religious life of its citizens. These two dimensions probably account for the success of their campaign and the vigor with which they opposed the new religious tendencies.

In 1884 they published the *Sabbath Sentinel* and 500,000 copies were circulated. It became the *American Sentinel* in 1886. Three years later, in February 1889, the Church appointed a State Press Committee which published books and brochures on religious freedom issues under the name of The Sentinel Library.[17]

Very active years led up to the 1889 launching of the National Religious Liberty Association. It was done during a meeting held in the SDA Tabernacle in Battle Creek, Michigan. In the declaration signed by 110 charter members, we read: "We deny the right of any civil government to legislate on religious questions. We believe it is the right, and should be the privilege, of every man to worship according to the dictates of his own conscience.[18]

The understanding of religious freedom is strongly based on the concept of Church-State separation. In 1890, the association collected 250,000 signatures against religious legislation presented both in the Senate and in the House.[19] As the activities of the association spread to other countries around the world, in 1893 the National Association became the International Religious Liberty Association (IRLA).[20]

Important Dates

The Department of Religious Liberty was organized in 1901 by the General Conference of Seventh-day Adventists. A few years later, in 1906, the department began publishing *Liberty, A Magazine of Religious Freedom*.

In the 1920s, the Sunday law issue came back to the 70th Congress in Washington DC and to several states. In 1926–1929, the Department of Religious Liberty secured eight million signatures to petition against various bills.[21] According the head of the department, C S Longacre, it was "the most vigorous and intensive campaign for signatures on petitions which had ever been launched in our history."[22] In the year 1927, there were approximately 250,000 Seventh-day Adventist members in the world (1930:314,253).[23] The National Reform Association which promoted these bills said the only opponents were "The motion picture interests, the atheists, and the Seventh-day Adventists."[24]

In one year 9,351,000 books, magazines and leaflets were distributed.

A few years later in 1931 the issue of Calendar Reform was brought before the League of Nations. A change in the calendar would have created a lot of problems for Sabbath-keepers. So 220,000 signatures were secured in the United States against the proposal, and 236,000 signatures came from other countries. Neither the Sunday law nor the Calendar Reform was implemented.

Before World War II the religious liberty leaders encouraged the creation of national and regional associations in Canada, Australia, the Philippines, and in Europe.[25] During the period of the war, *Liberty* magazine was still published.

Religious Liberty: An Official Ministry

The Seventh-day Adventist Church was the first Christian church to establish religious freedom as an official ministry. This explains why religious freedom has been present all these years as an important aspect of the life of the Church. Its popularity and visibility were really strong until War World II began.

A large part of the religious liberty ministry was done through *Liberty* magazine, which became the largest American magazine on this issue. With close to 200,000 copies distributed every two months today, it is still the largest one.

In 1980 the North American Division, one of the current 13 branches of the General Conference around the world, got the same status as the other divisions. It was detached from the direct administration of the world headquarters. The Religious Liberty Department split in two: one part for North American and one for the world church. *Liberty* became the magazine of the new North American Division Religious Liberty Department. Its articles were focused on the United States, Canada, and Bermuda; and the promotion of religious freedom in North America was mainly done through it.[26] Then in 1998 the North American Religious Liberty Association (NARLA) was organized and covered all the territory of the North American Division. It worked closely with the IRLA.

The General Conference PARL Department was directly involved in sustaining and developing NARLA. James Standish, US Congressional Liaison from 2000-2008, reorganized it and worked closely with it in Washington DC until 2008 when he was asked to serve as Executive Director of the US Commission on International Religious Freedom. Barry Bussey kept the NARLA work going until he left in 2011. Then Melissa Reid, Associate Editor of *Liberty* magazine, was elected Executive Director of NARLA. The General Conference PARL Department continued to develop the activities of the IRLA and accomplished a large part of its religious freedom ministry through it.

The International Religious Liberty Association: The Second Breath

Since its creation in 1893, the IRLA had periods of great activity, depending on the issues and the international environment. After World War II, the IRLA was registered in the District of Columbia for educational purposes on August 16, 1946. It extended its influence in the world and, under the influence of Dr Dean Nussbaum from Europe, the IRLA opened its membership to those who were not Seventh-day Adventists.[27] It also facilitated the organization or the reorganization of partner associations around the world, like the International Association for the Defense of Religious Freedom (AIDLR) in Europe. Under the leadership of Dr Jean Nussbaum,[28] then Pierre Lanarés, AIDLR published in French the journal *Conscience et Liberte* which was translated into several languages and became one of the best resources in this field.[29] AIDLR received the support of Mrs Eleanor Roosevelt, who agreed to be its first President of Honor in 1948; followed by Nobel Peace Prize winner Dr Albert Schweitzer in 1966; and Rene Cassin in 1978, who, along with Mrs Roosevelt, had played a major role in the redaction of the *Universal Declaration of Human Rights* in 1948.

AIDLR obtained the Consultative Status of United Nations Non-Governmental Organization by ECOSOC, a status that the General Conference obtained later in 1982 and the IRLA in 2003.[30] AIDLR Secretary General, Dr Gianfranco Rossi, became the voice of religious freedom during more than 10 years at the United Nations Human Rights Commission. Dr Bert Beach, who was elected Director of the Public Affairs and Religious Liberty Department at the General Conference in 1985, worked closely with the European association. He associated it with the organization of the 2nd and 3rd IRLA World Congresses in Rome and London.

With the *United Nations Declaration of Human Rights* in 1948, then the *Declaration on the Elimination of All Forms of Intolerance and Discrimination Based on Religion or Belief*, proclaimed in 1981, and several international documents which followed, religious freedom received the official label of human rights. The UN facilitated and encouraged the work of the IRLA and AIDLR. These organizations got credibility and visibly at the United Nations Human Rights Commission and were able to welcome a number of people to their ranks who were not Adventists.

The IRLA around the World

Beginning in 1980, the PARL Department under the charisma and talent of Dr Bert Beach developed a new and successful activity, Interchurch Relations, without neglecting the diplomatic work with governments and embassies. The General Conference Council of Interchurch Relations was organized in 1980. The work of the PARL Department went beyond the borders of religious freedom and became the *de facto* External Affairs Department, which dealt with the diplomatic work of the World Church.[31]

The IRLA succeeded in building a tradition on the World Congress. The three IRLA World Congresses—in Amsterdam 1977, Rome 1984, and London 1989—were intentionally held in Western Europe. They offered the possibility of inviting government officials from the East. They also gave opportunity to develop a diplomatic activity and to make the Adventist Church more visible in the communist regime's territories.

In 1997 the IRLA decided to hold its 4th World Congress in Rio de Janeiro, Brazil. As the newly elected Secretary General, I wanted to open new territories. Europe, which now had an anti-sect climate, was no longer an attractive venue for such an international event. In Brazil the Adventist Church was well known and religious tolerance was a reality. As could be expected, it was at this time that the largest congress organized by the IRLA was held. Experts came from Europe, Russia, the United States, and, of course, South America. Officials from new European democracies attended and Cuba sent one of its Religious Affairs Vice-Directors. The media was interested in this event, as was the government of Brazil which sent its Minister of Justice who read a message from his President.

On Saturday following the congress, the first Festival of Religious Freedom was held in an Adventist church in Rio de Janeiro.

The idea was that such an important event should also have a connection with the local community. To organize a world congress the General Conference (GC) administration had to be involved. The Manager, Don Robinson, was the IRLA Treasurer, but also the GC Undertreasurer. The regional and local Adventist leadership, led by Siloe Alameida, cooperated very well in supporting their local religious liberty association. Several trips to Brazil were made to promote the congress and, as a result, public lectures were given and officials were met. A few years later, the Brazilian Religious Freedom Association (ABLIRC)[32] was organized and became one of the most active partner associations of the IRLA. Congresses and symposiums were held in the following years in Peru, Chile, and Argentina—including two South American Religious Freedom Congresses. In 2006, the first mega Festival of Religious Freedom was held in Sao Paulo. This major event was organized by the union conference of the Church and supported by the South American Division. It was attended by 12,000, but according to the police 20,000 additional people were not able to find a seat and they stayed outside. It was the beginning of a new way to promote religious freedom and it opened a new page in the history of the IRLA and, in some ways, in the history of the Church.

A similar work was done to prepare for the 7th IRLA World Congress. Roberto Herrera, the IRLA General Secretary for Inter-America, was very much involved. I visited the countries covered by the association since 1998; then after 2005 the number of meetings and training seminars continued to increase. Many prejudices about the work of religious freedom had to be overcome. In 2009 Roberto Herrera organized the first Inter-American Congress on Religious Freedom in the Dominican Republic. It was followed by the largest Festival of Religious Freedom in the capital city of Santo Domingo. This was attended by 13,000 people. The congress received strong support from the Dominican Republic Association of Religious Freedom and the Festival was organized by the Adventist Church there. The cooperation went very well. It encouraged us to hold the 7th IRLA World Congress in Punta Cana.

Mass Meetings of Religious Freedom

Promoting religious freedom has very often been seen as an academic activity. The Festival of Religious Freedom brought religious freedom to the people.[33] When there is no freedom, ordinary people suffer—not only experts or religious leaders. But the question was: How do we bring this issue to the people? I had experience when I was in France working in Pau as a pastor and then in Paris as a union department director. I organized the religious freedom public lectures for Dr Pierre Lanarés, the Secretary General of AIDLR. In both cities we filled the auditoriums. This was an exception because most of the meetings on this theme attracted a small number of attendees. I had the conviction we could do far better, and I began dreaming of filling stadiums.

To reach this goal, we needed a simple but very attractive concept which could convince the leaders of the Church and mobilize people. The motto was: "The time has come to say thanks for religious freedom!" The concept was: Religious freedom is a gift from God and from the country which protects it. When I spoke in churches I asked the members: "Is religious freedom a great gift?" The answer was "Yes!" Then, "What is the normal reaction when we receive a gift?" The answer was given with more or less conviction at the beginning: "It is to say: Thank you!" Since 2006, I have been traveling around the world asking these questions. Then of course the final question: "Have we said Thank You for the religious freedom we have?"

The international context became more favorable to this kind of popular campaign. Religious intolerance and persecution of Christians were increasing in some parts of the world. This made people more sensitive to the importance of this freedom.

Since 2006, 25 festivals were held on five continents, gathering thousands of people and leaders from all religions. They have attracted ministers of governments, ambassadors, and reporters. Some festivals were held in big cities like Cape Town, South Africa; Jakarta and Manado, Indonesia; Saint Petersburg, Russia; Honolulu, Hawaii; Bucharest and Bacau, Romania; Port of Spain, Trinidad and Tobago; Guatemala City, Guatemala; and Caracas, Venezuela. They were also held in Suriname, Guyana, Tobago, and North and South Mexico. The largest ones were held in Santo Domingo, Dominican Republic (13,000); Bogota, Colombia (15,000); and Luanda, Angola, (40,000). To keep the movement we proposed to hold a World Festival every five years. My intention was to build a new tradition similar to the World Congresses. In 2008, the Executive Committee of the General Conference voted the new event on its calendar of world activities.

The first World Festival was held in Lima, Peru in 2009 and attended by 45,000. At first I thought that the organization of such big events would annihilate other traditional events such as forums and symposiums. But it was just the opposite. Those who organized festivals wanted to also have an academic dimension. They organized symposiums, forums, and marches for freedom in the city. Before the festival in Lima, three important forums were held in Cuzco, Trujillo and Lima with officials and religious leaders. We observed a similar trend with congresses. They are now followed by festivals. At this point we don't know how long the tradition will last, but the idea is well received.

Several festivals are planned for 2013. The most important will be in Tuxtla Gutierrez, South Mexico; Yaoundé, Cameroon, following the 3rd Pan-African Congress on Religious Liberty; and the 2nd World Festival which will be held in Sao Paulo, Brazil, on May 25. The Brazil festival will be the climax of a number of other events: A symposium in the Latin American Parliament, a Religious Freedom Concert at the University; and, on Saturday morning, all Adventist churches in South America will focus their service on religious freedom. In the afternoon, 40-50,000 will gather in a public park in Sao Paulo with the presence of many officials including the mayor and the state governor, ministers and members of Parliament. Religious leaders are invited too.

Such events provide opportunity to meet the authorities, religious leaders and the media. It is a great way to promote religious freedom on a large scale. After the first mega festival in Sao Paulo in 2006—organized by my colleague in South America, Williams Costa, with the strong support of the Adventist Church in Sao Paulo—a law on religious freedom in the workplace was passed by the State Assembly. It became a model for Argentina. A similar law was voted in the Philippines after the 5th World Congress held in Manila in 2002. A law recognizing several churches in Peru was voted in 2010, a few months after the 1st World Festival in 2009. In the program of the 2nd World Festival, May 25 will be proposed by the City Council as Religious Freedom Day for Sao Paulo. It will be the day of the Festival.

The concept of the Festival of Religious Freedom is well received and 2014 will bring a number of large festivals around the world. One of the best outcomes would be to see other churches or interchurch or interfaith organizations organize such mass events and fill stadiums with 80,000 to 100,000 people celebrating religious freedom. It is part of our vision, and Adventists would be much honored to pass the concept to all believers who want to protect and promote religious freedom for all people everywhere. It would be the best answer to violent religious fanaticism and to the indifference we see in the world today. We can dream of one day having a large festival organized by the Mennonites, or the Baptists, or the Pentecostals, or the Mormons—or by all of us together, including Catholics, Buddhists, and Muslims.

IRLA and the Adventist Church

As we have explained, most of the religious freedom activities in the Seventh-day Adventist Church are run by the IRLA. But some are sponsored by the General Conference and the IRLA, and the Festival is a good example. Another example is the annual Religious Liberty Dinner held in Washington DC.[34] The General Conference, the IRLA, *Liberty* magazine, and NARLA are the official sponsors. The 10th dinner in 2012 was hosted by the Embassy of Canada and the speaker was the Honorable John Baird, Minister of Foreign Affairs for Canada. Previous speakers included Senators Hillary Clinton, John Kerry, and John McCain. The partnership between the IRLA and the Church was well accepted. This event, held for the first time in 2003, became a well-accepted tradition in the American capital city and a plus for the promotion of religious freedom.

The IRLA annual Meeting of Experts, which gathers approximately 25 of the best experts on religious freedom, is organized exclusively by the IRLA. This is probably the reason why this group is hosted by secular universities more than any other Adventist associations.

For most of the officials and experts who are in contact with the Church or the IRLA, there is no significant distinction between them. They see the IRLA as the non-sectarian arm of the Church. Even if it is an independent association, the link with the Church is strong and it is relatively well accepted as long the IRLA keeps focusing on religious freedom as Article 18 of the UN Universal Declaration of Human Rights defines it.[35]

Conclusion

The interest of Adventists in religious freedom probably has no equivalent in the Christian world. It has to do with their eschatological vision, their reading of history, and, of course, their theology; but also with their experience as a religious minority facing challenges as they try to live their beliefs—including resting on the Saturday Sabbath. It gives Adventists openness to those who are persecuted and discriminated against.

As their Church is recognized and accepted by governments and by interchurch and interfaith organizations, the temptation to slow down the enthusiasm for religious freedom may come. Fortunately, it is not happening yet.

These are the solid foundations of a ministry recognized, encouraged and promoted by the world Adventist Church—from the world headquarters to the most humble local church.

The best testimony comes from non-Adventists. The former Moderator of the European Conference of Churches and former President of the French Protestant Federation, Reverend Jean Arnold de Clermont, said in a book published about him: "I have a deep admiration for the Seventh-day Adventists. They have an important structure of defense of religious liberty on the international level."[36]

ENDNOTES

[1] At the 9th Annual Religious Liberty Dinner, April 5, 2011, Marriott Wardman Park Hotel, Washington DC.

[2] Bettina Krause, "Wilson Explores Clash between Secularism and Religious Belief," *Adventist Review*, May 17, 2012, 8. During the Festival of Religious Freedom which was held in Santo Domingo after the Congress, Wilson said that every Adventist member should become a champion of religious liberty.

[3] See "Religious Liberty," *SDA Encyclopedia*, vol 11, (Hagerstown, Maryland: Review and Herald Publishing Association, 1996), 430-433. We are very dependent on the information given by this article. It would be useful to have new research on this topic.

[4] Ellen G White, *The Great Controversy*.

[5] Revelation 13:11-16.

[6] Matthew 24:9.

[7] "Is it Lawful to Pay Tribute?" *The Religious Liberty Library*, November 1893, No 16, 63.

[8] John N Andrews, "Thoughts on Revelation XIII and XIV," *Review and Herald*, 1:83, May 19, 1851.

[9] *SDA Encyclopedia*, vol 11, 431.

[10] Ellen G White, *Testimonies*, vol 5, 713.

[11] See Niels-Erik Andreasen, "A Stranger in your Midst: A Biblical Perspective on Religious Freedom and Interfaith Understanding," *Building Bridges of Faith and Freedom*, John Graz, General Editor, Carol E Rasmussen, Managing Editor, Public Affairs and Religious liberty Department, General Conference of Seventh-day Adventists, Silver Spring MD, 2005, 67-75.

[12] See John Graz, "Seventh-day Adventists and Religious Freedom," *Issues of Faith & Freedom*, Public Affairs and Religious Liberty Department, General Conference of Seventh-day Adventists, Silver Spring MD USA, 2008, 119-131.

[13] Ellen G White, *The Acts of the Apostles*, (Mountain View, California: Pacific Press Publishing Association, 1921), 68-69.

[14] Revelation 14:12.

[15] John Graz, "Seventh-day Adventists and Religious Freedom," *Issues of Faith & Freedom*, 2008, 119-131.

[16] See the article which showed the admiration Adventists had for Jefferson. C S Longrave, Editor, "The Apostle of Individual Freedom," *Liberty*, Vol IX, No 1, First Quarter 1914, 9-10.

[17] "Religious Liberty," *SDA Encyclopedia*, Vol 11, (Hagerstown, Maryland: Review and Herald Publishing Association, 1996), 430-433.

[18] *SDA Encyclopedia* 430-433.

[19] *SDA Enclycopedia* 430-433.

[20] See the "Declaration of Principles of the International Religious Liberty Association," *The Religious Liberty Library*, No 7, March 1893, 23.

[21] See "Four 'Blue Sunday' Bills before Congress," *Liberty*, Vol XXI, Second Quar-

ter, 1926, Extra No 2.

[22] "Public Affairs and Religious Liberty Department," *SDA Encyclopedia*, op. cit.

[23] See *147th Annual Statistical Report–2009*, General Conference of Seventh-day Adventists, Silver Spring, Maryland, 84.

[24] See "A Famous Petition, Stanford University Faculty Opposed to Lankford Sunday Bill," *Liberty*, First Quarter 1929, no 1, vol XXIV, 10-11. We can also read: "Up to date, so far as we can estimate, about 7,000,000 individual protests have been sent to the Congress in opposition to the Lankford Sunday Bill," 10.

[25] *SDA Encyclopedia*, op cit.

[26] Internet site: www.Libertymagazine.org.

[27] In document "Home and Foreign Officers' Meeting," May 30, 1946, page 1, it was agreed "To ask the chair to appoint a committee to give study to the organization of an International Religious Liberty Association on a broader basis...." Dr Nussbaum gave a report about his meetings with religious leaders in France and mentioned projects of the IRLA in France.

[28] See Bert B Beach in *Bert B Beach, Ambassador for Liberty: Building Bridges of Faith, Friendship, and Freedom*, (Hagerstown, Maryland: Review and Herald Publishing Association, 2012), 45.

[29] See www.aidlr.org.

[30] See minutes of the IRLA Legal meeting, October 13, 2008, 1. See also John Graz, "Focused on Freedom," *Liberty* magazine, March/April 2007, vol 102, no 2, 25.

[31] Bert B Beach, op cit.

[32] See www.Ablirc.org.

[33] See John Graz, *Festival of Religious Freedom*, brochure published by the Public Affairs and Religious Liberty Department, General Conference of Seventh-day Adventists, Silver Spring, Maryland, 2008.

[34] Minutes of the IRLA Legal Meeting, October 13, 2003, 2. The First Religious Liberty Dinner was held in the US Senate Caucus Room on April 2, 2003, with about 200 participants.

[35] A book is scheduled to be published by a Professor of the University of Madrid about the IRLA journal *Fides et Libertas*. As the result of the 13th and 14th IRLA Meeting of Experts and the 7th IRLA World Congress, a book was published by two members or the IRLA Board of Experts. Jaime Contreras and Rosa Maria Martinez de Codes, Editors, *Trends of Secularism in a Pluralistic World*, Iberoamericana /Vervuert, 2013.

[36] Jean Arnold De Clermont, Une voix protestante, Entretiens avec Bernadette Sauvaget, Desclee de Brouwer, 2001, 172.

Reflections on Anabaptist Ecclesiology

Robert J Suderman

Although we have left this discussion for the last, the understandings of the nature, identity, and vocation of the church
will have permeated everything we have considered thus far.
Indeed, when we consider our church's origins in the Radical Reformation, ecclesiology needs to dominate the agenda.[1]

It is, perhaps, more appealing to some to talk about other priorities, but all those priorities are such only to the extent that they
reflect what is already real in the life of the church. It is in their
incarnation—becoming flesh—that each of these priorities gains
integrity and trustworthiness. For example:

- Peace is not simply activism; it is the way a community of
  Jesus lives its life.
- Discipleship is not simply learning to be a good Christian; it
  is learning to be a good church.
- Community is not simply sharing common things; it is to-
  gether sharing the mind of Christ as a witness to the world.
- Simplicity is not simply a matter of economic stewardship;
  it is demonstrating that as a Body it is possible to trust in

God's provisions for our lives.

- Baptism is not simply a public witness of our individual decision to accept Christ; it is a commitment to offer our gifts to the life of the Body of Christ, and to be nurtured and discipled by that community.

- Pacifism and non-violence are not simply ethical choices we make to be better people; they are creating a community that aligns with the path chosen by Jesus so that we can be worthy of being called His Body.

- Ethics are not simply a code of behaviour; they are a mirror of the habits of God's people and how they treat each other and learn to live together as a paradigm of reconciliation.

- Nonconformity is not simply difference from the directions of the societies around us; it is a demonstration that there is another Empire present in the same territory, and this community marches to the beat of that Empire, and has granted it supreme authority over who we are and want to become.

- The church is not simply other than the state because it has different functions; it is not the state because it recognizes a different Lord as the "head of state."

- Salvation is not simply rescuing individual souls from eternal destruction; it is the on-going vigorous presence of a community that invites others to enlist in an alternative cause that has as its agenda the promise of setting things right—the way they were meant to be.

- Evangelism is not simply proclaiming the truths of God; it is living the good news of the presence of the Kingdom and bringing its values into a visible, accessible and tangible reality for others.

Many have attempted to focus and summarize the Anabaptist theological contribution. H S Bender, often credited with helping our tradition recover itself, described the Anabaptist vision with three foci: discipleship to Jesus Christ; the formation of the church as a body of believers, and the ethic of non-resistance. Others have added the freedom of life in the Spirit, a community of common goods, the passion for evangelism, and the prophetic nature of its proclamation and life. Still others have emphasized the voluntary nature of faith and discipleship, the freedom of the church from the state, the pursuit of authentic personal faith, the hermeneutic nature of the community, and a commitment to live out the fruits of the Spirit.[2]

While these are indeed all significant contributions of the Anabaptist perspective, I would dare to filter them all through one foundational heart that served as their fomenting passion. That heart was the rediscovery of the nature, identity, and vocation of the church as a living, breathing, growing, and visible organism of the Kingdom of God that is already among us, but is yet to be fulfilled. The New Testament added two important nuances or ingredients to this essential focus. They are:

1. That the nature of the presence of God's Kingdom, and therefore the vocation of the church, is now best understood via the life, teaching, death, and resurrection of Jesus. That is, ecclesiology now is inseparable from Christology.

2. Jesus of Nazareth is now understood as the promised Messiah of God, the one charged with the on-going task of forming a people of and for God that would serve as the primary vehicle for the restoration of creation as intended by God. In other words, Christology now is inseparable from ecclesiology.

The biblical witness had always been understood as saying that transforming and restoring creation to its original design and purpose was best done via the formation of people-hood. This was not new, and it is evident from Genesis 1 to Revelation 22. Jewish and Christian scholarship agrees that this is the biblical witness and hope. And it had always been understood that this people-hood would somehow be the flesh and blood presence of God's coming Kingdom and God's Kingdom already present. Where consensus has not been reached is the insight that the Apostle Paul and others had, namely that Jesus the Jew, recognized now as Messiah, was the encapsulated paradigm of how such a people-hood would live, act, and believe. In other words, Jesus was not only the messenger, he was also the message.

Not only has there been no such consensus among Jewish and

Christian scholars, there has not been such a consensus within Christian scholarship itself. Very recently, the head of a major historical denomination in Canada told me: "Our church believes in Jesus too, but only as the source of our salvation, not as the primary source for our ethics." In other words, he is saying that Jesus creates people-hood, but is not the primary inspiration for the way this people-hood lives out its vocation.

This example, perhaps as well as anything, highlights the contribution of the Radical Reformation (Anabaptist Vision) to inter-ecclesial, ecumenical conversation. Anabaptists believe that proclaiming Jesus as both Saviour and Lord means that Jesus both creates a people-hood and that it will understand living out the Kingdom of God in the way he demonstrated. In other words, there is no conceptual separation between the purposes of creation and the intentions of redemption. Neither is there a conceptual distinction between the intentions of redemption and purposes of discipleship. And there is no significant way of talking about creation, redemption, discipleship, purpose, and intention without talking about people-hood. In other words, all these foci experience their warmest embrace in ecclesiology.

One could say that the Anabaptists have understood the nature and vocation of the church (ecclesiology) in terms of a three-legged stool, each leg essential for the stool to be useful or whole. The three legs are: Kingdom, Jesus, and Church. None is synonymous with the others, and none stands alone without the others. The Kingdom is active within and beyond the Church, but the Church functions as an intentional, invitational sign of what happens when the Kingdom approaches. The Church is the "body of Christ" but does not monopolize the reality of Christ's Lordship within itself. Jesus is the definitive paradigm of how the presence of the Kingdom must now be understood, and the life of the church must now be shaped. And so each one is inseparably intertwined with the others, but none is entirely absorbed in the reality of the other.

The temptation of the church worldwide is to align preferentially with one or two, but not three, of the legs of the stool, i.e., to create undesired dichotomies. There are the temptations of dual-focus:

- Some are enamoured with Jesus and the church, but don't understand either in terms of God's Kingdom.
- Others are inspired by the Kingdom and Jesus, without either becoming flesh in the reality of the church.
- Still others give their lives for the church as a kingdom community, but don't take Jesus seriously as the foundational paradigm of both.

Then there are the temptations of mono-focus:

- Striving for the Kingdom without a significant link to either Jesus or the church;
- Being a "Jesus-person" without any significant connection to the Kingdom or the church;
- Embedded in the church without understanding it in the power of Jesus and the presence of the Kingdom.

In this holistic understanding of the nature and vocation of the church, the other elements we have already discussed are natural and needed components.

- Discipleship is personal and individual, but designed for community.
- Ethics is Christological and therefore reconciliation and non-violence are foundational.
- The presence of the Holy Spirit is connected to teaching us more about reflecting God's purposes embodied in a Christological community.
- The gifts of the Spirit, while given to persons, belong to the body.
- The church is a hermeneutic community, under the power and guidance of the Holy Spirit, always with the Bible open, together discerning faithfulness for our times.
- Baptism is based on confession of faith and a decision to accept Jesus as both Saviour and Lord of our individual and communal lives.
- Governance and organization are heavily shaped by local communities of faith each of which, however, is willing to teach and learn from others.
- Doctrine is defined, but must always be revisited and rede-

fined if needed.

- Liturgy is based on the participation of all the gifts of the Spirit given to each of the participants.

The primary sacrament is the grace extended by God to the world through the presence and life of the community in its context, i.e., the church is understood to be the sacrament of God's multidimensional grace. It is in the visible community of Christ where the presence of God's grace can be seen, touched, and experienced. It is also an invitational and hospitable place where those seeking and experiencing life in God may come and live out God's mission with the brothers and sisters of the community and together in the larger world. In this life together the Gospel is discerned and exercised, which implies that the Body is disciplined to live out its vocational purposes. The church thus becomes the preferred and primary vehicle for the transformation of the world so passionately desired by God.

How do these understandings translate into the nitty-gritty of organization, authority, and mission? We will touch on just a few of these understandings.

1. We understand scriptural authority as foundational in the life of the church. The Bible's authority comes alive when Scripture is open, in the midst of the church, with the presence of the Holy Spirit. The fruit of such discernment guides the life and faith of the church.

2. We understand that the gifts of the Holy Spirit are given to each disciple for the purposes of strengthening the Body in its vocation as agent of God's redeeming and reconciling purposes. These gifts are all important, with no evident hierarchy; perhaps the most important one being the one that at any given moment appears to be missing.

3. Both the immediate context of the local community and the organic realities of regional and world Bodies are critically important in the life of discernment and faithfulness. It is too much to talk about "autonomy" of the local congregation, just as it is too much to suggest pyramidal authority from regional or world bodies. Autonomy gives way to the wisdom of the whole, and the wisdom of

the whole is gleaned from life of discipled congregations.

4. The Church as a hermeneutic community is visible in a particular time and place, but is shaped by other times and places. In other words, the experience and wisdom of God's people throughout history, in multiple cultural contexts, and in geographical diversity are critical to the hermeneutical task of discerning faithfulness today. No congregation or church-body is an isolated and autonomous island.

5. Defined doctrines and formal Confessions are authoritative in the sense that no part of the Body should proceed without consulting, knowing, and assuming that faithfulness in each particular aspect of faith and life indeed has a foundation. But they are not the only or final authority when local or regional bodies, due to the dynamics experienced in different contexts, discern a need to digress from the authoritative whole. Structural mechanisms that assure faithful adherence to defined doctrine are contextually designed and applied.

So how are we doing? The challenges are daunting. We are mystified, in a good-natured and humble kind of way, that such good and helpful biblical/theological understandings are not igniting fires of commitment and rapid growth throughout the world. The identifiable Anabaptist world is small in numbers. But there is powerful Anabaptist influence present in denominations that do not overtly use the language of Anabaptism. We are, at times, tempted to think that growth is slow and methodical because the integrity of holistic discipleship we represent is attractive to only the few who are truly serious about following Christ. But such temptations quickly evaporate when we engage the sincerity, commitment, and faithfulness of other traditions. We vacillate between discouragement and optimism; between a sense that we need to change, and a sense that what we have is too valuable to give up.

We see ourselves as custodians of a pearl of great price that needs to be both protected and exposed to continuous scrutiny and made accessible to all who want it. We are already a people, but we struggle hard to become more of what we already are and of what we would still hope to become. We are a part of the Body of Christ.

ENDNOTES

[1] The oldest Confession of Faith emerging from the Radical Reformation (the *Schleitheim Confession*, 1527) does not have a separate article about ecclesiology. Yet within the seven topics addressed (Baptism, the Ban, the Lord's Supper, Separation, Pastors in the Church, the Sword, and the Oath), the assumption is that these themes are important because the Church is meant to be the Church and not something else. In this sense the absence of the church as a separate item actually highlights the importance of the church as a foundation that needs no defense.

[2] *The Confession of Faith in a Mennonite Perspective,* Adopted by the delegates of Mennonite Church General Assembly, and of the General Conference Mennonite Church Tricentennial Session, July 28, 1995, Wichita, Kansas, (Scottdale, Pennsylvania: Herald Press, 1995).

Article 9, The Church of Jesus Christ: "We believe that the church is the assembly of those who have accepted God's offer of salvation through faith in Jesus Christ. The church is the new community of disciples sent into the world to proclaim the reign of God and to provide a foretaste of the church's glorious hope. The church is the new society established and sustained by the Holy Spirit. The church, the body of Christ, is called to become ever more like Jesus Christ, its head, in its worship, ministry, witness, mutual love and care, and the ordering of its common life."

SECOND MEETING

Early Anabaptist Eschatology

Valerie G Rempel

Radical Beginnings

Some 45 years ago theologian Vernard Eller suggested that the "radical churches are those which have consistently seen themselves from an eschatological perspective."[1] Eller was trying to identify a unifying theme that might characterize the radical tradition that arose first in the 16th century reformation period and then in later movements as well.[2] What was radical, he argued, was the attempt to "restore and preserve the eschatological dynamic so central to the career of Jesus and the life of the early church," a distinction made evident in its ecclesiology. "The radical church sees itself always as being 'on the way,'" he wrote, "in process of becoming, pointed toward the new age which is its true home, held in the dialectic tension between the Already and the Not Yet."[3]

That eschatological perspective emerged in a larger context of impulses and ideas that were prevalent in the years leading up to the Protestant Reformation. Historian Carter Lindberg, for example, has noted what he terms the "vivid eschatological currents" that swirled about in the late medieval period, shaping art, literary works, and the visual representations carved into medieval church buildings.[4] Apocalyptic imagery was frequently employed, especially in the tracts and woodcuts that began to circulate as part of the increasing criticism of Roman Catholic clergy. There were some who were preoccupied with end-time prophecies, others were increasingly anxious because of the ongoing threat presented by the Turks. For many, it seemed as if the end of the world was at hand.[5]

Like many Christians, early Anabaptists lived with an expectation of Christ's soon return. The political turmoil of the day and the persecution they experienced because of the way they lived out their faith in Jesus, only reinforced this sense of living in the end times. Their approaches varied, however. The Swiss Anabaptists, those who articulated their theology in the 1527 statement known as the *Schleitheim Confession*, sought to separate themselves quite thoroughly from society.[6] As C Arnold Snyder puts it, "the Schleitheim group did not hope to reform the world according to a utopian pattern: they had given up on the world and were withdrawing from it, awaiting the divine Judgment of the Last Days which they believed was imminent."[7]

By contrast, others who were adopting more radical expressions of faith studied the prophetic books of the Bible and, in at least one instance, sought to create the New Jerusalem. The events at Muenster are often considered a stain on the Anabaptist story and much has been written to either distance it from the larger movement or to acknowledge the events as part of the varied movements that eventually died out or coalesced into the form of Anabaptist expression we see today.

The northern German city of Muenster was particularly caught up in reformation fever during the early 1530s. It was the seat of a Catholic bishop but also had strong Lutheran presence and later was home to radicals with some ties to Anabaptist communities in the low lands. Numerous Dutch Anabaptists attempted to migrate to the city which was increasingly being seen as a refuge for those persecuted by Catholic authorities, especially when preachers began referring to it as the "New Jerusalem." Jan van Leyden eventually emerged as a leader but his views were increasingly fanatical. He attempted to adapt Old Testament practices to the present context, taking up arms in defense of the city, instituting elders, the community of goods and even polygamy. Setting himself up as king, van Leyden "ruled" Muenster and held off opposition until the bishop's troops reclaimed the city. The leaders of the movement were tortured, put to death and their bodies placed on display in cages that remain to this day on the towers of St Lambert's Church.[8]

The events at Muenster, as well as an earlier armed defense that was defeated near the Dutch city of Bolsward, shaped the early Anabaptist movement in two important ways. First, it added to the perception that the Anabaptist movement was dangerous. Both Catholic and Lutheran leaders characterized the radicals as just that—radical. There was some truth to the accusation. Melchior Hoffman, an early leader in Dutch and North German Anabaptism, was chiliastic in his reading of the Bible; Jan Matthijs predicted the end of the world at Easter 1534. Both of these had influenced, directly or indirectly, the events that took place in that region. As a result, church and civil leaders increased the persecution directed at those who were separating from the established church.

The second way the Muenster debacle shaped Anabaptism was to heighten the commitment to use only the ban as a means of dealing with sin, and to refuse taking up arms as a way to "pass sentence in worldly disputes and strife."[9] Menno Simons, whose brother may have been one of those defeated at Bolsward, began to emerge as the leader of the Dutch and northern German movements. He strongly rejected "all revolutionary and mystical fanaticism," and helped shape the nonresistant practices that came to be more universally accepted as an identifying mark of the Anabaptist tradition.[10] The early attempts at armed resistance on the part of a few "fanatics" were viewed as highly misguided and outside of proper Christian understanding and practice. Indeed, many have refused to consider these events as a legitimate part of the Anabaptist story.

From "Then" to "Now"

In the intervening centuries, Anabaptist eschatology continued to be lived out primarily in its ecclesiology and understanding of discipleship. Anabaptists were to live in the world but not be of it, for they were citizens of a new kingdom. There is little evidence of a conscious attempt to define a distinct eschatological perspective that stood outside of prevailing trends in the Christian tradition. This last point is important: Anabaptists, especially those drawn to the more pietistic or evangelical tradition, were at times caught up in movements that had a heightened interest in the prophetic passages of the Bible. This can be seen, for example, in the trek to Asia during the 1880s by about 600 Mennonites who were anticipating the appearance of the Antichrist and, some years later, in the fascination of some with dispensationalism.

The Great Trek occurred under the leadership of Claas Epp Jr, who had been deeply shaped by the writings of the German pietist J H Jung-Stilling. Epp began teaching that the Antichrist was soon to appear and that the place of refuge for Christians was to be in the east toward China.[11] Beginning in 1880 about 600 Mennonites living in southern Russia and in the area of the Volga River, relocated to Turkestan. Some of these followed Epp while others followed an elder by the name of Abraham Peters so that the colony which was founded was divided in its leadership. Epp himself grew increasingly fanatical, eventually naming the day of the Lord's return and even claiming to be the son of Christ and the fourth member of the Trinity. He was excommunicated.[12] The Great Trek clearly bears some resemblance to other millennial movements of the nineteenth century. It remains a kind of footnote, however, in the Mennonite story because it was a highly regionalized event.

Dispensationalist understandings of biblical prophecy were somewhat regionalized as well. They were most likely to be adopted by North American Mennonites though they were also present among some Russian Mennonite communities[13] and, in some cases, were taken via missionary work to other parts of the world.[14] North Americans were exposed to dispensationalism through the many Bible Institutes that arose in the late 19th and early 20th centuries. As students returned to their home communities or assumed pastoral duties, some began preaching about the Last Days from a dispensationalist perspective. A number of traveling evangelists were particularly strong advocates of the system and, for a time, parts of the Anabaptist community in the United States and Canada were quite impacted. Other church leaders were quite troubled by this and a number of publications were written to, as one writer put it, "discourage the preaching of speculative, controversial prophetic themes, and encourage the preaching of the certain eschatology on which the Bible speaks with clarity and authority."[15]

That "certain eschatology" has rested on the Christian affirmation that Christ died, Christ arose, and Christ will come again. Outside of that, the events of our past have generally discouraged the main bodies within the Mennonite tradition from indulging in too much speculation about the Last Days. As one of our confessional statements reminds us, "The final destiny of all things lies in God's hands. In God's time, creation will be renewed in Christ. The kingdoms of this world shall become the kingdom of our Lord, and He shall reign forever."[16]

ENDNOTES

[1] Vernard Eller, "Protestant Radicalism," *Christian Century* 84, No 44 (1967): 1391, accessed May 19, 2012, ATLA *Religion Database with ATLASerials*, EBSCOhost.

[2] Eller identifies these as "Mennonites, Quakers and Brethren (plus Moravians, Schwenkfelders and such), then the Baptist bodies, and to a lesser extent the Methodists and Congregationalists." *Christian Century.*

[3] *Christian Century.*

[4] Carter Lindberg, "Eschatology and Fanaticism in the Reformation Era: Luther and the Anabaptists," *Concordia Theological Quarterly*, 64, no 4 (2000): 260, accessed May 19, 2012, ATLA Religion Database with ATLASerials, EBSCOhost. The great reformer Martin Luther is illustrative of the power of these images. His fear of God's wrath and judgment was profound and only relieved when he began to understand salvation as a free gift of God. Only then could he begin to look forward to the day of Christ's return.

[5] *Concordia Theological Quarterly*, 262. Lindberg particularly notes the way these themes appear in artwork of the period that seems to reflect the general uneasi-

ness of the times.

[6] The *Schleitheim Confession* is one of the earliest Anabaptist confessions of faith. Article IV reads: "From this we should learn that everything which is not united with our God and Christ cannot be other than an abomination which we should shun and flee from. By this is meant all Catholic and Protestant works and church services, meetings and church attendance, drinking houses, civic affairs, the oaths sworn in unbelief and other things of that kind, which are highly regarded by the world and yet are carried on in flat contradiction to the command of God, in accordance with all the unrighteousness which is in the world. From all these things we shall be separated and have no part with them for they are nothing but an abomination, and they are the cause of our being hated before our Christ Jesus, Who has set us free from the slavery of the flesh and fitted us for the service of God through the Spirit Whom He has given us." *The Schleitheim Confession*, accessed May 25, 2012, http://www.anabaptists.org/history/the-schleitheim-confession.html.

[7] C Arnold Snyder, *Anabaptist History and Theology: An Introduction*, (Kitchener, Ontario: 1995), 61-62.

[8] There are many accounts of these events. For a brief summary, refer to Cornelius Krahn, Nanne van der Zijpp and James M Stayer, "Münster Anabaptists," *Global Anabaptist Mennonite Encyclopedia Online* (1987).

[9] *The Schleitheim Confession*.

[10] Cornelius Krahn and Cornelius J Dyck. "Menno Simons (1496-1561)," *Global Anabaptist Mennonite Encyclopedia Online*, (1990), accessed May 25, 2012, http://www.gameo.org/encyclopedia/contents/M4636ME.html.

[11] Epp, like Jung-Stilling, was reading Daniel and the book of Revelation with attention to Revelation 12:6 and its reference to fleeing into the wilderness. Fred Richard Belk, *The Great Trek of the Russian Mennonites to Central Asia, 1880-1884*, (Scottdale, Pennsylvania: Herald Press, 1976), 1.

[12] See also Franz Bartsch and Richard D Thiessen, "Epp, Claas (1838-1913)," *Global Anabaptist Mennonite Encyclopedia Online*, (April 2005), accessed May 25, 2012, http://www.gameo.org/encyclopedia/contents/E6595.html.

[13] A J Dueck, "How our fathers understood the hope of Christ's coming." *Direction* 5, No 2 (1976), 20-25, accessed May 25, 2012, ATLA Religion Database with ATLASerials, EBSCOhost.

[14] The Japanese Mennonite Brethren Church, for example, continues to be dispensationalist in its understanding of the Bible as a result of missionary teaching during the 1950s.

[15] Paul Erb, *The Alpha and the Omega: A Restatement of The Christian Hope in Christ's Coming*, (Scottdale, Pennsylvania: Herald Press, 1955), vii. See also Ira D Landis, *The Faith of Our Fathers on Eschatology*, (Lititz, Pennsylvania: self-published, 1946).

[16] "Eternal Hope and Judgment," *Articles of Faith and Doctrine [Brethren in Christ]*, accessed May 27, 2012, http://www.bic-church.org/about/beliefs/eternalhope_judgement.asp.

Eschatology as Understood by Mennonites Today

Thomas R Yoder Neufeld

I would like to continue from where Valerie G Rempel left off and focus on the present. In keeping with the spirit of this dialogue, in which we are engaging in conversation and coming to a deeper understanding of each other, I will begin with description and then go on to evaluation, identifying some areas to which Mennonites might give attention.

I invite my colleagues in the Mennonite delegation to offer correction or insights from their own perspectives and settings so as to more fully represent the current status of eschatology among us. I do so because it is difficult to say what a Mennonite view on eschatology might be, given that even the MWC, comprising approximately 100 church bodies and denominations, does not encompass the whole range of Mennonite, let alone Anabaptist, churches and denominations. Giving a fair account is complicated further by the fact that within the same denominations, even within local congregations, there is a wide spectrum of views. We intersect with quite disparate segments and directions within the wider church (e.g., some of us identify with Evangelical and Pentecostal emphases, others with various expressions of liberation theology), we read the Bible through diverse lenses (some of us read it "literally," whereas others take a critical approach), and we have quite varied understandings of the church and its mission (evangelism and church planting on one hand, and engagement for peace and justice, socially understood, on the other). These all impinge on eschatology.

1. Confessions and/or statements of faith and/or conviction
Let me begin with a brief discussion of some of our recent and presently operative statements and confessions of faith. I will address only those statements that explicitly address or contain eschatology.

a. *Shared Convictions* (Mennonite World Conference, 2006)[1]
While such eschatologically loaded subjects as salvation, resurrection, Holy Spirit, and the church and its mission are addressed in the seven listed convictions, they are not related explicitly to eschatology. The only reference to eschatology comes in the very last sentence in the document, following the seven shared convictions: "We seek to walk in his name by the power of the Holy Spirit, as we confidently await Christ's return and the final fulfillment of God's kingdom." In other words, an eschatological stance is taken as a given, but it is not identified among the seven convictions "we hold ... to be central to our belief and practice." We might wonder whether this is an indicator of where eschatology is located in the corporate confessional imagination.

Alfred Neufeld, Paraguayan chair of the Faith and Life Commission of the MWC, has written a book-length commentary on the *Shared Convictions*, entitled *What We Believe Together*.[2] As in the *Shared Convictions*, there is a clear acknowledgement of the future hope of Christ's return (147) and a recognition of Christ's role in judgment (Acts 10:42; WWBT, 49). For the most part, however, when eschatology is emphasized it is in relation to the church's stance in the present.

Eternal life is parsed in light of John 3:36 ("Whoever believes in the Son has eternal life," WWBT, 50, 51). In short, "eternity begins here and now" (50). The church participates *now* in eternal life, "because the eternal Christ is in its midst already" (50). Neufeld stresses that believers have already been raised with Christ (Eph 2:6). The church is the ongoing visibility of the resurrection, through which "God started the restoration of the world in a visible way" (45). Placing the stress on the present task of the church, Neufeld speaks of this as "the time of the church and the Holy Spirit," and of God having "placed his whole redeeming project on behalf of humanity into the hands of the church" (56).

Just as *Shared Convictions* ends on a future oriented note, Neufeld cites the Swiss theologian Bernhard Ott's *God's Shalom Project*[3] to the effect that whereas "the new" has begun, it is still, as Romans 8 reminds us, "in the delivery stage." The Holy Spirit is the "down payment toward the coming world" (WWBT, 145). So, while the church serves as "the showcase and vanguard" (146) of the coming reign of God, it lives in the hope-filled tension between the already and the not yet.

Neufeld's and Ott's books are not official Mennonite statements, but they were specifically written for and adopted by MWC for the global Mennonite community to express the shared perspective of the global Mennonite community. These statements together reflect a future dimension in their eschatology, but much more strongly a stress on the present. The church is not simply the waiting and enduring community, even if suffering is very much part of what it means to participate now in the age to come in the midst of a still broken world. The church is what we might call a "colony of the future," fully engaged in the present as God's means of realizing his reign. There is little sense of urgency in relation to the *parousia* of Christ, unless Christ is understood largely as the church as His body, and *parousia* is understood, as it can be, as "presence." There is thus no stated interest in speculating on the how and when of that acknowledged future event of Christ's return. Perhaps that is largely because it is seen not as disruption but as culmination and fulfillment of what is already underway in and through the church.

Moving beyond the MWC documents, and the global reality they reflect, I can do little more than reflect on a limited sample of statements mostly from the North American context.

b. *Mennonite Church Confession of Faith in a Mennonite Perspective* (1995)[4]

Article 8 on "Salvation" stresses what is already available to the believer in Christ. There is an acknowledgment that "...the salvation we already experience is but a foretaste of the salvation yet to come, when Christ will vanquish sin and death, and the redeemed will live in eternal communion with God." This point is, however, not elaborated on, nor supported with biblical references, as is otherwise typical of the articles in the Confession.

Article 24 on "Reign of God" reflects what we just saw in the MWC statements, namely, that since "in Jesus' ministry, death, and resurrection, the time of fulfillment has begun," the church already lives "under the reign of God according to the pattern of God's future." The church is to be "a spiritual, social, and economic reality, demonstrating now the justice, righteousness, love, and peace of the age to come." While we are to "place our hope in the reign of God and in its fulfillment in the day when Christ our ascended Lord will come again in glory to judge the living and the dead," the stress falls again at least as much if not more on the present and on the church as a kind of "colony of the future."

At the same time, Article 24 concludes with an assertion of the importance of the resurrection and judgment to come in conjunction with the appearing of Christ, resulting in eternal life for those who have done good and condemnation to hell and eternal separation from God for those who have done evil. The article ends with themes from John's Apocalypse with a promise of a new heaven and a new earth and a quotation of Revelation 5:13-14, praising the Lamb seated on the throne.

The immediately following commentary on Article 24 acknowledges that for many Mennonites the stress on judgment is problematic, given the emphasis on God's wrath. While punishment is acknowledged as an aspect of God's justice, an effort is made to parse judgment more as God's unwillingness to coerce persons into a relationship with Him than as punishment, even if that too is acknowledged.

With respect to the state of the faithful dead between their death and the resurrection,[5] the commentary asserts that the New Testament "speaks much less frequently and clearly about the state of persons between the time of their deaths and the resurrection." The question is evidently quite deliberately left unanswered, but responded to with a reference to Romans 8:38-39: "Yet, we who are in Christ are assured that not even death can separate us from the love of God."

The commentary concludes with a word of caution not to engage in end-times speculation but rather to await "in hope the coming of our Lord and Savior Jesus Christ."

    c. *Mennonite Brethren Confessions*

There are two confessional statements for the second largest Mennonite body, Mennonite Brethren. They are the 1999 *Confession of Faith* serving both the US and Canada,[6] and the statement adopted by the International Community of Mennonite Brethren (ICOMB) in 2004 by 18 MB national conferences around the globe.[7]

First, the 1999 *Confession of Faith*. With respect to eschatology, Article 5 on "Salvation" speaks of God completing at the coming of Christ "the plan of salvation" when sin and death are no more and "the redeemed are gathered in the new heaven and the new earth." Article 18 on "Christ's Final Triumph" asserts that "Christ will return visibly and triumphantly at the end of the present age," with the church "living in expectation of his imminent return." "New creation" is identified with "a new heaven and a new earth."

On the question of what happens to believers who pass away prior to the resurrection, they are said to "go to be with the Lord when they die," even as they await the resurrection of the body which will be "fit for life in God's eternal kingdom." Christ's return will bring judgment, with the destruction of all evil, and the consignment to hell of those who have rejected Christ.

The ICOMB *Confession of Faith* has affinities with the *Shared Convictions* document of the MWC, in particular with the commentary by Alfred Neufeld (himself MB), in that the emphasis falls on associating eschatology with the present mission of the church: "The church is God's new creation, the agent of transformation called to

model God's design for humanity." The future element is present
as well, however, in that the "new creation will be completed when
Christ returns," which will be marked by resurrection and judgment.
In the present time the church "belongs to the in-breaking kingdom
of God," modeling an "alternative community," all the while "empowered by the certainty that God will create a new heaven and a
new earth."

The ICOMB *Confession of Faith* does not address the question
of the fate of the dead between their passing and the resurrection to
come.

    d. Brethren in Christ *Articles of Faith and Doctrine* (1986)[8]

The Brethren in Christ statement brings the promise of resurrection and "life everlasting" in direct connection to the experience
of dying in this life. "We believe that following death, the believer's
spirit is present with the Lord.... Those who die in Christ, along
with the faithful believers alive at His return, will rise and will
receive a new, glorified body, which will be free from infirmity and
death. The lost, however, await a resurrection unto condemnation,"
and "will be punished with everlasting destruction in hell." With
clear allusions to 2 Peter 3, Revelation 21, and 1 Corinthians 15,
"The people of God anticipate God's promise of a new heaven and
a new earth under the rule of Christ. Evil will be destroyed and ultimately Christ will deliver all things to the Father."

Observations Regarding Mennonites and Eschatology

These statements on eschatology are quite clear, if sparse. They
essentially attempt to capture the unarguable presence of explicit
eschatological statements within the New Testament, while cau-
tioning against speculation as to the when and the how; and, more
importantly, a majority of recent confessional statements place the
stress on the present stance and mission of the church as living
the "new age" in this still very much old world. In some cases, the
church is identified as God's agent of eschatological change, speaking of Christ's return as completing the process the church is already
engaged in, rather than being a disruptive intervention in an ever-
worsening world, as is more typical of apocalyptic scenarios.

While the confessional statements are fairly clear, we should be cautious about how much of a picture they provide of the views of the great variety of Mennonites who make up actual congregations. (That is not unique to Mennonites, but in some instances the polity and the "non-creedal" nature of the tradition permits that disparity to a much greater extent than in traditions in which the confessional statements are considered definitive for what "we believe.") My own observation of the Mennonite stance(s) on eschatology is based on my experience as a professor and pastor within a Canadian context.

First of all, I observe a turning away both from expectation of the imminent return of Christ and from speculative Dispensationalism (other than in those sectors which are heavily nurtured by the eschatology of conservative Christian media).

Second, I observe a turning toward an ethicized "realizing" rather than "realized" eschatology. For example, there is a notable stress on Kingdom of God ethically and socially understood, whose realization is related to the mission of the church as much or more than on a future coming of Christ (accompanied by a growing prominence of missional rhetoric). The work of service and peace-making is hardly accompanied by more than a vague sense of hope (the Mennonite Church's slogan of "healing and hope" is largely left undefined). Eschatology has simply ceased in many circles to be much of a point of discussion or interest, as may perhaps be reflected in the *Shared Convictions*.

Third, there is among many, perhaps especially among younger and more educated Mennonites, an assumption that the cosmos is very old and that the human community has evolved over many millennia. They view the future as one in which humans may end their sojourn on earth via nuclear catastrophe or global warming, but that the earth, and indeed the cosmos, still has an indefinitely long future. Little effort is made in teaching and preaching to bridge the gap between the church's biblically informed ways of conceptualizing the present and the future (apocalyptic) and contemporary scientifically informed ways of viewing reality. If apocalyptic language has a place in these circles, it is largely in relation to potential nuclear and ecological/environmental catastrophes.

Fourth, I observe a divide between those Mennonites who are oriented by biblical/evangelical ways of conceptualizing and articulating Christian convictions and those who are principally interested in a social peace and justice ethic more amorphously informed by tradition and spirituality. An end to war, to ecological degradation, and to social and economic inequities, are for many the nature of the future hope. At the same time, even in those circles in which evangelism is an urgent concern, it seems to me that the urgency is framed less eschatologically than in terms of church growth, fullness of life in Christ, and personal assurance of an afterlife in heaven.

Fifth, there is no clarity, let alone consensus, regarding what happens when a person dies. This comes to the fore at funerals: the deceased has "gone to be with the Lord" and may even be said to be "looking down on us;" but at the graveside we also hear the words "dust to dust...," including assurance of the future resurrection of the dead, with little need to sort out the admixture of Greek and Hebrew notions of death, soul, and immortality, and how that all relates to the eschatological hope of resurrection.

Sixth, among Mennonites nourished by popular dispensationalism (TV evangelists, *Left Behind* novels), one also finds so-called Christian Zionism, which tends to clash with the pro-Palestinian stance of those whose views are more oriented to peace and justice. In mainstream Mennonite churches this perspective tends not to have access to the denominational organs, and is not typically present in teaching venues and seldom in the pulpit. For that reason, it is difficult to assess the strength of these views.

Seventh, the eschatological foundation and context of biblical understandings of resurrection, Holy Spirit, salvation, and church—to say nothing of naming Jesus the "Christ/Messiah"—are not fully appreciated by many Mennonites. Peace is too often a social project rather than viewed as central to the work of Messiah and the mission of His body, the church, and thus to be viewed in relation to eschatology, indeed to soteriology more generally. Certainly theologians and biblical scholars appreciate the eschatological framework within which it makes sense to speak of Jesus as risen Messiah, of gospel, salvation, and church.[9] John Howard Yoder's highly influential peace perspective, for example, is informed by the eschatologically framed notion of the "reign of Christ," marked off from the full appearing of the "reign of God" by the fact that it is engaged dynamically in the present in the struggle against the powers that, while in actuality already defeated (Col 2:15), continue to resist the full realization of God's reign. It is my strong impression, however, that while Yoder's thoroughgoing pacifism has continued to be championed, his grounding in biblical eschatology has been retained much less.

In short, it would be difficult to identify a shared eschatological orientation among Mennonites and Brethren in Christ. It may even be that sophistication in biblical analysis has contributed to such lack of clear consensus. Biblical scholars in our seminaries share roughly a mix of evangelical theology and critical methodology in the study of the Bible. This means that they/we would share a sense that to remove eschatology from the Bible, most especially the New Testament, would render the Bible mute. At the same time, we have come to take for granted that the New Testament does *not* speak with one voice on the question, but reflects both the early intense anticipation that the resurrection of Jesus would find its completion in his *parousia* in the immediate future, on one hand, and apparent adjustment to a protracted future, on the other, in which both patient waiting and growing appreciation for *parousia* as present reality are encouraged responses.

To illustrate, in 1 Thessalonians 4 and 5, likely the earliest writing in the New Testament, Paul reassures believers of the day of the Lord's arrival with the assumption that some will be alive when it happens (4:17; cf. also Matt 16:28 and parallels). Texts such as these clearly reflect apocalyptic ways of understanding the consummation of the process begun with Jesus' resurrection as imminent.[10]

At the same time, other texts (John, Ephesians, Colossians) reflect a willingness to speak of the future as already present where to "know God" is already to have "eternal life" (John 17:3), to have already passed from death to life (John 5:24), to have already been raised and seated with Christ in the heavenly places (Eph 2:6), echoing Paul's breathtaking "if anyone is in Christ, there is New

Creation; the old things have passed, the new things have come" (2 Cor 5:17).

Alongside such "realized" or "realizing" eschatology are texts that presuppose a longer, more protracted future before the culmination of the reign of God, requiring less urgent anticipation than endurance and patience. In 2 Thessalonians 2:2 there is an explicit warning about pseudo-Pauline letters claiming the day of the Lord has already happened. Hebrews is essentially a sermon calling for an enduring faithfulness so that believers might not miss out on arriving at the "rest." In 2 Peter 3:8-9 the apparent delay of the day of the Lord is tied to the patience of God, reminding readers that God's reckoning of time does not match ours.

In more recent years Mennonite and Brethren in Christ scholars have come to interpret the Revelation of John as a prophetic critique of its own Roman imperial time rather than as a code for predicting the coming of Christ, as was the case in dispensationalism.[11]

Rather than reading it as predictive prophecy, it is read as proclamatory critical prophecy, akin to the writing prophets of the Old Testament. Its figurative language is not a code for a determined future, but code that intends to expose the true nature of the present. It is addressed first and foremost to the churches of Asia Minor, attempting to wake them up to the true state of reality, both criticizing and encouraging them in their faithful witness. Revelation 5 is deemed key to Mennonite interpretation. Jesus is the "lamb that was slain" (5:6), and thus alone "worthy" to open the scroll and to break its seals (5:6-7).[12] The conclusion of the book with the New Jerusalem coming down from heaven, with the gates open and the kings of the earth going in and out, is seen as a peaceable vision and serves often as a way of capsulizing the hope of the church.

To this array of eschatological signals we might add the way in which believers are drawn into the divine activity associated in apocalyptic texts with God's intervention. Paul, for example, applies the depiction of God in Isaiah 59, as a warrior in full armor, to believers already in 1 Thessalonians 5:8, but then again in Romans 13:12, and most dramatically in Ephesians 6:10-20. Believers are not bystanders in the divine drama of the day of the Lord.[13]

Given this bewildering variety of eschatological conceptions, Jesus' words in Luke 17:21 are worth heeding, even if they also complicate matters further, especially if placed next to Mark 13 and Matthew 24: "Don't look here or there, the Kingdom of God is in your midst." It may be enough to say: God's future is certain, but unpredictable. At same time, the future is already present and impinging on the life of the church. The church lives in the *kairos* of a present loaded with the future and is summoned to participate in its coming. By being the body of the Messiah, God's eschatological agent, the church is in essence an eschatological reality.

It is clear that such an approach to biblical scholarship and interpretation leaves little room for a clear system. We might welcome that. On the other hand, it can leave laypersons confused and perhaps even discouraged from taking eschatology seriously. That is not to be welcomed.

Challenges

I wish to conclude by identifying some challenges for us in the Mennonite community:

1. We dare not neglect eschatology, which is constitutive of our faith as rooted in Scripture.

2. We need to recover a sense of the church as "colonies of the future" in which the future unity is already being forged in socially concrete ways that transcend class, gender, and tribe. At the same time we should not confuse our efforts with anything more than participation by God's grace in the "coming of the day."

3. We need to guard against polarizing either into individualized "realized" eschatology ("hope" as personal renewal/rebirth) or into social "building the kingdom or the city of God" largely as vision of more peaceable world. Otherwise we will have competing or even mutually exclusive eschatologies, rather than pieces of a recoverable whole.

4. Can we recover the eager expectancy of early believers that afforded them the courage to open themselves to the convulsive presence of the Spirit without determining what the fulfillment looks like?

5. Can we/Should we recover a sense of eschatological urgency that contains a sense of the judgment of God within a framework of a loving and gracious God who will not allow creation to drift beyond the reach of righteousness—a righteousness that is expressed not only in justice and judgment, but also in mercy (Rom 3:21-26; Eph 2:4; 2 Peter 3:9)?

6. Without defining what it will look like, or when it will happen, can we share with our SDA sisters and brothers some of the joyous anticipation in Christ's coming we saw reflected in the sculpture in the atrium of their Silver Springs headquarters?

7. Can we anchor our hope, not in our own individual or corporate positive disposition, nor in optimism about our own individual or corporate capacity for success, but in God's promise to bring to completion the revolution begun in the resurrection of Jesus? And can we leave the time and the nature of that completion open, given the diversity of the biblical witness, without sacrificing faith in its certainty and in its shaping of our faithfulness?

ENDNOTES

[1] "In an historic action, MWC's General Council approved a statement of shared convictions to give members around the world a clearer picture of beliefs Anabaptists hold in common. This is the first statement of beliefs adopted by leaders of the global Anabaptist community. The statement is not meant to replace conferences' official confessions of faith. Nancy Heisey, Mennonite World Conference President in 2006, said 'groups are free to use it for theological conversations.' It can also be used by those who do not have a formal confession. It is also intended to help define Anabaptism to others.
The discussion of shared convictions started in 1997 in Mennonite World Conference's Faith and Life Council. After collecting faith statements from member churches, the council brought a first draft to the 2003 MWC assembly in Zimbabwe. Revisions were made based on responses from member churches over the next three years, leading to adoption at Pasadena, California.
See http://www.gameo.org/encyclopedia/contents/shared_convictions_mennonite_world_conference_2006.
[2] Alfred Neufeld, *What We Believe Together: Exploring the "Shared Convictions" of Anabaptist-Related Churches* (Good Books, 2007).

[3] Bernhard Ott, *God's Shalom Project: An Engaging Look at the Bible's Sweeping Story*, Timothy Geddert, translator, (Intercourse, Pennsylvania: Good Books, 2004).

[4] http://www.gameo.org/encyclopedia/contents/C6652_1995.html.

[5] This issue has been raised specifically by our SDA conversation partners, and is thus specifically taken up in this presentation, as requested.

[6] www.mbconf.ca/home/products_and_services/resources/theology/confession_of_faith/detailed_version/.

[7] www.mbconf.ca/home/products_and_services/resources/theology/confession_of_faith/icomb_confession_of_faith/.

[8] http://www.bic-church.org/about/articlesoffaith.asp.

[9] See Yoder's *Politics of Jesus*, second edition (Grand Rapids, Michigan: Eerdmans, 1994), and also his essays "To Serve our God and to Rule the World," and "Peace without Eschatology?" in *The Royal Priesthood: Essays. Ecclesiological and Ecumenical*, Michael Cartwright, editor, (Grand Rapids, Michigan: Eerdmans, 1994), 127-167. Yoder's thinking has had a significant impact on the kind of loading of the present with God's future we see in Alfred Neufeld's commentary on the *Shared Convictions*. E.g., "The ultimate meaning of history is to be found in the church," which, to be sure, participates in the victory of the lamb (151). "The most effective way to contribute to the preservation of society in the old aeon is to live in the new" (165).

[10] Among Mennonite authors addressing eschatology, in particular apocalyptic eschatology, see my *Ephesians* essay on "Apocalyptic;" BCBC; (Waterloo, Ontario/ Scottdale, Pennsylvania: Herald, 2002), 339-341; *Recovering Jesus: The Witness of the New Testament* (Grand Rapids, Michigan: Brazos, 2007), 134-36. See also, Jacob W Elias, 1 & 2 Thessalonians essays on "Apocalyptic," and "Eschatology," BCBC, (Waterloo, Ontario/Scottdale, Pennsylvania: Herald, 1995), 354-57, and the bibliographical items listed there.

[11] See the work of J Nelson Kraybill, *Apocalypse and Allegiance: Worship, Politics, and Devotion in the Book of Revelation* (Grand Rapids, Michigan: Brazos, 2010); Loren L Johns, *The Lamb Christology of the Apocalypse of John: An Investigation into Its Origins and Rhetorical Force* (WUNT 2/167; Tübingen: Mohr Siebeck, 2003); John R Yeatts, *Revelation*, BCBC (Waterloo, Ontario/Scottdale, Pennsylvania: Herald, 2003); John Howard Yoder, *Politics of Jesus*, 228-47; my own *Killing Enmity: Violence and the New Testament* (Grand Rapids, Michigan: Baker Academic, 2011), 122-35.

[12] This perspective has received considerable echo in the scholarship of Richard Baukham, Jacques Ellul, Michael Gorman, Christopher Rowlands, etc.

[13] As I have argued for both 1 Thessalonians 5:1-11 and Ephesians 6:10-20 in *'Put on the Armour of God': The Divine Warrior from Isaiah to Ephesians* (Sheffield, United Kingdom: Sheffield Academic, 1997); *Ephesians*; *Killing Enmity*.

The Role of Eschatology in Seventh-day Adventist Thought and Practice

William G Johnsson

That eschatology plays a major role in Seventh-day Adventist thought and practice quickly becomes apparent to even the casual observer of the movement. Adventists commonly refer to themselves as "a people of hope," and their hymnody from the beginning has featured songs of the Second Coming, such as "Lift up the trumpet and loud let it ring; Jesus is coming again," or the more recent and exceedingly popular "We have this hope.... hope in the coming of the Lord."

Beyond such manifestations from Adventist life and worship, two facts make abundantly evident the centrality of eschatology—the very name, and the Fundamental Beliefs of the church.

In 1860, at the outset of the movement, the early believers faced the question of what name they should adopt. They considered generic designations such as "Church of God," but quickly rejected them. Seeking a name that would proclaim to the world their distinctive characteristics, they settled on "Seventh-day," which points to the observance of Saturday, the Sabbath; and "Adventist," which embodies their conviction that Jesus Christ will soon return to this earth. Christians for centuries have believed and proclaimed the Second Coming; the difference with Seventh-day Adventists is belief in the *imminence* of Jesus' return.

If the very name "Seventh-day Adventist" declares the central role of eschatology, the official body of doctrine voted by the general assembly of the church—the General Conference Session—reinforces the fact. This body of doctrine, known as the *Fundamental Beliefs of Seventh-day Adventists*, consists of 28 articles. Among them, the last four focus on final events. These articles are:

25. Second Coming of Christ
26. Death and Resurrection
27. Millennium and End of Sin
28. New Earth

In addition, the 24th article, "Christ's Ministry in the Heavenly Sanctuary," has a large eschatological component. While it expresses Christ's ongoing intercessory ministry—a doctrine taught by other Christians over the course of the centuries—it focuses on His work in the pre-Advent judgment.

Each of these five statements warrants careful examination. That is a task that would extend this paper far beyond the needs of this conversation; indeed, it would call for book-length treatment, not a presentation. Here our concern must be kaleidoscopic rather than detailed. I aim to set forth a birds-eye view of Seventh-day Adventist eschatology, attempting to explain in three stages:

1. How eschatology came to be so important for Seventh-day Adventists,
2. The theological factors that shape Adventist eschatology, and
3. The role of a particular aspect of eschatology—apocalyptic—in the New Testament and among Seventh-day Adventists.

I.   The Origins of Seventh-day Adventists

The Seventh-day Adventist Church finds its immediate roots in the 19th century revival in the United States, known as the Second Great Awakening. In the early part of the century many preachers in Europe and other parts of the world proclaimed the soon coming of Jesus Christ, but the impact was by far the greatest in North America.

A Baptist layman named William Miller played a major role in the movement in the United States. Miller had abandoned his Christian upbringing for deism, but subsequently he turned back to the Bible as the Second Great Awakening revitalized the churches.

Miller became an ardent student of Scripture. With the help of *Cruden's Concordance*, he worked through the Bible comparing Scripture with Scripture in a methodical manner. His investigation led him to conclude that in about 25 years—in 1843—Christ would return to this earth.

Key to Miller's findings were the prophecies of the book of Daniel, and in particular Daniel 8:14: "Unto two thousand three hundred days; then shall the sanctuary be cleansed." Miller operated on a commonly accepted interpretation that a day in Bible prophecy stands for a year (Num 14:34; Ezek 4:5-6); he also interpreted the sanctuary of Daniel 8:14 as this earth and its cleansing as by fire at Christ's coming (2 Thess 1:7-10; 2 Peter 3:10-12).

Miller's conclusion that Jesus would come *before* the millennium ran counter to the theology of the day, which had Him returning after the millennium. Conscious of this tension, Miller for several years was reluctant to share his findings with others. Eventually, however, he came under conviction that he needed to warn the world of its danger. Before long Miller had a stream of invitations to preach in the churches of several denominations. By the end of the 1830's several ministers had been persuaded that Jesus would return about the year 1843.

Miller's cause received a major impetus with the enlistment in 1834 of Joshua B Himes. Himes, the influential pastor of a church in Boston, was an activist. Within four years he made *Millerism* and *Adventism* household words in the United States. Himes' efforts spread Miller's message even further, however. Historian George R Knight notes: "Beyond North America, Himes' ingenuity saw to it that by 1844 the advent doctrine had been heard around the world."[1]

Himes launched a media blitz to get out the message of the soon Second Coming. Through periodicals, pamphlets, tracts and books, he spread the word everywhere. He launched the periodical *Signs of the Times* and a two-cent daily newspaper, *The Midnight Cry*, to warn the people of New York City. In five months in 1842, more than 600,000 copies were sold by newsboys or given away.

In addition to publishing, Himes organized a series of general conferences of Christians Expecting the Advent. He also initiated Adventist camp meetings: between 1842 and 1844 more than 130 such meetings convened, with a combined attendance of more than 500,000 (one out of every 35 Americans). To accommodate the large crowds, Himes pioneered the use of a large tent with a seating capacity of about 4,000.

As the Millerite movement mushroomed, attitudes in the popular churches changed. Pulpits and church buildings were no longer open; the Millerites were ridiculed; they were forced to decide between belief in the soon return of Christ and church membership.

The passing of the year 1843 brought the first disappointment to the Millerites. However, the movement found a new life through a recalculation of the prophecy of Daniel 8:14. It was now predicted that the cleansing of the sanctuary would take place on the Jewish Day of Atonement, which in 1844 was October 22.

Knight observes: "On October 22, 1844 an estimated 50,000 to 100,000 believers lingered in expectation of the appearance of Jesus in the clouds of heaven, while countless others waited in doubt, fearing that the Millerites might be correct."[2]

The day came and went, leaving the Millerites shattered. Later Hiram Edson wrote: "Our fondest hopes and expectations were blasted, and such a spirit of weeping came over us as I never experienced before. It seemed that the loss of all earthly friends could have been no comparison. We wept, and wept, till the day dawn."[3]

In total disarray and discouragement, the majority abandoned hope in the Second Coming, but not Miller. On November 10, 1844, he wrote: "Although I have been twice disappointed, I am not yet cast down or discouraged. God has been with me in Spirit, and has comforted me.... Although surrounded with enemies and scoffers, yet my mind is perfectly calm, and my hope in the coming of Christ is as strong as ever."[4]

Out of such unpromising soil—blasted hopes, keenest disappointment—would emerge what would become known as the Seventh-day Adventist Church. It was the unlikeliest beginning for a worldwide movement.

Although most of the Adventists returned to their churches or fell into unbelief, some continued to hold onto hope in the soon return of Jesus. These fell into three groups:

1. Those who believed that they had been correct concerning the event, but wrong in the time calculation; Miller and Himes fit here.

2. Those who believed that they had been correct in both event and time, but that Christ's return had been a spiritual coming; this group fell into fanaticism.

3. Those who believed that they had been correct on the time but wrong in the event.

The future leaders of the Seventh-day Adventist Church came from the third group, which was the smallest of the three. Further study led them to conclude that the "Sanctuary" of Daniel 8:14 was not the earth but the Sanctuary in heaven mentioned in the book of Hebrews (see Heb 8:1-2; 9:11-12).

To this new understanding was shortly linked observance of the seventh day, the Sabbath. A few of those who expected Christ to return soon had already become Sabbath-keepers prior to the disappointment; now the practice spread among others in the third group.

The period 1844-1848 marked intensive Bible study by the Sabbatarian leaders. By its close the group, numbering only about 100, had reached agreement on five basic points of doctrine. These are the so-called "pillars" of the Seventh-day Adventist Church:

1. The personal, visible return of Jesus;

2. The cleansing of the sanctuary: Christ's ministry in heaven beginning on October 22, 1844 as the beginning of the antitypical Day of Atonement;

3. The continuing gift of prophecy, with its modern manifestation in the life and work of Ellen G White;

4. The Sabbath;

5. Immortality, not as inherent but received through faith in Christ.

These doctrines formed a unified package of doctrine and prophetic interpretation, encapsulated in the vision of the three angels in an end-time setting (Rev 14:6-14). The group was miniscule in numbers, but it began to see itself as called by God to a large mission. As the years passed, the vision expanded to eventually encompass the world.

I have dwelt at some length on the origins of the Seventh-day Adventist Church because it is impossible to grasp its ethos apart from consideration of the crucial role of eschatology from its earliest beginnings. Eschatology is in the DNA of Seventh-day Adventists. It isn't something to be merely studied as part of its history—eschatology lives and throbs in the Church.

To the onlooker, the stretch of time, now 169 years since 1844, might seem to negate expectations of Jesus' soon return by a massive cognitive dissonance. That is not the case with Seventh-day Adventists. To them, Jesus' coming is a living hope that tinges every new morning with joy. Their experience resonates with that of William Miller, who refused to abandon expectation as he wrote following the disappointment of October 22, 1844: "Brethren, hold fast; let no one take your crown. I have fixed my mind upon another time, and here I mean to stand until God gives me more light—and that is *Today*, TODAY and TODAY, until he comes, and I see him for whom my soul yearns."[5]

Seventh-day Adventists are not Millerites. The latter were not a denomination, but a movement of Christians from many denominations. Miller never accepted the Sabbath doctrine. Nevertheless, several aspects of the 1844 revival passed over into the life of the Seventh-day Adventist Church. Among them were the emphasis on the books of Daniel and Revelation; publishing (the *Signs of the Times* continues as an Adventist periodical); camp meetings; and the use of tents, including the "big tent."

II. Theological Considerations

In considering the role of eschatology in Adventist thought and life, two aspects are foundational.

First, while eschatology has been crucial in Adventist self-understanding, it is not the center of Adventism. That center is Jesus Christ, in His person and work. All other dimensions of Adventist thought derive from that center. The 28 Fundamental Beliefs of the church make this fact abundantly clear. While several articles relate to eschatology, these all appear at the very end of the list. The list of beliefs in the main follows the traditional order of doctrines in a systematic theology: the doctrine of God comes first, followed by articles on the person and work of Christ, then ecclesiology and articles on Christian life. Only then do the articles on eschatology appear.

Second, the articles on eschatology, while listed separately, show close inter-connections. In effect, they are a package. I list below these final articles and include also number 24, The Ministry of Christ in the Heavenly Sanctuary, because it includes ideas important to the package. Like all the 28 articles of the Fundamental Beliefs, each of these final articles at its close includes supporting biblical references; I include these references also to indicate the biblical basis for Adventist theological understanding.

"24. Christ's Ministry in the Heavenly Sanctuary: There is a sanctuary in heaven, the true tabernacle which the Lord set up and not man. In it Christ ministers on our behalf, making available to believers the benefits of His atoning sacrifice offered once for all on the cross. He was inaugurated as our great High Priest and began His intercessory ministry at the time of His ascension. In 1844, at the end of the prophetic period of 2300 days, He entered the second and last phase of His atoning ministry. It is a work of investigative judgment which is part of the ultimate disposition of all sin, typified by the cleansing of the ancient Hebrew sanctuary on the Day of

Atonement. In that typical service the sanctuary was cleansed with the blood of animal sacrifices, but the heavenly things are purified with the perfect sacrifice of the blood of Jesus. The investigative judgment reveals to heavenly intelligences who among the dead are asleep in Christ and therefore, in Him, are deemed worthy to have part in the first resurrection. It also makes manifest who among the living are abiding in Christ, keeping the commandments of God and the faith of Jesus, and in Him, therefore, are ready for translation into His everlasting kingdom. This judgment vindicates the justice of God in saving those who believe in Jesus. It declares that those who have remained loyal to God shall receive the kingdom. The completion of this ministry of Christ will mark the close of human probation before the Second Advent. (Heb. 8:1-5; 4:14-16; 9:11-28; 10:19-22; 1:3; 2:16, 17; Dan. 7:9-27; 8:13, 14; 9:24-27; Num. 14:34; Eze. 4:6; Lev. 16; Rev. 14:6, 7; 20:12; 14:12; 22:12.)

"**25. Second Coming of Christ**: The second coming of Christ is the blessed hope of the church, the grand climax of the gospel. The Saviour's coming will be literal, personal, visible, and world-wide. When He returns, the righteous dead will be resurrected, and together with the righteous living will be glorified and taken to heaven, but the unrighteous will die. The almost complete fulfillment of most lines of prophecy, together with the present condition of the world, indicates that Christ's coming is imminent. The time of that event has not been revealed, and we are therefore exhorted to be ready at all times. (Titus 2:13; Heb. 9:28; John 14:1-3; Acts 1:9-11; Matt. 24:14; Rev. 1:7; Matt. 24:43, 44; 1 Thess. 4:13-18; 1 Cor. 15:51-54; 2 Thess. 1:7-10; 2:8; Rev. 14:14-20; 19:11-21; Matt. 24; Mark 13; Luke 21; 2 Tim. 3:1-5; 1 Thess. 5:1-6.)

"**26. Death and Resurrection**: The wages of sin is death. But God, who alone is immortal, will grant eternal life to His redeemed. Until that day death is an unconscious state for all people. When Christ, who is our life, appears, the resurrected righteous and the living righteous will be glorified and caught up to meet their Lord. The second resurrection, the resurrection of the unrighteous, will take place a thousand years later. (Rom. 6:23; 1 Tim. 6:15, 16; Eccl. 9:5, 6; Ps. 146:3, 4; John 11:11-14; Col. 3:4; 1 Cor. 15:51-54; 1 Thess.

4:13-17; John 5:28, 29; Rev. 20:1-10.)

"27. Millennium and the End of Sin: The millennium is the thousand-year reign of Christ with His saints in heaven between the first and second resurrections. During this time the wicked dead will be judged; the earth will be utterly desolate, without living human inhabitants, but occupied by Satan and his angels. At its close Christ with His saints and the Holy City will descend from heaven to earth. The unrighteous dead will then be resurrected, and with Satan and his angels will surround the city; but fire from God will consume them and cleanse the earth. The universe will thus be freed of sin and sinners forever. (Rev. 20; 1 Cor. 6:2, 3; Jer. 4:23-26; Rev. 21:1-5; Mal. 4:1; Eze. 28:18, 19.)

"28. New Earth: On the new earth, in which righteousness dwells, God will provide an eternal home for the redeemed and a perfect environment for everlasting life, love, joy, and learning in His presence. For here God Himself will dwell with His people, and suffering and death will have passed away. The great controversy will be ended, and sin will be no more. All things, animate and inanimate, will declare that God is love; and He shall reign forever. Amen. (2 Peter 3:13; Isa. 35; 65:17-25; Matt. 5:5; Rev. 21:1-7; 22:1-5; 11:15.)"

Looking over these five articles on Eschatology, the last four bear resemblance to positions commonly held by other Christians. That holds true also for #26 Death and Resurrection. When the pioneers of Adventism arrived at this understanding of Bible teaching, that was not the case—theirs was a distinctly minority position. Biblical scholarship in the 20th century, however, has arrived at the same conclusion. Oscar Cullmann in, *Immortality of the Soul or Resurrection of the Dead? The Witness of the New Testament,* convincingly showed the idea of immortality of the soul as a Greek, not Hebrew, idea and that the New Testament teaches instead resurrection from the dead.

The 24th article, however, is uniquely Adventist. While its elements of Christ's high-priestly ministry and final judgment connect with traditions of other churches, the introduction of the time aspect sets it sharply apart. The article is a construct built on several ideas:

1. The earthly Sanctuary system prefigured the work of Christ

in the heavenly Sanctuary;

2. Just as the earthly Sanctuary involved two phases of ministry, a daily and a yearly, so Christ's ministry in heaven embraces both intercession and judgment;

3. Christ's yearly (Day of Atonement) phase of ministry deals with making cosmic reconciliation for the sin problem, and

4. Parallel lines of prophecy in the books of Daniel and Revelation converge on the 19th century as the time when God sets in motion the final events of the age-long struggle between good and evil.

This article is carefully worded so as to avoid any distortion of doctrine that would diminish the only-ness and all-sufficiency of the blood of Christ as our only hope. It also safeguards our assurance of salvation by emphasizing that our relationship to Him is the basis of hope.

III. Reflections on Apocalyptic in the New Testament and in Adventism

Adventist eschatology is largely apocalyptic in nature. Therefore, an overview of Seventh-day Adventist eschatology would not be complete without further consideration of the apocalyptic element. The treatment here is of necessity brief.[6]

During the past half-century *apocalyptic* has attracted considerable interest and study among New Testament scholars. They sought to trace the extra-biblical roots of *apocalyptic* and to determine the role it played in the life and thought of the early Christians. In spite of the large literature that has been developed on the topic, no clear definition of *apocalyptic* has been arrived at. Instead, *apocalyptic* has been described according to features that are customarily found associated with it. Perhaps the most central mark of *apocalyptic* is its focus on the end of the world—that is, of the *world* understood as the immediate environment such as a city or nation, or the *world* in the larger sense, of the cosmos.

Apocalyptic literature emerges in times of peril and distress. It gives hope for hard times because it speaks of the direct intervention of God to save His people. Apocalyptic is often associated with visions and dreams given to the agent of the message. Its language frequently is laced with symbols, colorful images, and calculations involving time. Apocalyptic is esoteric: it conceals the portrayal of what is about to happen in language that carries import to "the wise"—those who understand.

Apocalyptic runs counter to the post-Enlightenment thought that dominated the 19th and early 20th centuries. During this period much of New Testament scholarship focused on attempts to discover the "historic Jesus," that is, Jesus as He really was, stripped of ecclesiastical accretions. A series of "lives" of Jesus came from the pens of German and French scholars, each sketching a person who fit comfortably into the liberal thought of the age.

These efforts, however, were brought to a screeching halt by the publication of Albert Schweitzer's *The Quest of the Historical Jesus* in 1910. Schweitzer reviewed and critiqued the "Lives," devastatingly revealing their inadequacies. Then he briefly set out his own historical Jesus: an apocalyptic figure utterly out of step with the optimism of 19th century liberal thought.

Schweitzer's insights gradually won the day among 20th century scholars. A key moment came in 1960 with a programmatic essay by Ernst Kasemann, which argued that apocalyptic was not merely peripheral to New Testament thought—it was central. Kasemann claimed that "Apocalyptic was the mother of all Christian theology."

Scholarly recognition and acknowledgment of the role of apocalyptic in the Bible by no means leads to acceptance of its ideas as true, however. One can accept that Bible writers, both Old Testament and New, believed in the end of the world without agreeing with them. One can acknowledge that even Jesus Christ, the central figure of Christianity, believed that He would come again, but deny the truth of the belief.

In this regard hermeneutics plays a critical role. One result of the Enlightenment was the development of a "scientific" approach to the study of the Scriptures. In its most thoroughgoing expression, this method excludes consideration of the supernatural in its analysis of the text. It does not necessarily deny the supernatural *per se*, but brackets it out as an explanation. Thus, it views history as a closed continuum of cause and effect; the possibility of miracles cannot be entertained, nor can any intervention from outside the continuum.

One result of this approach to the Bible—commonly termed the "historical-critical method"—is to rule out apocalyptic as furnishing accurate predictions of what is coming. The world will not come to an end, nor will Jesus Christ return. He *thought* that He would return, just as did the other writers of Scripture, but He and they were wrong. The world will continue as it always has.

Seventh-day Adventists reject the presuppositions of the historical-critical approach to the Bible. They believe that all Scripture was "God-breathed" (2 Tim 3:16) and gives us not only guidance for living but insights into what is coming. God, the Creator of heaven and earth, has not left us alone. God intervenes in human lives and events on earth. Because God is a God of justice, He will in His own time call a halt to the reign of sin and evil. He will bring the present world order to an end; He will create "a new heaven and a new earth, wherein righteousness dwells" (2 Peter 3:13). Jesus will come again—as He promised.

When William Miller began to preach that Jesus would soon return, he met ridicule and suffering. The idea of the end of the world ran counter to the optimism of 19th century thought.

Nearly 200 years later, a remarkable reversal has taken place. Apocalyptic is in the air we breathe. Some of the direst warnings about the end of the world come, not from Seventh-day Adventists, but from scientists and environmentalists who warn of over-population, global warming, and collisions with meteorites or comets. A new variety of time setting has taken root: so many years until we reach the age of perpetual famine, and so on. Hollywood has come on board. Movie and TV shows build on fears of apocalyptic disasters that depopulate the earth.

Today, Adventist scholars have achieved widespread recognition for their careful studies of the Bible. Their academic publications are numerous and well accepted. But the driving force behind their thinking—belief in the soon return of Jesus—remains as alien to most other scholars as was William Miller to his contemporaries.

An interesting development in today's world scene is the expectation of the near coming of a Saviour figure in non-Christian religions. The Qu'ran teaches that Jesus Christ will come again to this earth, and many Muslims, on the basis of statements in the Hadith, believe that the event is near. Followers of the Baha'i likewise expect Jesus to come soon, while, further afield, Hindu writings predict that Kalki, the tenth and final manifestation of Vishnu, who periodically is incarnated when the world is in distress, is soon to appear.

Against such a backdrop, Seventh-day Adventists continue to proclaim the soon return of Christ. We do not set dates—never have as a denomination—but simply wait in quiet confidence that God's Word cannot fail.

Adventist living parallels that of the early Christians. They also expected Jesus to return soon, as the New Testament makes clear (see John 21:20-23; Rom 13:11-12). Occasionally some became overly excited and ran to extremes like some of the Thessalonian believers (2 Thess 2:1-3). Others, however, began to give up hope as the years passed, arguing that all things continued as they had from the Creation (2 Peter 3:3-10).

Seventh-day Adventists have, and have had, their share of similar aberrations. Some Adventists spend much time and thought on prophetic interpretation in an endeavor to be able to determine the date, or approximate date, of Christ's coming. They tend to fall into the error of making eschatology the center, instead of Christology. On the other side, the relentless passing of the years leads other Adventists to gradually abandon the expectation of Jesus' soon return.

Adventist ethics in relation to the Second Coming makes a fascinating study. Here the careful observer finds two apparently contradictory and competing impulses—a hope that would seem to lead to disengagement with society, and active involvement in the world. Conceivably, Adventism might have flamed out long ago like other apocalyptic groups that forsook society to await Jesus' coming. But it did not.

From the pioneer days, this Church on one hand preached that Jesus is coming again, but on the other planned long-term, establishing schools and hospitals. A startling example: by 1903 Seventh-day Adventists had built the Sanitarium in Battle Creek, Michigan, a huge facility that attracted the leaders of American society—including the President—to its state-of-the-art medical care.

Adventist involvement in society continues to grow as church membership explodes, especially in developing countries. Two members of the church serve in the US Congress, and the Senate Chaplain is a Seventh-day Adventist minister. Several ambassadors serving in Washington DC from other countries in the world are Adventists. Elsewhere in the world Adventists hold high offices from heads of state to prime ministers, cabinet ministers, and so on. Thus do Seventh-day Adventists, steeped in apocalyptic, confound the conventional ethical paradigms.

Conclusion

Seventh-day Adventists live in tension between the "already" and the "not yet." All Christians who take the New Testament seriously, of course, feel that tension. However, for Adventists it comes with a sharper edge because of our emphasis on time. We live on the knife-edge of time, poised between the finished work of Christ and the future, pregnant with meaning, imbued with hope.

For us, the tension is intellectual, not existential. We know the Lord and we rest in Him, confident that He is working to bring the Denoument in His own time and way. Scripture, from which our certainty of the Second Coming derives, teaches us to live in the existential moment.

" For,
   "In just a little while,
      he who is coming will come
      and will not delay."
"And,
   "But my righteous one will live by faith.
      And I take no pleasure
      in the one who shrinks back."
   "But we do not belong to those who shrink back and are destroyed, but to those who have faith and are saved."—Heb 10:37-39

On several occasions during Ellen White's long ministry she encountered Adventists who were preoccupied with the time of Christ's coming. In every instance she warned them of the danger of such tendencies. In a sermon preached at Lansing, Michigan, on September 5, 1891, she addressed the issue pointedly:

"Instead of living in expectation of some special season of excitement, we are wisely to improve present opportunities, doing that which must be done in order that souls may be saved. Instead of exhausting the powers of our mind in speculations in regard to the times and seasons which the Lord has placed in His own power, and withheld from men, we are to yield ourselves to the control of the Holy Spirit, to do present duties, to give the bread of life, unadulterated with human opinions, to souls who are perishing for the truth."[7]

Ellen White further stated, "You will not be able to say that He will come in one, two, or five years, neither are you to put off His coming by stating that it may not be for ten or twenty years."[8]

Even so, come, Lord Jesus.

ENDNOTES

[1] George R Knight, *Anticipating the Advent: A Brief History of Seventh-day Adventists,* (Boise, Idaho: Pacific Press Publishing Association, 1993), 10.

[2] *Anticipating* 17.

[3] Quoted in Richard W Schwarz and Floyd Greenleaf, *Lightbearers: A History of the Seventh-day Adventist Church,* (Boise, Idaho: Pacific Press Publishing Association, 2000), 49.

[4] *Lightbearers* 51

[5] *Lightbearers* 52

[6] For a thorough discussion, see William G Johnsson, "Biblical Apocalyptic," *Handbook of Seventh-day Adventist Theology,* Commentary Reference Series, vol 12, (Hagerstown, Maryland: Review and Herald Publishing Association, 2000), 784-814.

[7] Ellen G White, *Selected Messages,* Book 1, (Washington DC: Review and Herald Publishing Association, 1958), 186.

[8] *Selected Messages* 189.

Reflections on Seventh-day Adventist Ecclesiology and Church Organization[1]

Bert B Beach

In contrast to former centuries, the doctrine of the church has become a more central and recurring theological topic. This may be partially due to the influence of the modern ecumenical movement. Even the Roman Catholic Church waited until Vatican II before adopting a Constitution on the Church.

Hesitancy Regarding Church Organization

The early pioneers of the Seventh-day Adventist Church did not emphasize ecclesiology. In fact, they were more than hesitant in setting up a church organization (seeing it potentially as a "return to Babylon"). It was not until 1946 that a proper *Church Manual* was fully adopted.

Various Metaphors

There are many metaphors we can take from the Bible that characterize the church, such as the body, the bride, the temple, the remnant, and many others. Adventists are conversant with these metaphors and use them frequently, as do other Christian churches. The concept of the remnant is one that has resonated consistently in SDA ranks.

Church—Local and Universal

Adventists see the church as both local and universal—the local community of believers and also the totality or universality of the church. This is the model of the New Testament. The local church is not just a part of the whole church, but the local expression of the universal church, the fellowship of all the believers, the people of God.

Visible and Invisible Church

Seventh-day Adventists see the church as both a visible body or temple of Christ and as having an invisible dimension. We cannot clearly see the line that divides true and false believers. Unfortunately, the visible community is a mix of faithful believers and the unfaithful. Furthermore, Adventists believe that there are those who have a saving relationship with Christ without holding membership in the visible church. SDAs repudiate the thought that only they belong to God's people and church. All those who live in harmony with God's will, as they understand it, can be seen as "members-at-large" of the church.

When you believe that the universal church is currently composed of all those who believe in Christ, you are in effect affirming that this church is currently invisible. In this connection, I make three short statements:

1. Not every Seventh-day Adventist will be saved.

2. Not all, or only, Christians belonging to a church will be saved.

3. The Pauline principle: "For God does not show favoritism.... it is those who obey the law who will be declared righteous. Indeed, when Gentiles, who do not have the law, do by nature things required by the law, they are a law for themselves, even though they do not have the law. Since they show that the requirements of the law are written in their hearts, their conscience also bearing witness" (Rom 2:11-15, NIV).

Christ the True Light

In the Gospel of John, Christ is presented as "the true light" that comes into the world and illumines the existence of every human being.[2] The true light is at work even in gross darkness, and thus truth is found in other religions. However, Seventh-day Adventists believe salvation comes only in Christ, even though men and women may not know or acknowledge Him. The salvific value of a religion or church is in proportion to the extent it points its followers in the direction of divine truth and light, that is, in the final analysis, to Christ.

Agencies that Lift Up Christ Are Part of the Divine Plan for World Evangelization

It may help to point out here that in 1926, before ecumenism was in vogue, the General Conference Executive Committee voted a statement,[3] since then slightly revised, that includes the following: "1. We recognize those agencies that lift up Christ before men as part of the divine plan for the evangelization of the world and we hold in high esteem men and women in other communions who are engaged in winning souls to Christ.... 3. We recognize that true religion is based on conscience and conviction.... If a change of conviction leads a member of our church to feel no longer in harmony with Seventh-day Adventist faith and practice, we recognize not only the right but also the responsibility of that member to change, without opprobrium, religious affiliation in accord with belief."

Mission Is Vital

Though the church is not defined simply by her function, the mission of the church is vital to her nature and existence. Without mission, a church does not have a *raison d'être* as a church.

Instrument of Evangelism

The church is essentially an instrument of evangelism, but also of worship, instruction, and nurture, always proclaiming the good news of salvation. For Adventists this task is accomplished by a movement proclaiming and preparing the way for a soon coming Lord and returning Savior. Jesus said "this gospel of the kingdom will be preached in the whole world as a testimony to all nations, and then the end will come" (Matt 24:14, NIV). Adventists take this promise and injunction as their "marching orders," so to speak. Thus, there is an element of timely significance in Adventist eschatology: Making disciples of men and women from all nations, tribes, tongues, and peoples (Matt 28:19, 20; Acts 1:8). SDAs are encouraged by the thought that they now have a working presence in more than 200 of the world's political entities. On the other hand, they are concerned by the size of the unfinished task, especially in the 10/40 window of opportunity.

Service on a Parallel Track

While evangelism is the primary task of the church, *service* moves on a separate, but parallel track, promoting social, economic and educational welfare, healing, health, peace, and humanitarian service.

Expectancy and Urgency

So, discipleship, expectancy and a certain element of urgency are all part of SDA ecclesial identity.

Children of the Radical Reformation

In our dialog with the Lutherans (1994-98) we said that we saw ourselves as children of Luther. In fact, because of our very high view of Luther, I even had the audacity to say that in some ways we were more Lutheran than the Lutherans! Back in 1959, in a Reformation Day talk at what is now Washington Adventist University, I said that SDAs see themselves as children of the 16th century Protestant Reformation. In some ways that is quite true.

However, after the meeting one of the history professors spoke to me and pointed out that in many ways we are more children of the Radical Reformation. I think he was right. Our ecclesiology sees the Christian church—not as identified with society, its cultures, its power structures, and its public status, but as a minority—as a *faithful remnant* called out and identified as different. This favors and even requires separation of church and state.

An Anabaptist Element

Thus, there is an Anabaptist element in Seventh-day Adventism. This has not been clearly seen and articulated, probably because there were no significant or indicative contacts with Mennonites and related groups in the early, formative decades of the SDA movement. It is good that we are endeavoring to find and put in its rightful place this missing and neglected historical link.

The Remnant Motif

The concept of "the remnant" has been frequently used in the SDA church. In recent years there have been references in Adventist ranks to such terms as the "historical remnant," the "faithful remnant," and the "eschatological remnant."

Adventists are influenced in their ecclesiological identity by the motif of the end-time eschatological remnant of Revelation 12 and 14. Revelation identifies this remnant as a people with at least four characteristics:

1. They keep the commandments of God (12:17; 14:12);
2. They have the "testimony of Jesus," interpreted as "the spirit of prophecy" (12:17; 19:10);
3. They remain faithful in holding the faith of Jesus (14:12); and
4. They exhibit patient endurance (14:12).

An authentic remnant ecclesiology must face the relationship between the remnant and the fragmentation of the Christian church. Angel Rodriguez says that "the lack of unity prevalent in the Christian world should be interpreted as the presence of Babylonian elements in it." On one hand, Adventist ecclesiology cannot simply ignore this reality; but on the other hand, it must "emphasize the universal unity of the church...because the possibility of ecclesiastical oneness is presupposed in the mission of the remnant people of God....We could then suggest that the remnant ecclesiology is in a sense a revolt against the fragmentation of the Christian world."[4]

Christ the Head of the Church

As is well known, Christian churches have historically adopted in their ecclesiology various forms of church government, going the entire gamut from Congregational, Presbyterian, and Episcopal, to Papal. For Adventists, the fullness of the church does not reside in formal ecclesiastic or hierarchical organization, and external signs, such as "hands-on" apostolic succession, or forms of mutual recognition. Christ is, and must be, the head of the church. This means that His will, revealed in the biblical word, is the ultimate legitimacy, authority and standard to determine the church's standards, doctrinal teachings and decisions. While Christ's authority is exercised by chosen representative church leaders, this does not mean "that Christ has transferred His authority to His servants."[5]

Three Pronged Spiritual Leadership

The SDA Church has developed a three pronged leadership of the church: deacon/deaconess, elder, and bishop. The elders and deacons have leadership responsibilities in the local church. The bishop is the ordained minister appointed by and paid by the conference. In practice, the term *bishop* is never used in the SDA church, because of the use (we could say misuse) of the term in non-episcopal churches. However, in actuality and theologically, every SDA ordained minister can be said to be a bishop or presbyter (the NT doesn't really make a clear difference between the two), in the New Testament use and understanding of this terminology.

Charismatica

Ephesians 4:11 describes some forms of leadership in the church as gifts (charismatica), with obviously some authority of leadership. It is not always clear exactly how the institutional and charismatic leadership are to relate to each other. It seems obvious that they both exist and each needs to support the other, rather than thinking that they are mutually exclusive.

Local and Universal Church Authority

In the SDA church both the local church and the universal church have authority. Decisions by the world church carry weight everywhere and exert authority particularly regarding church doctrine, Fundamental Beliefs, the *Church Manual*, organization, world evangelism, and working policies. However, the local church also has specific and final authority, particularly regarding individual membership in the church, church discipline, and the appointment of all local church officers.

General Conference the Highest Authority

When meeting in world session, the General Conference becomes the highest authority in the organized SDA church. Between sessions (held currently every five years), the Executive Committee of the General Conference, especially its Annual Council of the full Committee, is the highest authority, except in matters reserved to the session.

Current Organization—A Little Bit of History

The current organization of the SDA church is based on the 1863 organization of the General Conference, which grouped together half a dozen or so local conferences which had been organized beginning in 1860. This was followed by the reorganizations of 1901, 1913 and 1922, with subsequent adjustments or changes in more recent years, particularly in the number and nature of the departments.

The 1901 reorganization did two main things: 1) Organized Union Conferences; and 2) brought church departments—which had been somewhat independent entities and located in different parts of the United States–to the General Conference headquarters and placed them more clearly under its control.

The 1913 and 1922 reorganizations created the Divisions–first called Division Conferences, but very soon changed to Divisions of the General Conference–operating clearly as sections of the General Conference, avoiding the possibility of Divisions gradually becoming separate General Conferences.

Four Separate Constituency Levels

The whole organization of the SDA church may seem to an onlooker rather complicated. Just think of it as an organization operating with four separate, but interlocking, constituency levels:

1. Local churches, with direct democratic participation open to all members.

2. Local Conferences/Missions, bringing together all churches in a given geographical area through elected representation from and for the local churches.

3. Union Conferences/Missions, bringing together, through representation, several Conferences in a larger given area or country.

4. The General Conference (GC), bringing together, through delegated representatives, more than 100 Unions, with a world headquarters, but also operating through (currently) 13 Divisions (branch offices of the General Conference). The Division is, in effect, the General Conference in that part of the world. A cursory view may seem to suggest that the Division is a fifth, separate level of administration, but that is not really so. The Division has no constituency of its own. One constituency serves both the GC and the Divisions.

Each of the above constituency levels elects its own officers (president, secretary and treasurer), department directors and Executive Committee. The Division Presidents are also Vice Presidents of the General Conference, thus underlining the unique and special relationship between the GC and Division. The quinquennial GC session elects the officers of both the GC and the Divisions, and the Department Directors of the GC.

Not CEO, but Executive Committee System of Governance

It needs to be pointed out that Presidents at all levels in the SDA church tend to have much influence (one could say "power" if this were not a suspect word). However, the SDA church does not operate under the CEO system of governance, though its hospital and educational systems generally do. Under the CEO form of operation, the chief executive officer is generally chosen by the board, and he or she in turn appoints the supporting subordinates and carries final authority or responsibility. In the SDA church the same constituency that elects the President also elects his fellow officers and department directors. On the Union and Conference levels department directors are increasingly appointed by the Executive Committees rather than the sessions.

At the 2010 GC Session in Atlanta it was proposed that the GC Associate Directors of departments no longer be elected by the session, but be appointed by the next Annual Council of the Executive Committee. This proposal was defeated. However, for some time now they have not been members of the Executive Committee. At all four levels the *elected* staff works under the authority and direction of the Executive Committee, of which they often are themselves members (always on the GC level).

Of course, the President is the first officer and chairman of the Executive Committee and in this capacity is respected and looked to for spiritual leadership and administrative guidance of the team. The Secretary is the second officer and serves as secretary of the Executive Committee.

A Closing Observation

In Raoul Dederen's key chapter, "The Church," he writes: "Like the Anabaptists, Seventh-day Adventists have stood traditionally equidistant from magisterial Protestantism (Lutheran, Reformed, Anglican) and Roman Catholicism. They have promoted the authority of Scripture, believer's baptism, separation of church and state, religious liberty, a deep concern for the Great Commission, and the conviction that the church, built as closely as possible to the pattern of the NT, transcends national boundaries and local cultures.

For them the church, whatever else it might be, is a community of baptized believers, rooted in the Scriptures and unrestricted in their missionary concern by territorial limitations."[6]

Limitations of These Reflections and Challenge

In these modest reflections on SDA ecclesiology and church organization I have obviously failed in three directions: I have been beset by *over*simplification, *over*sight (or incompleteness), and *over*-complexity of the difficult to explain or unexplainable. Much more can and should be said, when time and further opportunity permit. That is what dialog is all about.

To grasp the essence of Seventh-day Adventism, we need to realize and understand that this ecclesiology is an "end-time ecclesiology." This requires the church and her structures, institutions, organizations and members to go "from everywhere to everywhere," knowing that we need "understanding [of] the present time...because our salvation is nearer now than when we first believed" (Rom 13:11, NIV).

ENDNOTES

[1] In preparing these reflections I have been helped by four sources: Raoul Dederen, "The Church," *Handbook of Seventh-day Adventist Theology*, vol 12, Walter R Beach and Bert B Beach, *Pattern for Progress*; Angel Rodriguez, "God's End-time Remnant and the Christian Church," *Toward a Theology of the Remnant*; and my personal experience, having served for 45 years as a member of the General Conference Executive Committee.

[2] See John 1:5-9.

[3] "Relationships with Other Christian Churches and Religious Organizations," GC *Working Policy 2010-2011*, Policy O 110.

[4] Angel Rodriguez, "God's End-time Remnant and the Christian Church," *Toward a Theology of the Remnant*, 217.

[5] Raoul Dederen, "The Church," *Handbook of Seventh-day Adventist Theology*, vol 12, 554.

[6] Dederen 576.

Nonconformity

Henk Stenvers

Introduction

"My prayer is not that you take them out of the world but that you protect them from the evil one. They are not of the world, even as I am not of it" (John 17:15, 16, NIV). "Therefore, I urge you, brothers and sisters, in view of God's mercy, to offer your bodies as a living sacrifice, holy and pleasing to God—this is your true and proper worship. Do not conform to the pattern of this world, but be transformed by the renewing of your mind. Then you will be able to test and approve what God's will is— his good, pleasing and perfect will" (Rom 12:1-2).

"Dear friends, I urge you, as foreigners and exiles, to abstain from sinful desires, which wage war against your soul" (1 Peter 2:11).

"Do not love the world or anything in the world. If anyone loves the world, love for the Father is not in them. For everything in the world—the lust of the flesh, the lust of the eyes, and the pride of life—comes not from the Father but from the world" (1 John 2:15-16).

In literature two terms are used to describe the topic we are talking about today: *Separation* and *Nonconformity*. The way these two terms are used is sometimes confusing.

Separation, in the context of the discussion today, is standing apart from the world, excluding others and being excluded from others—others in this case being non-Christians—or from activities or behaviors considered "sinful." It is a more general term that also has different associations. Separation may or may not lead to nonconformity. You separate from someone, or groups separate from other groups.

Nonconformity, on the other hand, is the refusal to conform to accepted standards, conventions, rules, or laws. Groups can and often did separate on questions on nonconformity. Mennonite history is full of this kind of separation.[1]

A good illustration of the difference between the two is found in *The Declaration of Commitment in Respect to Christian Separation and Nonconformity to the World*, a statement adopted by the Mennonite General Conference in the USA in 1955.[2] It states that "Christian nonconformity to the world is based on the fact that God calls His children to a life of holiness, and to conformity to the character of Jesus Christ delivering them 'from this present evil world.'" On *separation*, the declaration states: "In reference to those who do not know Christ, the divine summons is, 'Come out from among them, and ye be separate, saith the Lord, and touch not the unclean thing....'"

Notwithstanding this difference in meaning, for many Mennonite groups separation was, and for some still is, one of the ways to be non-conformed.

History

It is almost impossible to talk about or understand nonconformity in the Mennonite family today without looking at history.

Of course, the concept of nonconformity is not unique for Anabaptists or Mennonites. In the medieval church, for example, the monastic tradition was a way to solve the problem of worldliness. The medieval sect in the Waldenses sought other ways, as did the Anabaptists in the Reformation period.

For Anabaptists and Mennonites, nonconformity has been a very important theme with very detailed application in different periods of time—like in Holland in the 16th and 17th centuries and in North America in the 19th and 20th centuries—especially among the more conservative groups. Although the practical answers have not always been the same, the general principle of nonconformity to the spirit, ideals and culture of the non-Christian world, or a seriously diluted Christian culture, and an attempt to mould life after the image of Christ, has been the same.[3]

The biblical teachings of purity of life, holiness, following Christ, and taking up the Cross of suffering, are the main motives behind the Mennonite understanding of nonconformity. The negative of nonconformity to the world and the positive of conformity to the holiness and purity of Christ or God are together in this. It is interesting that in most cases we tend to use the negative word instead of the positive.

The idea of being Pilgrims and strangers with no abiding city in this world, but with a citizenship in heaven, inevitably leads to rejection of many cultural ideas and expressions. Being a people of God implies separation from the world.

The persecution in the early days of Anabaptism in the 16th century made nonconformity all the more important. In the centuries that followed, Mennonites were not considered citizens or were treated as citizens with certain special privileges such as exemption from military service. The strong, bitter and often violent opposition from the ruling state church clergy, who called them sects, and the persecution by the state itself, made them all the more conscious of being a separate people and enhanced their sense of separation and nonconformity.

In these first centuries the emphasis of nonconformity for the Mennonites took the form of non-resistance, non-participation in the affairs of the state, and withdrawal from public political, though not economic, life.

Tradition, indoctrination and discipline are the three forces that carried the ideas of nonconformity in Mennonite communities. The congregation and the broader settlement groups have a strong solidarity and social control. There is usually a deeply rooted tradition with a clear sense of separation from the surrounding culture. Initially the rules are taken for granted without any written regulations or group discernment.

For the Amish, this isolation of the local congregation or settlement group and the absence of written regulations made it possible to have different rules for the different groups.

In Mennonite history, the concept of nonconformity has been, and sometimes still is, a cause for bitter arguments often resulting in schisms, sometimes even within families. Almost all schisms in the first centuries were caused by arguments about this topic. In North America the labels *conservative* and *liberal* refer most often to attitudes on nonconformity and separation.

The development of thought and practice regarding nonconformity has run along different lines in different parts of the world. We will look in succession at Europe, North America and the rest of the world.

Europe

In Europe we can discern two areas where there has been a different development—the Netherlands and Germany-Switzerland-France.

In the Netherlands, nonconformity today is no longer expressed in different clothing or lifestyle. Dutch Mennonites dress like others, have no problem with going to the theatre or cinema, and many do not refrain from alcohol or smoking. The church has no regulations whatsoever about this and leaves it to the individual member to make his or her own conscious decision about the way to live according to their faith.

Dutch Mennonites have never lived in closed separated communities. Although there were villages where the people were predominantly Mennonite, like in Friesland, they have always had contact with non-Mennonites.

In the years of persecution before 1572, the Dutch Anabaptists lived in an eschatological expectation of the end times. This, and the fact that being Anabaptist meant risking your life, made the line between this world and the coming Kingdom very sharp. They lived as plain people, with humility in furniture and clothing.

In 1572 (Unie van Utrecht) freedom of religion was recognized in the Netherlands. In 1796 church and state were officially separated. Thus, for most of their history Dutch Mennonites have lived in a relatively open and tolerant society and their hard work and honesty made them respected citizens. Nonconformity was visible, for example, in the fact that they did not work for the government. So many of them became traders or bankers or started businesses like textile factories. And because they had a strong work ethic, they did very well. Indeed, some Mennonites, especially in the bigger towns, became very wealthy. Because they wanted to live soberly they didn't spend too much and so collected vast amounts of capital. Another expression of nonconformity was that many of those wealthy Mennonites contributed a lot of money for social goals. For example the big park in Amsterdam, the Vondelpark, was given to the city for the well-being of the citizens by a Mennonite trader and banker.

In Friesland the Mennonites were well-known for their honesty. For instance, if you asked advice on which carpenter to choose to get something made, the advice could well be: "Go to him, he is a Mennonite, he won't cheat you."

With their integration into society, the apprehension of the state started to disappear. Even non-resistance became less important and many Mennonites were willing to join the army or to help finance it. Also, engaging in politics or working for the government was not frowned upon anymore.

In the beginning of the 20th century a revival movement brought the non-resistance issue again to the table. Since Cor Inja, the first Mennonite conscientious objector in World War I, was jailed for his convictions, many others have followed.[4] Many young men have found the Mennonites through their assistance to objectors. In the second half of the 20th century the peace witness again became important. The more passive non-resistance was increasingly replaced by advocating social justice and active peace work. The protest against the Vietnam War played an important role in this.

Today the casual observer will not see much nonconformity. Still the nonconformity is more in the way people think and live, rather than in regulations, written or unwritten, about clothing and lifestyle.

Germany-Switzerland-France

During the first three centuries of their history the Anabaptists in Germany, Switzerland, and France were severely persecuted. This, combined with their strong belief in the spiritual principle of nonconformity, meant that they tried to apply it in daily life through separation from the world. This expressed itself in rejecting civil office or other participation in government as well as all litigation and swearing of oaths. Participation in war or military service was also rejected. Other expressions were simplicity in clothing, home furnishing and manner of life. Being in a rural, often isolated, community made it easier to hold on to these principles. From the 19th century on society changed. Legal restrictions for Mennonites disappeared and Mennonites started to participate in the general culture. The external nonconformity started to disappear most rapidly among Mennonites in North Germany. In these regions participation in military activities became more or less accepted, although big differences persisted among Mennonites in various regions. The non-swearing of oaths survived these changes and still it is one of the characteristics with which Mennonites describe themselves.

It is interesting to note that the attitude towards alcohol and tobacco among Mennonites was not an issue until the 19th and early 20th centuries, probably under the outside influence of the temperance movement. It was only then that many Mennonite conferences started to prohibit drinking or smoking.[5]

North America

In North America it was, and still is, easier to live in closed communities where there is also strong social control. Today you can find a whole range of positions on nonconformity—from groups who strictly uphold regulations like the Old Order Amish or the Old Order Mennonites, to groups who are culturally more liberal and have little difference from the world, except perhaps on non-resistance, non-violence and rejection. And, of course, there are groups in between.

There has been a strong feeling that nonconformity applies to every area of life. In business it could mean not entering into business partnerships with non-Christians or even non-Mennonites, maintaining strict standards of honesty and integrity, being content with a small business and the rejection of litigation. In relation to the state it could mean not holding any office that would violate the non-resistance principle. In some groups fashion in clothing was rejected and jewellery was not worn, sometimes not even wedding rings. In recreation, many activities were forbidden—like card playing, visiting movie theatres, etc.

Among more conservative groups, the church service is held in a simple meetinghouse and the liturgy is simple and quiet. Musical instruments are not used.

A long list of examples can be given of rules that are usually unwritten, but none-the-less strict, especially among the Amish. The main motivation for these rules is to prevent one from putting him or herself above the other or above God. University education is frowned upon because it causes pride. Because these groups value community, activities that can have the effect of getting out of the community or having too much contact with the outside world are frowned upon or are forbidden. Different communities have different interpretations, sometimes leading to surprising differences.

Most examples in the present time are to be found with the Amish. There are groups who forbid the use of bicycles, but allow the use of scooters, because a bicycle can take you further than a scooter. Another example is the prohibition of the use of rubber tires on a tractor because you could go on the public road and use it to go into town. Although all these rules sometimes seem a bit silly, they are always motivated by the need to protect the community and the prevention of individual pride and vanity.

These strict rules are generally not set by group discussion or democratic principles. The bishops, chosen by and from the community, decide on them and their power is almost absolute. When people go outside of the boundaries set by the rules and are not willing to repent publicly, it can lead to the decision to ban and shun someone. How far shunning goes depends, again, on the strictness of the specific group. The ban and shunning are intended to protect the community, while also encouraging the banned person to acknowledge his sin and repent. If done so publicly, he or she is lovingly accepted back into the community.[6] It may be clear that it often doesn't work that way. Legalism, pettiness and arbitrary decisions are, of course, close at hand, and often people are lost to the community. In the best case, they become members of a different church community, often a less conservative Mennonite group.

Rest of the World

As within Europe and North America, there are substantial differences in nonconformity in the rest of the world.

In Latin America there are many groups that descend from Russian or German Mennonites. Because they live in relative isolation, at least until some decades ago they held on to nonconformity in many parts of their lives. Rules concerning dress, non-resistance, education and many others have been maintained. Only in recent decades have some of the groups seemed to move a bit, but other groups, such as in Bolivia, seem to be getting more strict than before.

Mennonite churches in Africa and Asia came into being after the 19th century, at first through missionaries from the Global North and later through their own missionary activity. For these Mennonite churches the issue of nonconformity is often much more spiritual than just rules of behavior. Following Christ is the focus. Most Mennonites or Brethren in Christ live in the midst of society; there are no groups living in isolation. They are active within society in many ways. Their nonconformity shows through their working for peace, education and health.

20th Century

In the Netherlands a revival of spiritual nonconformity emerged at the beginning of the 20th century. Although the Netherlands tried to stay neutral in World War I, the horror of this full scale war, with the atrocities in the trenches in Belgium and France where sometimes thousands of soldiers were slaughtered within hours, affected Dutch society very deeply. The Mennonite Cor Inja was one of the first conscientious objectors. For this he spent years in jail. The *Gemeentedagbeweging* (Congregation-day movement) started with a new focus on community and Mennonite identity. Its focus was on promoting social justice and peace more than passive non-resistance.

In the second half of the 20th century the scope of nonconformity changed also in North America. To define what nonconformity meant became more difficult since many boundaries were no longer acceptable. Gradually people started to conform to social customs, especially in regard to dress, recreation, cars, houses, etc. But at the same time many did succeed in finding new forms of nonconformity.

Central in all these new forms is the historic conviction that nonconformity is not primarily about keeping up the external way of living, but an attitude of heart and mind—a commitment to discipleship and the simplification of lifestyle amid a complex consumer-oriented society. It is understood and accepted that this has implications for the visible life.

This shift also included a shift from separation from society to participation in society. Gradually, for example, the emphasis on non-resistance changed to active peace witness and working for social justice.

In 1944 Harold Bender published "The Anabaptist Vision," a summary of core Anabaptist convictions that viewed non-resistance as a means of influencing the world for good. In his view, non-resistance is more a mandate to be pursued than a doctrine to be taught.[7] For North American Mennonites and others all over the world, the theology of social ethics of John Howard Yoder was a major factor in this change. His book, *The Politics of Jesus*, and many other books from his hand, changed the view of Mennonites all over the world. For Yoder, ecclesiology cannot be separated from a lived witness to the world, including social justice. Ethics is to be developed as the visible expression of the political and doxological community.[8] In one of his last books, Yoder cited five Practices that described the behavior of the Church.

"Binding and loosing" in Matthew 18. For Yoder this is the exemplary style of life that leads to reconciliation through forgiveness, with the goal of restoring a person to the community.

The universality of charisms. Since in the one body every person is the bearer of a distinctly identifiable charism, or "manifestation of the Spirit for the common good" (1 Cor 12:7), this spells the end of every form of domination and leads to equality of rights without uniformity.

The Spirit's freedom in the meeting. The function of the Spirit is ·
to initiate a social process resulting in discernment through open dialogue and in building consensus.

Breaking bread. The distribution of bread is an act of social economics. Yoder pleads for a sacramental view, understood not only as a sign in the sense of symbolic meaning. At the same time he rejects a sacramental view in the sense of transubstantiation. What is presented occurs in actual fact: distribution and participation in community, personal, particular and decentralized.

Introduction into the new humanity. Baptism as initiation rite transcends all previous identities.[9] Social differences are relativized in this new humanity without being disavowed. Their discriminating influence is rejected. [10]

The Confession of Faith in a Mennonite Perspective, published in 1995 by the then General Conference Mennonite Church and the Mennonite Church who merged to become the Mennonite Church USA, is exemplary of this changing focus. In Article 22 on Peace, Justice, and Non-resistance is written: "Led by the Holy Spirit, we follow Christ in the way of peace, doing justice, bringing reconciliation, and practicing non-resistance even in the face of violence and warfare." [11]

Conclusion

We can conclude that the way nonconformity has found expression in the Mennonite world has changed, especially since the second half of the 20th century. The focus has shifted from separation and nonconformity in many aspects of life to active participation in society, with nonconformity expressed in the nonviolent struggle for social justice and peace. In the Mennonite world we can find nonconformity both in the "old" way of separation and regulations regarding dress, marriage, use of cars, etc., and in the "new" way of cultural assimilation with the world but with nonconformity in the way people live their lives and discipleship expressing itself in working for peace and social justice, with care for environment and sustainability. Modern techniques are accepted, but usually not uncritically. There is almost a utility argument, seldom pure luxury.

It seems that the idea of nonconformity has lost a lot of its meaning. That might be true for the old concept regarding clothing, closed communities, use of modern machinery, etc. It is safe to conclude, however, that it has been replaced by other forms of nonconformity, more in the Spirit and demonstrated in active work for peace and justice on different levels within the secular society. The most important task of the Church is simply to be the Church— a visible serving community. The church has no social ethics in its visible life, it is social ethics. [12]

Various modern scholars, such as Stanley Hauerwas, Stuart Murray, David Augsburger and James Kennedy, all conclude that the future for the Christian Church in a post-Christendom world lies in the community where people live their lives according to the law of Christ and in contrast to the world. Augsburger speaks of the eight radical principles,[13] Stanley Hauerwas calls it a robust church,[14] Kennedy uses the word "contrast" community,[15] but all mean the same—a community of faithful Christians living in accordance to the teachings of Jesus Christ and seeking peace and justice. In the world, but still not of this world.

ENDNOTES

[1] Reuben Sairs, *Mennonite Nonconformity*, A thesis presented to the faculty of the school of Religion of the University of Mobile, 1977.

[2] Mennonite Church, "Declaration of Commitment in Respect to Christian Separation and Nonconformity to the World", *Global Anabaptist Mennonite Encyclopaedia Online*, 1951. Web 22 April 2012, http://www.gameo.org/encyclopedia/contents/D386.html.

[3] "Nonconformity," *Mennonite Encyclopaedia III*, 890-897.

[4] Alle Hoekema, Piet Visser (red), *Cor Inja Geen cel kent deze dromen*, (Hilversum: Verloren, 2001).

[5] Ibid.

[6] Donald B Kraybill, *The Riddle of Amish Culture*, revised edition, (Baltimore and London: The Johns Hopkins University Press, 2001).

[7] Ervin R Stutzman, *From Non-resistance to Justice*, (Scottdale, Pennsylvania: Herald Press, 2011), 101.

[8] F Enns, *The Peace Church and the Ecumenical Community*, (Kitchener, Ontario: Pandora Press, 2007), 126.

[9] See Galatians 3:28; Ephesians 2; 2 Corinthians 5.

[10] Enns, 127.

[11] *Confession of Faith in a Mennonite Perspective*, (Scottdale, Pennsylvania: Herald Press, 1995), 81.

[12] Stanley Hauerwas, *Een robuuste kerk*, (Zoetermeer: Boekencentrum, 2010), 108, (translation from *The Peaceable Kingdom*, 1983).

[13] David Augsburger, *Dissident Discipleship*, (Grand Rapids: Brazos Press, 2006).

[14] Hauerwas.

[15] James Kennedy, *Stad op een berg*, (Zoetermeer: Boekencentrum, 2010).

Some Thoughts on Nonconformity in the Adventist Ethos

Teresa Reeve

"In the world, but not of the world." This saying was so much a part of my religious upbringing that until very recently I simply assumed it was a verbatim quote from somewhere in the New Testament.[1] Often heard in support of this maxim was the King James version of 1 Peter 2:9: "But ye are a chosen generation, a royal priesthood, an holy nation, a *peculiar* people; that ye should shew forth the praises of him who hath called you out of darkness into his marvelous light..." In the view of those who gave me religious nurture, the word *peculiar* indicated that we ought to be noticeably different from the world so that at a glance it could be seen that we serve a different Master.

In juxtaposition to this theme, the Great Commission of Matthew 24:14 (KJV), "And this gospel of the kingdom shall be preached in all the world for a witness unto all nations; and then shall the end come" regularly rang out from the pulpit of church and campmeeting and Adventist media, calling us into sustained engagement with the world. The urgency of this commission was underlined by the strains of songs such as, "Lift up the trumpet and loud let it ring, Jesus is coming again" reminding us that His coming was even "at the door." The twin emphases of separation from the world and commitment to mission were not unique to Western Canadian Adventists of the mid-20th century. Rather, tied together and underlined by fervent hope in the soon coming of Jesus, they have been key themes in Adventism since its beginnings in the early 19th century.

The theological and practical dynamics of living nonconformity in a worldwide organization committed to mission are complex; but the tension is a potentially healthy and balancing one. This paper will discuss four aspects of Adventist life and thought which have contributed to the way in which this tension is dealt with: the Adventist historical experience, the shape of God's grace, the normative nature of Scripture, and the relationship between distinctive Adventist theology and praxis. These four factors have together led Adventism to deal with the mission-separation tension primarily through calling people out in significant ways from their dominant culture, rather than seeking to reorient culture or to merge into culture or participate in the local civil religion.

Historical Roots of Adventist Nonconformity

At the beginning, many of the commitments and behaviors Adventists considered essential to godly life and thought were shared with significant segments of Christianity, including the Pietistic, Anabaptist, and Revivalist traditions, all of which believed these ideas to be deeply grounded in Scripture. The particular religious environment in the American northeast out of which the Adventist church was born was the experience of the Second Great Awakening with its call to leave one's lackadaisical world-conformed lifestyle and return to "true religion" in both inward conversion and outward behavior. Many of the specific behavior traits identified by these early 19th century Christian revivalists as essential in separating from the world were, and remain, an important part of Adventist lifestyle expectations. Examples that carry on, to a greater or lesser degree, into present day Adventist practice include the eschewing of such activities as dancing, card-playing, jewelry, Sabbath (Sunday) work and the use of tobacco and alcohol.

Adventist pioneers, however, also faced other experiences which separated them in fundamental ways from their spiritual forebears. For many in the revivalist era of the early 19th century, William Miller's call to look more closely at Scriptural prophecies of the soon coming of Christ held a compelling force. Christians from all denominations flocked to hear him and threw their lives into the desire to "be ready for Jesus to come." This urgent hope only intensified the emphasis on reformation and separation from worldliness already present in the contemporary religious environment. Early advent believers were thus dismayed when many from their local churches did not share in their excitement about Jesus' soon coming, As the gulf intensified, many were mocked and disfellowshipped by their own church communities and inadvertently found themselves in a state of nonconformity not only relative to the "world" but also to those with whom they had previously enjoyed communion in Christ. [2]

As a result of these events, Millerites found themselves in nonconformity with the world and with many of their fellow Christians; and they sought to make sense of what was happening in light of previous reformations in the church during which sincere and biblically justified reformers, such as Martin Luther, Menno Simons, and John Wesley, had been rejected and persecuted by the established churches. [3] Seeking an understanding of their experience in Scripture, a growing number of Advent believers, especially following the Great Disappointment of 1844, identified with the loyal remnant that had remained faithful to God despite trouble and persecution throughout the centuries. In Revelation's descriptions of an eschatological remnant who were keeping "the commandments of God and the faith of Jesus" (12:17; cf. 14:12), they saw a portrayal of their own contemporary experience. They saw themselves as being called to join in the proclamation of the message of Revelation 14:6-7 to "Fear God and give Him glory for the hour of His judgment is come." The mainstream churches, on the other hand, who not only consciously refused the message of Jesus' soon coming but also rejected Advent believers, came to be understood as the fallen Babylon of Revelation 14:8-10.[4]

Though these events took place nearly two centuries ago, they continue to play an important part in Adventist identity and also in how Adventists relate to those outside their faith. Adventist schools, first established in the 1870's to protect children from worldly influence and prepare people for the Gospel work, now number 5,813 primary schools, 1,823 secondary schools, and 111 tertiary institutions worldwide.[5] While a smaller percentage of parents are now committed to Adventist education than was the case a few decades ago, research has demonstrated that the longer a young person is a part of the Adventist school system the more likely it is that he/she will remain an active member of the church.[6] Adventists have also been very careful about media consumption, traditionally avoiding, for example, novel-reading, worldly music, and attendance at theatres.[7] The ideal of country living, as an important means of separation from worldly influence, illustrates the continuing challenge of this tension, for the church still struggles to discover effective ways of ministering in an urban context. Their historical experience has also led Adventists to be especially wary of any temptation to use the state to accomplish religious ends. Generally in the past, this caution has extended to choosing to refrain from most forms of political involvement.[8]

Such practices of separation, growing out of the Adventist historical experience and their subsequent reading of Scripture, illustrate one factor in the strong ongoing Adventist commitment to nonconformity in relation to the world. Further, expectation of a future time of persecution just before the coming of Christ, based on their reading of the Synoptic Gospels and of Daniel and Revelation, continues to be a part of Adventist theology, reinforcing this ongoing ethic of separation.

Other Primary Factors Contributing to Nonconformity among Adventists Today

In addition to historical experience read through the lens of Bible prophecy, a second factor that can be seen to contribute to an Adventist emphasis on nonconformity with the world is one that is shared with all believers in Christ who have discipled themselves to Him as their Master and Lord. Most fundamentally, it is God's grace through His Spirit that makes us new creatures, filled with the desire to know and please Him. While believers live in a fallen world at war in fundamental ways with God and His government, in an on-going surrendered love-relationship with Christ, God's grace, rather than bent human desires, increasingly becomes the source and guide for the whole of the believer's life and thought.

A third factor at the core of Adventist nonconformity is the place of Scripture in Adventist thought and life. Whereas many denominations have moved away from reliance on Scripture and turned increasingly toward tradition and human reason, the vast majority of Adventists continue to read Scripture in accordance with the Reformation principles of *sola Scriptura* (the Bible as the final standard of truth and duty), *tota Scriptura* (all Scripture as inspired by God and thus fully authoritative), and *analogia Scriptura* (the harmony of Scripture). A commitment to accept all of Scripture—carefully understood through appropriate exegetical and theological means—as normative is seen as essential in avoiding the tendency to allow human thought and culture to determine one's understanding of God and His plan for our lives in relation to the world.

Several portions of Scripture have been particularly fundamental to Adventist nonconformity, in addition to those discussed earlier. The Law has been understood as an eternal expression of God's character and thus ever relevant to the Christian, whether in literal detail as in the Ten Commandments, in the principles behind the civil law, or in the ritual foreshadowing Christ's work through the sacrificial service and festivals.[9] The Old Testament experience of Israel and the repeated need for God to call His people apart from the nations is understood as instructive to the church today, in accordance with both the instruction of Paul (e.g. 2 Cor 6:14-18) and with the end-time call of Revelation 18:4 to "come out of her my people." The numerous parables of Jesus calling people to be ready for His coming have had especially strong resonance for Adventists, heightening their resolve to be ready to joyfully meet Him when He comes.

A final factor that might be recognized as playing a role in the ongoing Adventist ethic of nonconformity is the inseparable nature of theology and praxis in a number of Adventism's more distinctive beliefs. For example, the belief in the sacred nature of the seventh-day Sabbath is not fundamentally a concept to be believed so much as it is a space in time where living itself is reoriented. On the Sabbath, humans are invited to turn from the frantic and acquisitional pace of the world around them to rest wholeheartedly in the values and rhythms of the God of Creation. This is done together with one's family and the community of believers, as well as in solitude with Him. A *de facto* consequence of this kind of Sabbath-keeping is that many activities that take place during the Sabbath hours are thereby missed by Adventists. The fact that there are few other faith communities who gather for Sabbath worship on the seventh day adds some distance even between Adventists and the philosophical trends of other Christians.

The rejection of the Greek dualism between body and soul, which is evidenced doctrinally in the Adventist disavowal of immortality of the soul and an ever-burning hell, also has its natural working out in praxis. Because the body is understood to be inseparable from the soul, the way we care for our bodies has been an inseparable aspect of soul care and Christian discipleship. It is for this reason that Adventists not only carry on 19th century revivalist mores such as the avoidance of alcohol, but also have come to value healthy living as a spiritual practice including such activities as exercise and eating a healthy, vegetarian diet.

The vivid conviction of Christ's ongoing work of judgment and the imminence of His coming is also manifestly oriented toward praxis. The Adventist conception of the Great Controversy between Christ and Satan views judgment not only as an evaluation of individual human lives, but also as a final demonstration for all time that God's ways are indeed infinitely good and right. Adventists thus see believers' actions of faithful separation from the world as being like "a city set on a hill" in a universal sense, a part of a larger theater of the universe in which He is about to complete the final act in the creation of an earth made new. In this view there is little impetus for seeking to redeem human culture.

The pragmatic nature of the Adventist ethos is only enhanced by the major percentage of space and emphasis devoted to practical matters by Ellen White, who continues to be an authoritative spiritual guide for most Adventists. Much of her writing involved testimonies to specific individuals regarding specific discipleship issues, as well as to church and parachurch entities ministering in areas such as education, medical work, family, and evangelism. The fact that the distinctive aspects of Adventism are not a standard part of the general Christian tradition has itself tended, through the years, to drive Adventists to Scripture for understanding and clarification rather than to religio-cultural tradition.

Conclusions

As a result of their historical experience, appreciation of grace, understanding of Scripture, and theological commitments, Adventists are much more inclined, on a philosophical level, toward a critical stance toward culture, rather than toward either an easy acculturation with the world or a missional methodology of syncretism. Their emphasis on mission to prepare for and even hasten the Second Coming does, however, not allow them to engage in full retreat from the world.

Of course the very strengths which help Adventists avoid conforming or catering to culture *carte blanche* also bring with them corresponding challenges. As a conservative tradition with carefully delineated understandings of Scriptural truth and mores, hard-won by our pioneers, it is easy to cling to 19th century forms without considering their applicability and implications in the face of contemporary realities. One simple example is that while most Adventists will still not attend a movie theatre, they are often not as careful about the various forms of electronic media they bring into their own homes. Another anomaly caused by attention to the letter rather than the spirit of past practices is the continued disapproval of traditional jewelry such as rings and necklaces, while elaborate brooches and watchbands (not to mention homes and cars) receive little notice. Separation and distinctiveness have too easily become ends in themselves, organized around self-chosen identity markers that allow groups to sideline other important issues, forgetting the God-centered reasons behind these differences. Such attitudes can allow people to slip into a kind of spiritual legalism and arrogance.

On the other side of the picture, both ongoing and periodic actions against the temptation to legalism are a significant part of Adventist community life. Voices both at the center and the margins of Adventism through the years have made it their mission to live and lead in a Christocentric manner that makes lifestyle a principled response to grace. Particularly powerful emphases in this direction were heard in certain eras, including the 1880's and 1950's and 60's, in response to a perceived drift in the opposite direction. As might be expected, the reaction against a perceived legalistic focus on the specific behaviors has at times led to an over-emphasis on justification by faith that leaves no room for the call to biblical discipleship. Overall, the pull in one direction or the other has functioned to provide checks and balances which help to draw the center of Adventism towards balance on these issues.

A challenge of a slightly different kind is the aging Adventist population in North America. While older Adventists continue to hold to traditional Adventist lifestyle mores, many among the "younger" generations, raised in an era of ubiquitous media presence and postmodernity, do not see the importance of separation from the world in the same way as their predecessors. It is easier, in the face of evidence of inconsistent standards, to loosen one's standards to the lowest common denominator than to seek the principles behind the standards and apply them consistently to the new context. In the post-modern era, the place of any church institution in determining one's values and lifestyle choices is often questioned. The increasing lapse of time between the early Adventist proclamation of an imminent coming and the present day has diminished the sense of urgency and the eagerness to forego cultural preferences in order to retain one's unique Adventist identity. Thus the drift away from traditional Christian lifestyle standards by many churches since the 19th century, based in the argument that they are legalistic and distracting from what is really important, has not left Adventism unaffected.

Evidence of shifts in Adventist values in some circles includes acceptance and even celebration of military service, jewelry becoming almost the norm in some churches, and widespread acceptance of certain dietary choices once considered taboo. On the other hand, some young Adventists react to such trends by seeking to return to the thinking and values of the early Adventists, not always managing either to understand them clearly or to recognize their weaknesses. Bright spots include movements such as *The One Project* that have arisen among Adventist young people themselves to create a community of discipleship and mission that is vibrantly Christ-centered as well as actively submitted. The research of church entities such as the *Institute of Church Ministry* at the SDA Theological Seminary has also been very helpful by making it possible to address these issues in informed ways.

The historic strength of the call to come out of the world also means that Adventists' relationships to possibly neutral and positive aspects of culture have not always been carefully thought through. Adventist missiologists are among those who have thought deeply about these questions, recognizing and seeking to explore the place of contextualization in Adventist life and mission. The problem with seeing oneself as fundamentally in opposition to culture is not only that good things may be rejected along with the bad, but that one does not always recognize where one is, in fact, acting on the basis of culture rather than Scripture. While this is not a problem in areas where culture colors our lives in ways not circumscribed by Scripture, it can be significantly misleading when other actions and ideas are simply assumed to be Scriptural. Most Adventists have understood in a general way that human persons are shaped by factors of human nature and experience and by their culture and society; but fewer have explicitly considered the power of culture in their own lives, or the possibility that these factors have the potential to both contribute to and to eclipse the work of God.

A further challenge for the world church is that for generations many missionaries, while seeking to avoid syncretization, did not adequately distinguish between spreading the Gospel and reduplicating conservative Western cultural and worship styles. An interesting side-effect of this is that, in an era of rapid global communication and transportation, individuals retaining a 1930's and 40's view of what it means to be Adventist are rubbing shoulders regularly with those in rapidly changing cosmopolitan cultures who have different interpretations. The resulting tensions are at times painful, but also help each group to look again at things they might otherwise have assumed.

The exciting growth of the church in the developing world has brought with it both joys and challenges.[10] In some places the church is growing so fast that it is very difficult to provide for adequate discipling. This is especially problematic when bringing souls into the church is treated with more concern than discipling them as members of the body. The church has attempted to respond creatively to this challenge by building up its institutions of higher learning to train leadership on each continent and providing numerous Bible training conferences to assist pastors in each of the world divisions in dealing with key issues faced in their local areas. On a more grass roots level, the church provides the Hope Channel, with educational and inspirational programming, to many areas of the world by satellite, and the journal *Adventist World*, which is sent monthly at no cost to members around the world.

In short, the Adventist Church as a whole remains committed to the basic view that the ways of the world are in fundamental opposition to the ways of God, and therefore to the task of calling all people to a true and life-shaping commitment to Christ and the full teachings of His Word. The rich interaction of cultures and ways of thinking within the church continues to pull us to think carefully about what things are fundamental principles of Adventist discipleship to Christ and which are tied to a particular culture and therefore expendable. First and foremost we recognize that the ongoing challenge and solution underlying such a vision is to continually seek to allow Christ to be the center, the ground, and reason for every distinction that is made. At the same time we seek to honestly understand in a more nuanced way the place that we have in culture, and that the culture has in us, and to deal both self-critically and faithfully with what we find.

ENDNOTES

[1] The saying comes closest to John 17:15-18 (NASB): "I do not ask You to take them out of the world, but to keep them from the evil one. They are not of the world, even as I am not of the world. Sanctify them in the truth; Your word is truth. As You sent Me into the world, I also have sent them into the world." (cf. also 1 John 2:15-17)

[2] In North America at that time, "the world" would have generally referred to a careless or a rejected Christianity, rather than to a secular or pluralistic culture or society.

[3] The earliest Adventist pioneers belonged to a variety of Christian denominations including the Methodist, Christian Connexion, and Baptist faith traditions. An important element in the identity formation of each of these groups has been stories of founding reformers who called for a re-emphasis or rediscovery of particular Scriptural truths, along with corresponding lifestyle changes, and who then found themselves and their message rejected by the mainstream of the church.

[4] This is an identification not unheard of among other reform movements of the time. For example, a group of American abolitionists, identified as "come-outers," also took on the task of calling people out of the fallen Babylon identified as the mainstream churches. See Jordan Ryan. "Quakers, 'Comeouters,' and the Meaning of Abolitionism in the Antebellum Free States," *Journal of the Early Republic 24*, no 4 (Winter 2004): 587-608; William Lloyd Garrison, (1854), *No Compromise with the Evil of Slavery*. Speech presented to the Broadway Tabernacle, New York, NY.

[5] Numbers as of December 31, 2010. http://www.adventist.org/world-church/facts-and-figures/index.html

[6] Jerome Thayer, "Youth Retention Study Reanalysis," Unpublished manuscript, Andrews University, Berrien Springs, MI, 2008c; Roger Dudley and V Bailey Gillespie, *Valuegenesis: Faith in the Balance*, (Riverside, CA: La Sierra University Press, 1992), 247-249; Jerome Thayer, "The Impact of Adventist Schools on Students," *Fourth Symposium on the Bible and Adventist Scholarship*, March 16-22, 2008. http://fae.adventist.org/essays/iv_Thayer_Jerry.pdf

[7] Development of more sophisticated and far-reaching forms of media in more recent years has challenged these simple rules. At the same time, even today this

concern about the media includes, for many, a deep caution with regard even to the media of other Christian individuals and organizations.

[8] The one area where Adventists have traditionally been willing to get involved has been to advocate for religious freedom.

[9] This reverence for the law is not for the purpose of achieving one's salvation but for the instruction and discipleship of those already belonging to God.

[10] In some countries, growth has been successful to the point that Adventists have become a significant political factor, and increasing numbers holding significant public offices challenges our simple past political solution of remaining primarily uninvolved in government affairs.

Hermeneutics from an Anabaptist Perspective

Robert J Suderman

Introduction

It is difficult to represent Mennonite World Conference[1] on the theme of Anabaptist hermeneutics. This is due, at least in part, to the simple fact that a shared hermeneutic is not what unites us as a communion. The hermeneutical assumptions that inform the diverse parts of our communion cannot be contained in a single, identifiable, interpretive design.

This should not, of course, surprise us. Our historical roots also reveal a very broad diversity of hermeneutical assumptions that at some points seem incompatible with others in the same movement. This means that it is not only difficult to adequately represent our current faith family, it is also difficult to represent our faith tradition. Whatever is said here must be considered descriptive—not prescriptive, and partial—not exhaustive.

Starting Points

Where do we begin? Do we begin with the 16th century, thus exposing the multiple hermeneutical assumptions that marked that dynamic movement, some of which were not broadly accepted then and are even less acceptable now? Or do we begin with our current reality, attempting to portray commonalities that would likely not withstand the crucible of close examination in our multi-cultural communion?

Perhaps, to be most faithful to our tradition, we would not begin with the Bible at all. We would begin with an examination of how faith is lived out in our diversity and we would say that our actions and lifestyles are the clearest indicators of how we actually read and interpret the Bible. The sense that *orthopraxis* is the most reliable indicator of *orthodoxy* is not an invention of contemporary Liberation Theology: it is borrowed from the historic Anabaptist tradition. Then it was not known as *orthopraxis* but as *nachfolge Christi* (following after Christ). But it was assumed that faithful *nachfolge* was a pre-condition to any authoritative competence to interpret the Bible rightly. This emphasis embedded them in circular logic that, in turn, generated multiple solutions. For some, Christ needed to be present in our inner selves prior to our capacity to understand the Bible. This was a way of ensuring that biblical interpretation was indeed secondary to a transformational experience with the Holy Spirit in our lives, the Spirit of the living Christ. For others, confidence in the written Word was such that understanding it was a pre-condition to understanding the Spirit of Jesus at all. How, after all, would one recognize the Spirit of Jesus within us if we had not first been mentored by the Bible about Jesus? But for most, signs of radical obedience to Jesus made possible by the power of the Spirit in transformed lives were the best evidence available that the Bible was being interpreted correctly.

With these signs they identified three important hermeneutical lenses. One, often unspoken, was that it is by the power of the Holy Spirit working in transformed lives, a gift of grace from God, that we are ignited to yearn to be disciples of Jesus, members of his church, and worthy of reading and interpreting Scripture together. Second, also assumed without extensive defence, was that Jesus is the interpretive key to reading both the Old and New Testaments. The third was that obedience to Jesus was both a pre-condition for and the fruit of right interpretation.

Whatever else we may say about Anabaptist hermeneutics, this integral connection to spiritual transformation and obedience was at the heart of it all.

Three Windows to Anabaptist Hermeneutics

The comments above point to the difficulty of presenting something considered *authoritative* or *prescriptive*, either as it relates to our history and tradition or for Mennonite churches around the world today. Some would understand this difficulty to be a weakness. We can, however, take a *descriptive* look at what we have now and what our tradition included when it began. If, by chance or providence, we find common ground within this diversity, then what we have may not be weakness at all. It may demonstrate what we always hope for, namely, that the Holy Spirit indeed does lead very diverse peoples to some common understandings. We will turn to this *descriptive* exercise now by taking a look at two samples from the 21st century: one global, and one national, and then by reviewing some vignettes of the hermeneutics evident in our tradition.

I.   Sample One: *Shared Convictions* of MWC Member Churches

During the last two decades, one of the significant developments in MWC was the unanimous approval by all member-churches[2] of a document simply entitled *Shared Convictions*. This statement is neither creed, nor dogma, nor is it a formal confession of faith. Given the diversity of our communion, and given our commitment that this be a statement generated via the voice of the various member-churches, this was not an easy or quick process. It is not, directly, a statement on hermeneutics either. But it does shed significant light on hermeneutical assumptions that undergird the *Convictions*. We will look at the statement from this perspective.

The statement reads as follows:

"Shared Convictions

"By the grace of God, we seek to live and proclaim the good news of reconciliation in Jesus Christ. As part of the one body of Christ at all times and places, we hold the following to be central to our belief and practice:

"1. God is known to us as Father, Son and Holy Spirit, the Creator who seeks to restore fallen humanity by calling a people to be faithful in fellowship, worship, service and witness.

"2. Jesus is the Son of God. Through his life and teachings, his cross and resurrection, he showed us how to be faithful disciples, redeemed the world, and offers eternal life.

"3. As a church, we are a community of those whom God's Spirit calls to turn from sin, acknowledge Jesus Christ as Lord, receive baptism upon confession of faith, and follow Christ in life.

"4. As a faith community, we accept the Bible as our authority for faith and life, interpreting it together under Holy Spirit guidance, in the light of Jesus Christ to discern God's will for our obedience.

"5. The Spirit of Jesus empowers us to trust God in all areas of life so we become peacemakers who renounce violence, love our enemies, seek justice, and share our possessions with those in need.

"6. We gather regularly to worship, to celebrate the Lord's Supper, and to hear the Word of God in a spirit of mutual accountability.

"7. As a worldwide community of faith and life we transcend boundaries of nationality, race, class, gender and language. We seek to live in the world without conforming to the powers of evil, witnessing to God's grace by serving others, caring for creation, and inviting all people to know Jesus Christ as Saviour and Lord.

"In these convictions we draw inspiration from Anabaptist forebears of the 16th century, who modeled radical discipleship to Jesus Christ. We seek to walk in his name by the power of the Holy Spirit, as we confidently await Christ's return and the final fulfillment of God's kingdom."[3]

Annotated Commentary on the *Shared Convictions*

The *Conviction* that most directly identifies hermeneutical assumptions is #4. Five critical elements are identified: the authority of the Bible for faith and life; the locus of the hermeneutical community ("interpreting [the Bible] together"); the guidance of the Holy Spirit; the centrality of Jesus Christ; and the primal significance of obedience. These elements, perhaps inadvertently, provide a substantive framework for a hermeneutical stance.

1.   The activities of worship, including "to hear the Word of God" (#6), are characterized by "a spirit of mutual accountability" (#6). The assumption that all discernment is subject to the accountability of the gathered community is a key hermeneutical element that gives voice to all members of the community. Hermeneutical authority is not vested in a hierarchy of leadership, nor in a circle of scholars, nor in the closed Bible. Authority is vested in "hearing the Word" (#6) as a whole community, gathered around the open Word, guided by the Holy Spirit, and obedient to Jesus as Lord.

2.   Our capacity to obey is pre-determined by our openness to trust (#5). It is interesting to note that our ability to "renounce violence, love our enemies, seek justice, and share our possessions with those in need" (#5) is not based on hermeneutical complexities of reading and understanding the biblical text. It is determined by our willingness to "trust." This trust, in turn, is gifted to us by the "Spirit of Jesus."

3.   The primary strategy of God to "restore fallen humanity" (#1) is ecclesial: "by calling a people to be faithful in fellowship, worship, service and witness" (#1). The church is much more than a gathered community, a family of support, or an organization of ministry. Its calling is to embody the grace of God (introduction, #7), discern the will of God for obedience (#4), demonstrate mutual accountability for its discernment and action (#6), be empowered to trust (#5), unite in worship (#6), non-conform to evil (#7), witness to

the Lordship of Jesus (introduction, #1, #7), and not be contained by time, geography, or politics of our day (introduction, #7). The church is called to be already what God has in store for all of creation eventually.

4. All seven *Convictions*, as well as the introductory and closing statements, highlight Jesus as Christ, Lord, and/or Saviour. This underscores the central role of Jesus in the hermeneutical enterprise. Regardless of what the area of discussion may be, it must somehow be informed by God's revelation in Jesus of Nazareth. One writer describes the 16th century Anabaptists similarly:

> For the Anabaptists, Jesus Christ ceased to be a "correlation point" in the evaluation of alleged Revelation. He is a person to be obeyed. Knowledge of Christ comes in walking with Him, and only then can one understand what is written about him. A large part of "interpreting" the Bible is imitating it. Therefore they allowed it to shape the way they spoke and the way they lived, following Christ to suffering and death.[4]

It should be noted that this vibrant emphasis on Jesus as the key to biblical interpretation raises the troubling question of the ongoing canonical status of the Old Testament in interpretation. This was already a hotly contested discussion in the 16th century, and it continues to be so in our time.

II.   Sample Two: 21st Century - Mennonite Church Canada

Mennonite Church Canada[5] has recently initiated a process to understand more fully how the Bible informs the discernment and life of its congregations. By deciphering the responses we wish to determine if there is solid, common, hermeneutical ground to stand on. It is hoped that this will help the national church in discerning difficult issues as a hermeneutic community. A survey tool requested stories and examples of how the Bible is helpful or not for discernment. There was significant response from congregations, groups, individuals, and a group of biblical scholars of the church. These responses have been compiled and categorized. It seems as though there is, indeed, an emerging framework that can be used to demonstrate hermeneutical transparency for future discernment. This framework uses the image of a communal hike on which we try to stick to the paths and avoid the ditches. We present this emerging framework as another contemporary window into the hermeneutical life of Mennonites. Twelve hermeneutical paths were identified.[6] These, with some commentary, are:

Paths to Stay On:

1.   The life, teaching, death, and resurrection of Jesus are central and serve as the critical lens of interpretation that helps us understand all of Scripture.[7]

2.   Context makes a difference in how Scripture is interpreted, understood, and applied for faith and life. Context refers not only to the importance of understanding the time and place out of which Scripture emerged and to which it was addressed. It also refers to our time and place and how that impacts our understandings of Scripture.[8]

3.   Scripture already interprets Scripture. It is very important to pay close attention to this inter-textual interpretation, because this already gives us essential clues in the ways we need to understand how various passages relate to each other.

4.   Jesus also interprets Scripture. One response focused exclusively on trying to understand the "hermeneutics of Jesus," i.e., how the Gospel writers portray the way Jesus uses and interprets the Old Testament. It is evident that we can learn much from that in our own reading of Scripture.[9]

5.   It is important to take the entire canon of Scripture as our base of operations for healthy hermeneutics. The fact that Scripture already interprets Scripture compels us to use the whole of Scripture in order to better understand each part.

6.   Scripture persistently hopes that the letters of its words will become a living Word in a world in need of redemption. This does not diminish the authority of Scripture, but sharpens it and makes it real in our community and to the world. This pathway indicates that other sources can illuminate what Scripture also teaches.

7.   It is the Holy Spirit who guides the interpretive community in faithfulness and in faithfully understanding Scripture for our

lives. This means that we must continually open our hearts and minds to the work of the Spirit within and among us. Without this, "the text is just black marks on the paper."

8. Scripture calls us to remember that we are a part of a larger story of "God's love affair with the world." The Gospel's command to go and baptize and the invitation to remember the Lord's Supper are prime examples of when we "do not forget" how God has accompanied us. The yearning to know God is inseparably connected to "remembering" the story of God, a story that we now acknowledge as our own.[10]

9. "Knowing" is inseparable from "doing," "hearing" is inseparable from "acting," and "*praxis* [practice] is indispensable for *gnosis* [knowledge]." Jesus' hermeneutic also repeatedly indicates this critical connection between "works [*erga*] and faith [*pistis*]." In other words, on a hike we need to walk and not just sit on the path and contemplate the map.

10. Scripture is a "delight" that serves also for devotional refreshment and daily inspiration. The delight of Scripture is even greater when we can hike together rather than going out on a lone trek.

11. We need to see our interpretive community as larger than the people we can see around us. The hiking trail we are on has already been forged by many who have gone before us.[11] They have left markers on the trail to help those who come after. And we will leave markers for those coming behind us. This does not mean that we can't make the trail better, create short-cuts where advisable, remove obstacles for better mobility, and so on. But the interpretive community extends geographically beyond those in our hiking group; it is not restricted to our choice of time and schedule; and it is not constrained by our particular agenda. We must affirm the critical importance of those on the trail with us at this time,[12] those who have gone before, and those who are hiking at the same time, but on trails that may be geographically and culturally distant from us. The awareness of other hikers should not, however, close our eyes to the contextual dangers lurking on *our* hike and the scenic beauty that may highlight something new for *us*.

12. Jesus is portrayed as "consistently interpreting Scripture in

reference to, and with regard for, the needs/realities of 'the least'—the most needy and vulnerable (the poor, the sick, the foreigner/outsider, women, social outcasts...)." God's intention through Scripture is to bring wholeness to creation, justice to the orphans and widows, sight and healing to the blind and the lame, reconciliation and salvation to the sinners.

Ditches to Avoid:

Each of the paths indicated above inherently hints at a ditch that we would wish to avoid. For example, we enter ditches when Jesus is not a central lens to interpretation, if we ignore context, if we diminish the extent of the canon, etc. We will, therefore, not repeat them all. We will highlight only a few that were specifically identified as potentially problematic ditches.

1.   The desire to keep Jesus central to hermeneutics at times leads some to disconnect him from his own Scriptural roots (The Hebrew Bible) and his own social/political context in 1st century Palestine. We need to avoid both of these ditches and not leave Jesus without a context.

2.   We should avoid the temptation to set the Old Testament aside. The Old Testament is part of our Scripture for at least two reasons: a) The New Testament is grounded in Old Testament language, images, quotations, and assumptions and therefore the two Testaments cannot and should not be separated; b) The Old Testament speaks to things that the New Testament may not highlight. "All of Scripture witnesses to God's revelation." "Both Testaments carry a living word of God for us." "Our task is to attempt to discern how all of Scripture might function as a word from God to us."

3.   We need to avoid proof-texting. "Proof-texting is essentially the use of a text to support or reject a position without giving sufficient attention to the meaning and function of that text in its historical and literary setting in the Bible and without bringing it into dialogue with other texts particularly relevant to the issue." This definition highlights the importance of both context and canon for healthy interpretation.

4.   We need to avoid generalizations without having immersed

ourselves in particular texts. This is the opposite of proof-texting and is equally detrimental to theological discernment. Some of the most common generalizations are: "the Bible says," or "all we need is love," or "let's just focus on justice." Each of these generalizations needs to be understood from particular texts.

5. "We should not assume that our own context is either static or normative when interpreting the Bible." The Apostle Paul says that "now we see in a mirror dimly... now I know only in part" (1 Cor 13:12). This is an important reminder that we live in a changing context, and our understandings are partial.

6. We should not try to subject God to our ideology. The gift of Scripture is that it may challenge rather than support our preferences.

Some Observations

While no effort was made to shape MC Canada responses to the MWC *Convictions*, we do note some remarkable similarities. Both have a strong sense of Jesus being an interpretive key to the whole Bible. Both emphasize the important role of the church as the authoritative hermeneutical community. Both understand the community to be non-hierarchical in its calling. Both emphasize the critical role of the Holy Spirit in guiding discernment. Both connect interpretation to obedience and faithfulness. Both speak of the importance of accountability in community processes. Both acknowledge the importance of the broader community in determining faithfulness. Both indicate the critical concern that biblical wisdom, however discerned, needs to address the welfare of the "least of these."

While the MC Canada document is more intentionally addressing issues of hermeneutics more narrowly defined, it is noteworthy how close the two documents are in their basic perspectives. We emphasize again, that both of these documents are *descriptive* in nature, but in spite of the diverse contexts, they demonstrate very significant common ground. We suggested above that if such compatibility should emerge, this changes apparent weakness into significant spiritual strength.

III. Sample Three: Vignettes from Anabaptist History

It is not in the scope of this paper to provide a thorough analysis of the hermeneutical tendencies of the Anabaptists movements of the 16th century. Excellent studies for this are available. We can only provide some brief vignettes of the debates and tendencies that are evident in the movements.

A.   The Rule of Christ

The role of the then designated "rule of Christ," as an agent of hermeneutical influence, can hardly be overstated.

> If another member of the church sins against you, go and point out the fault when the two of you are alone. If the member listens to you, you have regained that one. But if you are not listened to, take one or two others along with you, so that every word may be confirmed by the evidence of two or three witnesses. If the member refuses to listen to them, tell it to the church; and if the offender refuses to listen even to the church, let such a one be to you as a Gentile and a tax collector. Truly I tell you, whatever you bind on earth will be bound in heaven, and whatever you loose on earth will be loosed in heaven (Matt 18:15-18).

John H Yoder identifies four key implications of the "rule of Christ" for the hermeneutics of the Anabaptists:[13]

1.   The context for the discernment of what Scripture says to us is not scholarly objectivity; it is congregational involvement in offense and reconciliation.

2.   Discerning the intention of God is related to the offended, the offender, and the whole congregation. It is not delegated to official disciplinarians or scholars.

3.   The community's hermeneutic authority is binding for that time and place, but remains open to review which can be initiated by anyone in the congregation.

4.   The central mark of the church is its capacity to gather together to discern and to do the will of God.

B.   The Rule of Paul

> Let two or three prophets speak, and let the others weigh what is said (1 Cor 14:29).

One of the remarkable things about the early Anabaptists was that simple, often uneducated folk, articulated their faith in compelling ways even on the road to martyrdom. This sense that ordinary people, with the help of the Holy Spirit, and without the mediation of the hierarchy of the church, can understand enough to be faithful was a key conviction of the Anabaptists. The importance of the Holy Spirit to guide the hermeneutic community in its understanding of faithfulness according to Scripture was foundational.

John H Yoder states: "It is a basic novelty in the discussion of hermeneutics to say that a text is best understood in the congregation. This means that the toils of literary analysis do not suffice; that the Spirit is an interpreter of what a text is about only when Christians are gathered in readiness to hear it speak to their current needs and concerns."[14] In the same essay, Yoder articulates five implications of emphasizing that the Word is best discerned in the congregation:

1.   The common person becomes a full member of the church.

2.   The congregation must not be bound by tradition or former creedal statements, nor by the supervision of governing authorities, nor by specialized theologians or hierarchical authorities.

3.   Revelation moves beyond theory to an obligation to make very strong and specific statements about our actual congregational activity.

4.   The process of finding truth in the Church was a rejection of all kinds of visionary enthusiasm.

5.   Discernment could lead to the unity that permitted them to say with the early church: "It seemed good to the Spirit and to us" (Acts 15:28).

C.   *Christ the Foundation*

For no one can lay any foundation other than the one that has been laid; that foundation is Jesus Christ (1 Cor 3:11).

The Anabaptists had a strong sense that Jesus was the interpretive key to understanding all of Scripture. The foundational verse for Menno Simons was 1 Corinthians 3:11. Every time he wrote (which was often) and everything he wrote (which was substantial) began or ended with this key verse. In 1539 he wrote the classic Anabaptist phrase, "No doctrine is profitable or serviceable to our salvation but the doctrine of Christ Jesus and His holy apostles."[15] Dirk Philips, another Anabaptist leader insisted that "the only touchstone and the only measuring rod is God's word, and the only foundation is Jesus Christ. Jesus with his doctrine, life and example is our Teacher, Leader, and Guide, him we must hear and follow."[16]

1. Stuart Murray, author of *The Naked Anabaptist*, has identified six hermeneutical principles essential in 16th century Anabaptists.[17] These are: The Bible as Self-interpreting; Christocentrism; The Two Testaments; Spirit and Word; Congregational Hermeneutics; Hermeneutics of Obedience. Without investigating these in detail, it is again remarkable how closely these resemble the statements from MWC and from MC Canada.

2. The Global Anabaptist Mennonite Encyclopaedia Online (GAMEO) identifies some of the key hermeneutical similarities and differences between 16th century Anabaptists and other Reformers. It states, "Scripture interpretation among the Anabaptist resembled that of the other Protestant reformers in many ways:

- All Protestant and Anabaptist leaders agreed that the Bible is the final authority.
- All emphasized the literal-historical method of interpretation—in contrast to the allegorical method in use since the 2nd century A.D.
- All followed the Christ-principle and used Scripture to interpret Scripture.

"Significant areas of disagreement were:

- The understandings of the relation between the testaments, which were correlated with the Christ-principle;
- The understanding of the relation between the letter and Spirit, and inner and outer word;[18]
- The role of all believers in interpretation and testing of interpretation (priesthood of all believers);
- Perhaps most important of all, the relation of discipleship and obedience to insight and knowledge."[19]

3. Some 16th century Anabaptists understood Scripture to be the most authoritative source for Christian faith and life. Indeed,

they borrowed from other Reformers the idea of *sola scriptura* to in-dicate that other sources that claimed to be authoritative really were not. Their passion, however, was not so much to keep *scriptura* pure, but to maintain the faithfulness and obedience of the Church con-nected to our transformation by the Spirit and to God's revelation in Scripture.

4. As indicated above, some Anabaptists, however, had an interesting sense of the "living Word," or the "inner Word," that could be present quite apart from Scripture—indeed, that needed to be present apart from Scripture in order to fully understand Scrip-ture. This understanding did not eliminate the sense of *sola scriptura* but relativized it slightly. However, John H Yoder indicates that even in these cases: "the only court of appeal is the text of Scripture. No congregation and no prophet may claim with any authority to have heard the Spirit, unless in the testing of that Spirit Scripture can be appealed to."[20]

Closing Comments

Mennonite/Anabaptist hermeneutics are characterized by a profound three-legged paradox. One leg is fierce suspicion. The Mennonite ethos is deeply suspicious of any pretence toward author-itative creed, any assumption of the trustworthiness of dogma, and any commitment to prescriptive norms. This suspicion has, from the inception of our movement, contributed to innumerable quarrels, splits, divisions, and doctrinal nuances—too many to mention.

The second leg of the paradox is surprising adherence to tradition. There is, for example, little evidence that 16th century Ana-baptists deviated in any significant way from the foundational creeds of Christendom: the Apostles' Creed and the Nicene Creed. Nor is there evidence that at any point they did not embrace the traditional understandings of Trinity. They embraced these traditions, insisting that their new understandings were indeed deeper expressions of the authoritative traditions, creeds, and dogmas of the church. It was the Christendom church, they argued, that was no longer true to its own creeds and dogma.

The third leg is profound coherence. The three samples we

have touched on above: two contemporary—one global, the other national, and one historic, indicate how much coherence there is at a descriptive level. This foundational coherence is not simply the happy and comfortable agreement of good buddies enjoying each others' company in the lap of luxury. It is a broadly-based, deeply held coherence across cultures, traditions, and languages. Its breadth and depth span geographies and plumb the vagaries of centuries of history. The coherence has weathered storms of suffering and martyrdom, affluence and accommodation. In spite of the pervasive evidence of a splintering spirit, a deeper analysis reveals persistently profound common ground: a coherence of faith, life, and under-standing that is undeniable and remarkable.

I mentioned earlier that if, by chance or providence, a descriptive analysis might reveal such coherence spanning time, space, culture, and experience, then the apparent weakness of the Body begins to feel like the substantial strength of God's Spirit working through the flaws and failings of human obedience. It seems to be evidence, for those whose eyes are willing to see, that God's strategic design of working through peoplehood in order to restore creation is still pertinent, relevant, and real.

May it be so.

ENDNOTES

[1] We will use "MWC" as the abbreviation for Mennonite World Conference.

[2] At present there are 101 national church bodies that are members of MWC.

[3] Adopted by Mennonite World Conference, General Council, Pasadena, California (USA), March 15, 2006

[4] Ben C Ollenburger, "Hermeneutics of the Obedience: A Study of Anabaptist Hermeneutics," *Direction*, April 1977, vol 6, no 2, 19-31.

[5] MC Canada is one of the 100 member-churches of MWC. This summary is used here with permission.

[6] This document will be processed by the MC Canada Delegate Assembly in July 2012. Quotation marks in these points indicate direct quotes taken from respondents.

[7] John Howard Yoder, noted Mennonite theologian, states forcefully what the respondents also point to, namely that the experience with Jesus represents: "a

cosmos shaken by the cross.... a universe being re-ordered by the Word of the resurrection" (John H Yoder, *To Hear the Word*, 2nd edition, [Cascade Books, 2010], 135). Such a cosmic understanding of Jesus will impact the way Scripture is read and understood among God's people.

[8] We must be aware of all the contexts that have touched Scripture, including those of choosing and forming Scripture, preserving it through the centuries, and translating it.

[9] This response identified 21 key things about the ways in which Jesus is portrayed as using Scripture. These are very helpful. The first thing is that Jesus used Scripture a lot and is described as being creatively and provocatively engaged in conversations about and interpretation of Scripture. For example, the respondent identifies up to 25 Old Testament quotations, images, allusions, and echoes in a single chapter of Matthew. This demonstrates that there is already a very significant "hermeneutical ferment" in Scripture itself.

[10] One scholar suggests the following four important points: "The Bible has a persistent 'present tense' (it does not only address people long ago, but continues to address communities of faith throughout the ages), it functions as a 'witness' to divine revelation, it is linked to human writers, and it is sufficient rather than exhaustive."

[11] For a brief look at how our responses correspond to key elements of 16th century Anabaptist understandings, please refer to Appendix I.

[12] Mennonite Church Canada people are a tapestry of cultural and ethnic diversity, regional loyalties, and congregational histories. These are the people hiking together now.

[13] John H Yoder, *To Hear the Word*, second edition (Eugene, Oregon: Cascade Books, 2010), 232-234.

[14] Yoder 228.

[15] Stuart Murray, *Biblical Interpretation in the Anabaptist Tradition* (Kitchener: Pandora Press, 2000), 71.

[16] Murray 75.

[17] Murray.

[18] Willard M Swartley, Editor, *Essays on Biblical Interpretation: Anabaptist-Mennonite Perspectives*, (Elkhart, Indiana: Institute of Mennonite Studies, 1984).

[19] Hans Denck, a noted Anabaptist leader, indicated that "No one can know Christ except by following him in life, and no one can follow him except by knowing him." Hence, only the person "who is committed to the direction of obedience can read the truth so as to interpret it in line with the direction of God's purposes" (Swartley 27).

[20] John H Yoder, *To Hear the Word*, 2nd edition, (Cascade Books, 2010), 135, 227.

A Perspective on Seventh-day Adventist Hermeneutics

Denis Fortin

The preamble of the Seventh-day Adventist statement of Fundamental Beliefs states: "Seventh-day Adventists accept the Bible as their only creed and hold certain fundamental beliefs to be the teaching of the Holy Scriptures." Along with other Christians, Adventists share a high view of Scripture and accept it as the Word of God to humankind, and their beliefs and lifestyle are formulated as a result of the study of the Bible.

The first Adventist Fundamental Belief is about the Bible.

"1.   The Holy Scriptures

"The Holy Scriptures, Old and New Testaments, are the written Word of God, given by divine inspiration through holy men of God who spoke and wrote as they were moved by the Holy Spirit. In this Word, God has committed to man the knowledge necessary for salvation. The Holy Scriptures are the infallible revelation of His will. They are the standard of character, the test of experience, the authoritative revealer of doctrines, and the trustworthy record of God's acts in history. (2 Peter 1:20, 21; 2 Tim. 3:16, 17; Ps. 119:105; Prov. 30:5, 6; Isa. 8:20; John 17:17; 1 Thess. 2:13; Heb. 4:12.)"

The Nature and Authority of Scripture[1]

Seventh-day Adventists believe the Old and New Testaments are the Word of God and the revealed will of God to humanity. We make this claim because we also believe the writers of the 66 books that form the Bible were inspired by God to write these books. Given their supernatural inspiration, which goes beyond mere natural insights or intuition, these books therefore have an intrinsic authority located in God Himself. The uniqueness of the Bible is based on its origin and source. The writers did not claim to originate the messages they wrote but often referred to divine revelations for the truths they passed on (Isa 1:1; Micah 1:1).

The Bible has divine authority because in it God speaks through the Holy Spirit. Throughout His ministry, Jesus stressed the authority of the Scriptures. When tempted by Satan in the wilderness, He quoted Scripture in His defense (Matt 4:4, 7, 10). When discussing with opponents He referred to Scripture (Luke 10:26; 20:17) and He readily placed the Bible above human traditions and opinions (Mark 7:7-9). Jesus also believed in the authority of the prophetic word and revealed that it pointed to Him (John 5:39, 46). Repeatedly, Jesus and the apostles issued warnings against false prophets and false teachers who would seek to displace the Word of God as found in the Scripture with their own teachings (Matt 15:1-9; Acts 20:29-30; 2 Tim 4:3-4; 2 Peter 2:1; 1 John 4:1). Such warnings are evidence that Jesus and the apostles upheld the authority of Scripture and any exaltation of human teachings above the teachings of Scripture undermines the authority of God's Word.

The Interpretation of Scripture

A number of foundational presuppositions undergird an Adventist interpretation of Scripture.[2]

1. Adventists believe that God is a personal being who took the initiative to reveal Himself to humanity and the Bible provides us

with the knowledge to enable us to enter into a saving relationship with Him.

2.   The entrance of sin into the world radically altered the relationship between God and humanity and affects how people understand God's will for them. In the interpretation of Scripture, the effects of sin are obstacles that prevent a clear understanding of God's will. Pride, self-deception, doubt, distance and distortion are such obstacles that require the guidance of the Holy Spirit to overcome them (cf. Isa 59:2).

3.   The same Spirit who inspired the Bible writers has been promised to illumine the minds of those who seek to understand the meaning of Scripture (John 14:26).

4.   Those who read the Bible need a disposition of mind and heart that leads to understanding God's will. Such a disposition cannot be attained only through proper hermeneutical skills and techniques. Foundational attitudes include openness and honesty, faith and humility, obedience and prayer (1 Cor 2:10-14).

Obstacles created by sin also require the use of various rules of hermeneutics to comprehend the meaning of Scripture. Distance from the original authors of the Bible, separation in time, geography, languages and culture necessitate the interpretation of Scripture to our modern context. Already in the Old Testament, priests and Levites had the responsibility of teaching God's Word to the people (Lev 10:11; Deut 33:10) and interpreting the law of God in different situations (Deut 17:8-11; Eze 44:23-24). In the days of Ezra and Nehemiah, the Levites "read from the Book of the Law of God, making it clear and giving the meaning so that the people could understand what was being read" (Neh 8:8). The New Testament also provides examples of this: Philip explaining the book of Isaiah to the Ethiopian eunuch (Acts 8: 30-31) and Paul instructing Timothy to be sure he is "rightly handling" the Word of God (2 Tim 2:15).

Principles for Biblical Interpretation

Adventists find in the Bible some key principles of biblical interpretation.

1.   One key fundamental principle for biblical interpretation

that Adventists have repeatedly referred to is Isaiah 8:20, "To the law and to the testimony! If they do not speak according to this word, they have no light of dawn." The two words *law* and *testimony* point to the two loci of authority in Isaiah's time: the Pentateuch (Torah) and the testimony of the prophets to the previously revealed will of God in the Pentateuch. Jesus referred to these two loci of authority when He spoke of the law and the prophets in the Sermon on the Mount (Matt 5:17), to which Paul added the authoritative revelation given by Jesus and the witness of the apostles (Eph 2:20; 3:5).

Thus both the Old and New Testaments form the authoritative Word of God to humanity. For Adventists this means the Bible, as God's revealed Word, is the *sole standard* of beliefs and practices. While the Bible holds primacy over other means of epistemology, such as nature, reason, and tradition, the Bible has no other comparable or equivalent standard of authority in Christian life.

2. This principle also implies the corollary of the *sufficiency* of Scripture (2 Tim 3:15). The Bible stands alone as the unerring guide to truth and life; it is sufficient to lead one to salvation and it is the standard by which all doctrines and experiences must be tested. All additional pathways to knowledge, experience, or revelation must build upon and remain faithful to the all-sufficient revelation found in Scripture.

3. Another important principle of hermeneutics is the *totality* of Scripture. Adventists affirm with the apostle Paul that *"all* Scripture is inspired by God and profitable for teaching, for reproof, for correction, and for training in righteousness" (2 Tim 3:16). As the standard for doctrine and experience, *all* of Scripture is accepted and not only some sections of it. In this context, Adventists believe that the Bible *is* and does not only *contain* the Word of God. Although we recognize human elements in the Bible, the record of God's revelation is nonetheless trustworthy and an accurate representation of the divine message.

4. The *analogy* of Scripture is a fourth principle of hermeneutics. Since all Scripture is inspired by the same Holy Spirit and all of it is the Word of God, there is a fundamental unity, coherence and harmony among its various parts. Many New Testament authors

supported their points by citing several Old Testament sources. For example in Romans 3:10-18, Paul cites from Ecclesiastes (7:20), the book of Psalms (14:2, 3; 5:10; 10:7), and Isaiah (59:7, 8). This principle also claims that neither Testament supersedes the other, although the later revelation is tested by the former. The Bereans are a good example of this approach (Acts 17:11) and Jesus Himself insisted that the conviction of His disciples be based on the Scripture (i.e. the Old Testament; Luke 24:25-27).

5.   A corollary principle to the analogy of Scripture is the principle of Scripture being *its own interpreter*. The underlying unity among the various parts of Scripture allows one portion to interpret another, becoming the key for understanding related passages. Jesus demonstrated this principle during His conversation with the disciples on the road to Emmaus and later that night when He appeared to His disciples in the upper room (Luke 24:27, 44, 45). "And beginning at Moses and all the Prophets, He expounded to them in all the Scriptures the things concerning Himself" (Luke 24:27).

6.   Another corollary principle to the analogy of Scripture is the *consistency* of Scripture. Since the Bible has one divine Author, through the inspiration of the Holy Spirit the various parts of Scripture are consistent with each other. By this principle we mean that the interpretation of individual passages will harmonize with the totality of what Scripture teaches on a given subject. While the different writers may provide different emphases on the same subject or event (e.g. the four Gospels), this will be interpreted without contradiction. Each writer may contribute aspects of the topic or event that are needed to obtain a full and balanced picture. In the end, though, we admit that not all passages of Scripture may be interpreted satisfactorily and some ambiguity may remain (e.g. Peter speaking of Paul's writings, 2 Peter 3:15, 16)

7.   One last principle of interpretation is the *clarity* of Scripture. The Bible is perspicuous and does not require any ecclesiastical magisterium to clarify its meaning. Numerous times in the Bible, readers are encouraged to read the Bible for themselves in order to understand God's messages to them (e.g. Deut 30:11-14; Luke 1:3-4; Acts 17:11; Rev 1:3). Consequently, the meaning of Scripture is clear and

straightforward and to be taken in its plain, literal sense, unless a clear and obvious figure is intended. Naturally, Adventists recognize that the Bible has a variety of literary genres and structures each requiring a different literary hermeneutical approach. Nevertheless, we believe the intended meaning of the message is clear and contains an objective truth intention, rather than a subjective multiplicity of meanings.

While scholars, Christians and non-Christians, will readily expound on hermeneutical principles and claim that the intended meaning of Scripture can be ascertained by the rigorous applications of these principles, the apostle Paul offered another perspective. Since the original meaning of Scripture and its present application involves the thoughts of God, spiritual things are spiritually discerned. Without the illumination of the Holy Spirit, and without approaching the text of Scripture in a spirit of prayer, humility and confession, the true meaning of Scripture may never be found. "For what man knows the things of a man except the spirit of the man which is in him? Even so no one knows the things of God except the Spirit of God. ... But the natural man does not receive the things of the Spirit of God, for they are foolishness to him; nor can he know them, because they are spiritually discerned" (1 Cor 2: 11, 14). There is no "neutral" meaning when it comes to Scripture. However good and accurate tools of exegesis and principles of hermeneutics may be, the Bible cannot be studied like any other book. At every stage of the process, spiritual discernment is necessary. God's Word must be approached with reverence.

Philosophical Presuppositions

An important element in understanding Adventist hermeneutics is its philosophical presuppositions. In his 1998 Encyclical *Fides et Ratio*, Pope John Paul II argued that Christian philosophical presuppositions for a proper understanding of Scripture need to be within the Aristotelian and neo-Platonic philosophical presuppositions we have inherited from early Church Fathers, that such a basic philosophical framework is essential to maintain the faith inherited from the Apostles through centuries of Christian history and theological formulations. In many ways, John Paul II described the philosophical assumptions of much of Christianity when he argued this point, for most of Protestant theological formulations are also framed to a large extent within these philosophical presuppositions.

In contrast, Adventist theology rejects most of these philosophical presuppositions. Adventism from its beginning did not conceive its theological system within the neo-Platonic presuppositions of the Augustinian and Reformed systems of thought in which an immovable and impassible God exists only in timelessness, or that ultimate reality (i.e. heaven and the inheritance of the saved) is timeless or that the descriptions of redeemed life as found in Scripture are metaphors of this ultimate reality. Adventist theology attempts to make as strong a case as possible in saying that biblical writers did not have this worldview when they wrote Scripture and thus Aristotelian and neo-Platonic philosophical assumptions cannot be part of a faithful hermeneutical approach to Scripture. A couple theological examples should help explain what I mean.

Adventist soteriology is basically Wesleyan Arminian combined with what many Christians believe is a peculiar doctrine of the heavenly sanctuary where Christ is currently active in the forgiveness of sins and judgment. For Augustinian and Reformed theologies, all events of the plan of redemption are the results of decrees God has proclaimed through all of eternity, nothing new as such can be done by God, and the entire plan of redemption is predetermined in God's eternal foreknowledge. However, likely unintentionally at first, Adventism adopted a different system of thought in which God actually interacts with humanity within time and space in various events of salvation history. In this system, God's foreknowledge of future events is only descriptive of human responses and not prescriptive. This important difference in philosophical and theological presuppositions allowed Adventist writers to see all the events of the plan of redemption, as described in Scripture, as truly happening within time and as a linear process in which God is genuinely engaged rather than only a series of preordained punctiliar events shaped in the mind of God in eternity past. Since the Epistle to the Hebrews states that we have a High Priest who is interceding in heaven for His people on earth (Heb 7:23-28; 9:24-25), Adventists believe this is really happening; it is not a metaphor of salvation which is a necessary conclusion if neo-Platonic timelessness is accepted as a basic philosophical presupposition when interpreting Scripture. The same goes for the description of heavenly scenes of worship in the book of Revelation (chapters 4-5). When Christians say heaven is real, what do we really mean by this? When pushed to its logical conclusion this expression, if understood within a neo-Platonic frame of reference, is only a metaphor, along with descriptions of worship and music in heaven.

The Adventist doctrine of the non-immortality of the soul is also framed within a rejection of neo-Platonic reality. We believe human life and existence cannot be without a physical body; that thought processes as well as emotions require a physical body. When the physical body dies, human existence enters a state of "sleep" until the day of the resurrection when human existence is reestablished or recreated. At death the breath of life God gives at birth returns to God until the resurrection. This breath of life, however, is not a self-existent ontological entity that represents the ultimate reality of human existence. Human beings don't have a self-existent timeless soul that survives or yearns for a better life without a physical body, as if God's creation of the body had been a mistake, an afterthought, or a temporary necessity to experience salvation. In its own way Adventist theology is non-conformist at a very basic level of philosophical thought.

The Role and Ministry of Ellen G White

Any discussion of Seventh-day Adventist hermeneutics, of necessity, must engage the role and ministry of Ellen G White.

Adventists believe that God bestows upon all members of the church in every age spiritual gifts that are to be employed in ministry for the common good of the church and of humanity. These gifts are apportioned by the Holy Spirit to each believer and provide abilities and ministries needed by the church to fulfill its divinely ordained mission and functions. Adventists believe these gifts are to function for the perfecting of the saints and for the edification of the body of Christ until His return (Eph 4:8, 11-13). Just as they were needed in the early church to confirm the work of the apostles and to provide guidance to the young congregations, these gifts are also needed today. While Adventists recognize the unique position of the Bible as the sole criterion by which all claims to spiritual gifts must be evaluated, the Bible itself points to a continuing manifestation of spiritual gifts in the Christian Church until the return of Christ and particularly at the end of time. On the basis of Revelation 12:17 and 19:10, Adventists hold that the gift of prophecy is an identifying mark of the people of God in the last days. This gift they believe was manifested in the life and ministry of Ellen G White.

Adventists have argued that while Ellen White's ministry and writings are valued as a genuine gift of the Spirit, her authority is considered secondary to the Bible. Adventists see a similarity between the ministry of non-canonical prophets and that of Ellen White. The Bible describes the work of many prophets who did not write any portion of Scripture. Enoch, Gad, Nathan, Huldah, and even John the Baptist are such non-canonical prophets. Although genuine prophets and empowered by the Holy Spirit to minister to Israel during a particular period of time, these prophets did not write any section of the Bible. Yet their ministry is considered genuine, valid, and authoritative. Adventists perceive the role and ministry of Ellen White in a similar way. Her ministry is believed to be a spiritual gift to the church in the last days to provide guidance to Adventists in the fulfillment of their mission and to help prepare God's people for the second advent of Christ. But her writings are viewed as secondary to Scripture.

During her lifetime Ellen White provided prophetic guidance to the denomination through her influence, sermons, and numerous books and periodical articles. It is estimated that she wrote over 100,000 pages of manuscripts during her 70 years of ministry and addressed a wide variety of subjects and interests. She wrote on many biblical themes, church organization and pastoral ministry, lifestyle issues, education, health and temperance, home life, and mission.

Ellen White's numerous books fall into two major categories.

First, she wrote extensively on biblical themes and stories. Her best known books are part of a series called the "Conflict of the Ages" series which includes five books on the story of the conflict between good and evil, from the fall of Lucifer to the new earth.[3] She also authored *Steps to Christ* (1892) on themes related to the doctrine of salvation, *Thoughts from the Mount of Blessing* (1896) on the Sermon on the Mount, and *Christ's Object Lessons* (1900) on the parables of Jesus.

Much of her writings also dealt with various aspects of church ministry and Christian life. Often the contents of her letters, manuscripts, sermons, and periodical articles were reshaped to form books on particular subjects. Such is the nine-volume series of *Testimonies for the Church* published between 1855 and 1909, and books on *Education* (1903), *Ministry of Healing* (1905), and *Gospel Workers* (1915). In her last will and testament she made provision for her estate to continue the publication of her books and also print compilations of her writings as church leaders would see fit. Thus through the years many other books have been published from her published and unpublished letters and manuscripts files. All of Ellen White's published writings are available on CD-ROM and on the Ellen G White Estate website.[4] Her unpublished letters and manuscripts are available for consultation at many research centers in the United States and overseas and are currently in the process of being published by section. Ellen White is the most prolific American woman author in the history of the United States thus far. She is also the most translated author with her book *Steps to Christ* translated into more than 120 languages.

One of the earliest and clearest statements regarding what Ellen White believed to be her relationship to the Bible is the following in 1851, "I recommend to you, dear reader, the word of God as the rule of your faith and practise [sic]. By that word we are to be judged. God has, in that word, promised to give visions [i.e. a reference to her own ministry] in the 'LAST DAYS'; not for a new rule of faith, but for the comfort of His people, and to correct those who err from Bible truth."[5]

Ellen White believed in the supremacy and ultimate authority of the Word of God. The following comment was written in 1888 when many Adventist ministers were debating the concept of righteousness by faith. What I find enlightening in this statement is her understanding of the issues related to critical scholarship and her own strong faith in the Word of God.

"I take the Bible just as it is, as the Inspired Word. I believe its utterances in an entire Bible. Men arise who think they find something to criticize in God's Word. They lay it bare before others as evidence of superior wisdom. These men are, many of them, smart men, learned men, they have eloquence and talent, the whole lifework [of whom] is to unsettle minds in regard to the inspiration of the Scriptures. They influence many to see as they do. And the same work is passed on from one to another, just as Satan designed it should be, until we may see the full meaning of the words of Christ, 'When the Son of man cometh, shall he find faith on the earth?' (Luke 18:8)....

"Brethren, cling to your Bible, as it reads, and stop your criticisms in regard to its validity, and obey the Word, and not one of you will be lost. The ingenuity of men has been exercised for ages to measure the Word of God by their finite minds and limited comprehension. If the Lord, the Author of the living oracles, would throw back the curtain and reveal His wisdom and His glory before them, they would shrink into nothingness and exclaim as did Isaiah, 'I am a man of unclean lips, and I dwell in the midst of people of unclean lips' (Isaiah 6:5)....

"Men of humble acquirements, possessing but limited capabilities and opportunities to become conversant in the Scriptures, find in the living oracles comfort, guidance, counsel, and the plan of salvation as clear as a sunbeam. No one need be lost for want of knowledge, unless he is willfully blind. We thank God that the Bible is prepared for the poor man as well as for the learned man. It is fitted for all ages and all classes."[6]

Perhaps one of the subjects concerning Ellen White's ministry that brings up the most inquiries has been in regard to her involvement and influence in the development of Seventh-day Adventist doctrines. Many believe that her visions were the origin of the distinctive doctrines of Adventism. However, a brief look at the historical development of the distinctive doctrines of Adventism reveals a different picture. Adventist pioneers accepted a set of distinctive doctrines based on their study of the Bible, and Ellen White's influence in these early years was often limited to confirmation and clarification of these doctrines. Never was she the initiator of these doctrinal beliefs.

Seventh-day Adventists certainly value the writings of Ellen White and give them a measure of doctrinal and theological authority, albeit secondary to Scripture. But I wonder to what extent the way Adventists use the writings of Ellen White is different from what other evangelical denominations do with the writings of their founders. I've been told that Lutheran pastors are required to affirm their assent to the Book of Concord before they are ordained. Reformed Christians hold in high esteem the writings of John Calvin and the canons of the Synod of Dort. Methodists value the writings of John Wesley and an Arminian theological framework. The Westminster Confession of Faith is an authoritative document for Presbyterians. For Mennonites, the Schletheim Articles hold a special place. Although these Christian denominations do not categorize these writings as inspired, in contrast to what Adventists do with the writings of Ellen White, nonetheless these documents hold authoritative value in these denominations and serve as a compass for doctrinal orthodoxy and theological education. Yet all these denominations also claim to have Scripture as their sole authority in matters of faith. Perhaps this is one way to see how Adventists perceive the influence of Ellen White in their church.

In conclusion, Adventists understand the Bible to be the revealed Word of God to humanity and seek to understand it faithfully by giving it the ultimate authority: only the Scripture is the standard of faith and experience; it can be read and understood by all people and it is sufficient for salvation. Although we realize we cannot read Scripture without some interaction with Christian history and tradition, Adventist hermeneutics has strong affinities with the hermeneutics adopted by churches of the Radical Reformation and with those of the Restorationist and Primitivist Christian movements in the United States in the 19th century. The writings of Ellen White certainly hold a measure of doctrinal guidance and authority, but they are perceived as a secondary authority, under that of Scripture and are used as a theological compass rather than an ultimate magisterium.

ENDNOTES

[1] Much of the first half of this paper is adapted or summarized from Richard M Davidson, "Biblical Interpretation," in *Handbook of Seventh-day Adventist Theology*, Raoul Dederen, Editor, (Hagerstown, Maryland: Review and Herald Publishing Association, 2000), 58-104. Other recent publications on Adventist biblical hermeneutics are George W Reid, Editor, *Understanding Scripture: An Adventist Approach*, Biblical Research Institute Studies, vol 1, (Silver Spring, Maryland: Biblical Research Institute, 2006); and Gerhard Pfandl, Editor, *Interpreting Scripture: Bible Questions and Answers*, Biblical Research Institute Studies, vol 2, (Silver Spring, Maryland: Biblical Research Institute, 2010).

[2] See Frank M Hasel, "Presuppositions in the Interpretation of Scripture," *Understanding Scripture*, 29-35.

[3] The "Conflict of the Ages" series includes the books *Patriarchs and Prophets* (1890) which covers the fall of Lucifer to the reign of king David; *Prophets and Kings* (1916) from the reign of Solomon to the end of the Old Testament; *The Desire of Ages* (1898) on the life and ministry of Christ; *The Acts of the Apostles* (1911) on the early church; and *The Great Controversy* (1911) from the fall of Jerusalem to the new earth.

[4] The official Seventh-day Adventist website about Ellen White and her writings is found at www.whiteestate.org.

[5] *The Christian Experience and Views of Ellen G White* (1851), 64; reprinted in *Early Writings* (Hagerstown, Maryland: Review and Herald Publishing Association, 1945), 78.

[6] Manuscript 16, 1888 published in *Selected Messages* (Hagerstown, Maryland: Review and Herald Publishing Association, 1958), vol 1, 17-18.

SUMMARY
STATEMENT

Living the Christian Life in Today's World: Adventists and Mennonites in Conversation, 2011-2012

I n 2011 and 2012, representatives of the General Conference of Seventh-day Adventists and of the Mennonite World Conference met together for official conversations. In many respects the meetings proved to be a journey of mutual discovery.

Background

Mennonites and Adventists have had frequent contacts during the past forty years, particularly through their participation in the annual meetings of the secretaries of Christian World Communions. These periodic encounters, along with other contacts, gradually led to the conviction on both sides that an official conversation might be both instructive and valuable.

Adventists and Mennonites have distinct identities that are critically important to them. From the outset of discussions leading to the conversation, it was understood that organic union was not the objective. Rather, the dialogue would provide an opportunity for learning about each other's history, beliefs and values, clarifying misunderstandings, and removing stereotypes. Out of the discussion, therefore, might emerge areas where Mennonites and Adventists can join forces in selected areas of mutual concern.

The two communions, viewed superficially, might appear to have little in common.

Mennonites

The history of Mennonites stretches back 500 years, that of the Adventists' only about 160 years. Mennonites arose out of the religious ferment of the 16th century, Adventists out of the Second Great Awakening in the United States in the 1830s and 1840s.

Consideration of the Reformation of the 16th century customarily focuses on Protestants and Roman Catholics. However, there was a third movement that, while accepting the Protestant emphasis on salvation by grace through faith, had unique teachings. This movement, the Anabaptists, understood the church to be made up of disciples of Jesus who were baptized upon their declaration of wanting to follow Jesus by becoming part of this committed body of Christ. In effect, this challenged infant baptism. The term *Ana*baptist is a reference to this act of rebaptism (*ana*, in Greek, means again). Given that church and state were considered as one unit, making membership in the church an option based on personal decision was thus perceived as threatening the authority and unity of the state. The Anabaptists insisted that obedience to Christ take precedence in all circumstances of Christian life, including when it meant disobeying the demands of the state. Nonviolence, based on the example of Jesus, also became an important characteristic of this movement.

This movement in the Reformation is frequently called "The Radical Reformation." The Anabaptists were persecuted by both Catholics and Protestants. Since "Anabaptist" was from the beginning a designation of opprobrium, many adopted the term

"Mennonite" after the name of Menno Simons, a Dutch leader and writer, who stressed a renewed vision for the church, including the call for followers of Jesus to reject violence and seek peace.

Over the course of the centuries, Mennonites, along with other branches of the Anabaptists, suffered ongoing persecution, including imprisonment and death, because of their beliefs and practices. They frequently found it necessary to uproot and move on, seeking a more tolerant environment. Many eventually migrated to Canada and the United States where they established communities.

In 1925 European Mennonite churches came together to form the Mennonite World Conference (MWC). Today Mennonites are frequently known as a "peace church." They are active in building congregations as disciples of Jesus—the Prince of Peace, living and promoting reconciliation, mediation, justice and peace in all aspects of life. As a consequence of active missionary and evangelistic engagement over the last century, MWC is presently made up of 101 national churches, in 53 countries, with 1.3 million members.

Seventh-day Adventists

The first half of the 19th century witnessed a widespread expectation that Jesus Christ was about to return in person. While the anticipation was global in nature, it reached prominence in the United States under the preaching of Baptist layman, William Miller. From studies of Bible prophecies, especially those in the Book of Daniel, Miller predicted that Jesus would come again around 1843-1844.

Miller's proclamation had huge impact, ranging from enthusiasm to scorn. Eventually the Millerites settled on October 22, 1844 as the date of Jesus' return. When Jesus did not come on that date, they were subjected to ridicule and mocking.

Probably 50,000–100,000 people expected Jesus to come on October 22, 1844. With the failure of their hopes, the Millerites fell into disarray. The movement splintered; many people abandoned belief in Jesus' coming.

Out of this unpromising milieu arose the Seventh-day Adventist Church. A small group of Millerites, perhaps about one hundred people, restudied the prophecies. They concluded that, while they had been wrong in believing that Jesus would come in 1844, they should continue to expect His imminent return without setting a date for the event. To this belief the Adventists also concluded from Bible study that the seventh-day Sabbath should be observed as a day of rest and worship.

In 1860, this small group adopted the name "Seventh-day Adventist." Three years later it formally organized; its members numbered about 3,000. From these small beginnings, the church has grown to a membership of about twenty million in more than two hundred countries. Driven by a strong missionary impulse, it understands its mission to tell the world about "the blessed hope"—the soon return of Jesus.

Participants

The same participants were involved in both conversations. From the MWC they were:

Robert Suderman (Canada), Valerie G Rempel (United States), Henk Stenvers (The Netherlands), Patricia Urueña Barbosa (Colombia), Danisa Ndlovu (Zimbabwe), and Thomas R Yoder Neufeld (Canada).

From the Adventists they were: Bert B. Beach (US/Switzerland), Gary Councell (US), Denis Fortin (US/Canada), John Graz (US/Switzerland), William Johnsson (US/Australia), Peter Landless (US/South Africa), and Teresa Reeve (US/Canada).

Structure of the Conversation

The first conversation was held June 28-July 1, 2011, at the Seventh-day Adventist world headquarters in Silver Spring, Maryland, USA; the second, May 27-31, 2012, at the Study and Conference Center Bienenberg, near Basel, Switzerland.

Each day's discussion began and ended with worship, the worship leader alternating between the two communions. The theme, "Living the Christian Life in Today's World," focused both conversations, which were built on papers prepared on selected topics by representatives from each side. These papers, while theological in nature, endeavored to show the practical outworking in the life of the community.

During the first round of conversation, each group presented an overview of their communion's history. Papers followed on the topics of peace; non-violence and military service; discipleship and non-conformity; health, healing and ecology; and the nature and mission of the church.

In the second dialogue, major papers were presented from each side on eschatology, non-conformity, and hermeneutics. In addition, shorter discussions took up questions raised by each communion prior to the meeting in Bienenberg. Mennonites responded to issues of pacifism, Sabbath, salvation and obedience, personal lifestyle, hermeneutics, and eschatology. Adventists addressed questions of military service, Sabbath, contextualization, justice and discipleship, the role of women in ministry, church discipline, Ellen White, and eschatology.

During the second conversation, participants took time out to visit Swiss sites of significance to each group. They visited the grave of John Nevins Andrews, the Adventist Church's first missionary, and the first Adventist church constructed outside America—a simple wooden structure dedicated by Ellen White. From there they traveled to a Mennonite farming community on the plateau high above the town of Tramelan, Switzerland (Mennonites were initially not permitted to settle in the valley). Participants heard a lecture on the history of the community, visited its archives, and were welcomed to a fellowship meal.

Features in Common

Participants in the conversation quickly realized that they have much in common. They share a desire to recover the authenticity and passion of the New Testament church, a similar understanding of Christian history, and a strong commitment to be followers of Jesus in their personal lives and in their corporate witness to the world. Each communion brought to the conversation a deep experience of what it means to live the Christian faith, often as a minority voice in the world, and stressed the importance of discipleship and the practical living out of the Christian life. Together they understand that Christians live "in the world" but are not "of the world."

Areas of different understandings were also discussed in order to understand each other better. These areas include: the day on which the Sabbath is celebrated, eschatology, the status given to the writings of Ellen G. White by the Adventist church, the ministry of Jesus in the heavenly sanctuary, and the state of the dead.

Areas of resonance in belief and practice are:

1. The centrality of Jesus.

2. Relation to the state: As Christians we seek to live as responsible citizens, but we place obedience to God above obedience to the state.

3. Peace and non-violence: Both communions understand Jesus' teachings and example to reject the use of violence, even in military situations, realizing that the consequences may mean suffering and death, as they also did for our Lord. It was acknowledged, however, that this emphasis is not uniformly practiced.

4. Ordinances: Both communions teach and practice baptism of believers, not infants; they have a non-sacramental view of the Lord's Supper, and have a history of the practice of foot washing as an expression of humility and service to each other.

5. Ministry to humanity: Mennonites and Adventists are strongly committed to helping humanity. Mennonites stress peace and justice initiatives, community development and relief in disasters, while Adventists focus on health and healing through a large network of hospitals and clinics, as well as public health; they also operate agencies for relief and development, and advocate for religious freedom throughout the world.

Learning from One Another

Mennonites listed the following areas where the conversation with Adventists challenges them to growth and development:

1. A more robust commitment to observing the intentions of Sabbath that is part of Anabaptist/Mennonite heritage of celebrating Sunday as a day of rest and worship.

2. More attention to the importance of health and physical healing as integral parts of discipleship and God's intentions for his people.

3. Emphasizing a stronger sense of hope, confidence, and anticipation in the assured coming of God's reign in the world.

4. Exploring more deeply issues of religious freedom and Christian commitment to advocating for freedom of religious thought and practice where these are not present.

5. Focus more attention on theological formation and leadership development for the needs of the communion.

6. Learning together how a diverse global church can be nourished and strengthened at local, national, and international levels.

For Adventists the corresponding list for growth and development resulting from the conversation with Mennonites was:

1. Addressing the dilution of the church's historic stand concerning non-combatancy as an alternative to military service.

2. Strengthening theological education to ensure vibrancy of the church's ministry and service.

3. Keeping Christ central in witness, theology, and praxis.

4. Defending Christians and other religious minorities against persecution and discrimination.

5. More intentionally tying hermeneutics to practical Christian living.

Recommendations

Participants in the conversation offer the following recommendations to their respective authorizing bodies:

1. Continue contacts between our two communions.

2. Each authorizing body consider how to disseminate papers presented in the conversation.

3. Explore possibilities of cooperating together in joint endeavors such as the promotion of religious liberty and the promotion of non-violent approaches to social issues.

4. Explore ways to work together in areas of health and social justice.

5. Explore ways to cooperate in Seminary education.

Concluding Remarks

These encounters between brothers and sisters of two global Christian communions were formally designated as "conversations." In fact, they became much more than that. The conversations have been remarkable and palpable evidence of the truth of the Apostle Peter's teaching, when he says that each has received gifts (*xarisma*) flowing out of the "manifold" (*poikilos*) grace (*xaritos*) or graciousness of God (I Peter 4:10). Truly, the gifts and the graciousness of God are manifold: varied and diverse. And yet they flow from the same God and for the same intentions of God. More than conversations, these encounters have reminded us that God is active in human history, and that God's patience will not be exhausted by human frailty and failures. The conversations encourage us because of the unity we have in foundational understandings even while we identify the diversity in other understandings. These conversations have been testimony to the critical role of historical context in shaping values, beliefs, and ethics, but in each case they have been founded on the sincere desire to affirm the authority of scripture and the centrality of Jesus Christ for faith and practice. They have been an opportunity to acknowledge the need for humility as we have vulnerably and transparently tested each other in the ways we perceive ourselves and in ways that we may be perceived by others.

While organizational and structural unity was not the goal of these conversations, we have achieved a deeper sense of the unity of the Body of Christ, woven together with "sinews" of peace (Eph 4:3, 16). This unity is not something we are called to create: God has already done that for us. But it is something we are called to "maintain," to guard, and to preserve (Eph 4:3), so that we may truly say with the Apostle:

"There is one body and one Spirit, just as you were called to the one hope of your calling, one Lord, one faith, one baptism, one God and Father of all, who is above all and through all and in all" (Eph 4:4-6).

May it be so; to God be the glory.

APPENDICES

Frequently Asked Questions:

Mennonite Questions/ Adventist Answers

Questions about Ellen White

Question 1: Ellen White figures prominently for the Seventh-day Adventists. Do you have theologians who play a role similar to the role J H Yoder plays at present, for example, or is your theology beholden in some ways to "exegeting" White's theology? This is related to the authority questions, but also to ecclesiology, and pneumatology. In short, how much listening happens to "ordinary" folks in the ongoing development of SDA understandings and doctrines?

Answer 1: Adventists do not have, and never have had, a single person or persons who play a role similar to that of J H Yoder in their theological development. The Adventist way from the beginning has been a cooperative process that involves many minds. We believe strongly that "in the multitude of counselors there is safety" (Prov 11:14), and that the Holy Spirit guides through various individuals.

Any changes to the Fundamental Beliefs can only be made at a meeting of the General Conference Session. This is a large gathering of more than 2,000 delegates from all over the world who meet once every five years. But prior to a suggested change coming before a GC Session, it is circulated to members worldwide through the Church's media network, with input invited from all Adventists.

The Biblical Research Institute oversees theological matters for the Church. It is a group of six or seven scholars who respond to doctrinal questions, arrange Bible Conferences for pastors, and so on.[1] The Biblical Research Institute Committee, composed of about 50 scholars from all parts of the world church, convenes annually.

Ellen White's voluminous writings in the main provide counsel for daily living. They are not the basis of Adventist theology—only the Bible is.

Question 2: Are the hermeneutics of Ellen White updated with the passage of time, with advances in biblical sciences in the field of exegesis and hermeneutics, and the development of theology and of Adventist thought?

Answer 2: A brief answer to this question could simply state that there has in the last century been little development or change. While SDA scholarship has given serious attention to biblical hermeneutics, noticeably less attention has been directly paid to "Spirit of Prophecy" hermeneutics. One issue that has in recent years been discussed in SDA ranks is Ellen White's use of sources in some of her writings. One can endeavor to give several reasons why there is this lack of substantial attention to hermeneutics:

- Seventh-day Adventists hold the biblical Word of God in such high esteem that thinking about Ellen White and her writings in *hermeneutical* terms might seem to diminish the unique role of the biblical Canon.
- There is a long history of biblical hermeneutics. With the many authors, the complex historical developments, cultural and language changes, and theological trends, the understanding and interpretation of biblical literature has become a necessary science, though we would add under the necessary guidance of the Holy Spirit. In contrast, Ellen White was a single writer who lived comparatively recently and it is

obviously much easier to read and understand her in a more direct and simple way.

- For many decades, Ellen White was active through both voice and pen (until about World War I, the time of her death). She was able to provide, so to speak, her own explanation—hermeneutic, if you please—regarding her role as a messenger and the meaning of what she wrote. Naturally, with the passing of time, it becomes quite normal to ask whether the hermeneutical question does not increasingly deserve more thoughtful and even gradually more urgent attention.

- In any hermeneutical discussion regarding Ellen White, her role must obviously be looked at. She always made unmistakably clear that her role as a prophetic messenger was essentially to provide comfort, guidance, instruction, and even correction. She emphasized that the Bible is the only standard by which any teaching and prophetic experience must be tested. She taught that her writings need to be tested by the biblical standard, and only the Bible can serve as the final authority of doctrine and faith. This has to be part of the basis of any SDA hermeneutic of her writings.

- Finally, in view of the brotherly atmosphere of this meeting, I dare to state that I see two future hermeneutical issues that we as Adventists must face: a) Since SDAs believe that the quality of inspiration does not differ, how do we interpret and deal with extra-biblical inspiration (the promised biblical prophetic gift) that is inspired, but not canonical? b) In the future, if time lasts, there must come the time (probably a difficult issue, in practice perhaps more than in theory) when our hermeneutical studies will need to come to grips with the question of what parts of Ellen White's voluminous writings are inspired for the church, indeed a "lesser light" pointing to the "greater light" (Holy Scriptures)? And then what parts of her writings are, perhaps, simply a mother or godly woman writing and giving spiritual options or useful advice to her children, friends, and co-workers?

About Eschatology and Related Understandings

Question 3: What role does apocalyptic millenarian eschatology play in SDA ethics (e.g., nonviolence; nonparticipation in baring arms, economy/simplicity of living)? How do Adventists make themselves at home in our world in terms of simple living and long-term planning when the expectation of the coming of Jesus is that it will be "soon?"

Answer 3: The expectation and hope of the soon return of Jesus plays a major role in SDA ethics. Our Lord Himself tied together eschatology and ethics in a series of parables, especially those that focus on His coming. In particular, the apocalyptic discourse of Matthew 24 is followed by:

- The parable of the faithful and the evil servants (Matt 24:45-51). The faithful servant continues at his post of duty, fulfilling his appointed tasks and continually expecting the master's return. His life and work reflect his hope. But the evil servant says in his heart, "My master is delaying his coming," and falls into bad behaviors.

- The parable of the wise and foolish virgins (Matt 25:1-13). The wise virgins prepared for a waiting time, the foolish ones did not. Some were ready to meet the bridegroom, others were not. If the first parable above emphasizes duty, this one focuses on individual preparation for the Second Coming.

- The parable of the talents (Matt 25:14-30). Here our Lord calls us to use every opportunity and develop every gift in His service. Life is serious. What we are and have are to be employed for the Master's honor and glory. In this endeavor no one is excluded; no one can say he or she has not been given at least one talent.

- The parable of the sheep and goats (Matt 25:31-46). Here we have a striking judgment scene in which Christ calls the nations to account. The bottom line is not theology—what we know—but what we have done. Jesus identifies with the hungry, the thirsty, the stranger, the naked, the sick and the prisoner. What we do on behalf of those on the margins of society we do to our Lord. But the actions of the "sheep" do not constitute righteousness by works: they are spontaneous unremembered acts of kindness and love, so they are surprised to receive the King's commendation.

Question 4: It is clear that a theology of hope is foundational to the SDA movement. What happens to a church (theologically and even organizationally) as they approach their 150th anniversary as a denomination (2013) and the bicentennial of the great disappointment (2044) if hope continues to be postponed?

Answer 4: My larger paper takes up the tension between the "already" and the "not yet." To me it is an intellectual tension, not a spiritual one. Every day that goes by puts us that much closer to the Second Coming, which will come to pass in God's good time. While we wait, there is a world to be warned and to serve as we seek to carry on Jesus' loving ministry of healing, teaching, and preaching.

About Death as Sleep

Question 5: Seventh-day Adventists have a notion of "sleep"—to refer to the state after death—that seems to be different than common Protestant and Catholic beliefs and seems much closer to the Jewish thinking of New Testament writers than to what we hear at most Mennonite funerals. Another twist on this question: How does the issue of resurrection figure in their view of death, or in their view of the present life?

Answer 5: I have commented on this in my larger paper. The Adventist view, which developed in the earliest days of the movement, is now widely held by biblical scholars, even if the majority of Christians may not agree with it.

The Adventist understanding is part of a package that rejects the idea of an eternally burning hell—a concept that we find not only unbiblical, but one that does not comport with a loving God.

Resurrection plays a huge part in our thinking. As Jesus died and rose again, so will those who rest in Him. Resurrection and the Second Coming occur together (see 1 Thess 4:13-18), making Jesus' return something even more to be longed for. The Second Coming will be the day of reunion with departed loved ones.

About Military Service

Question 6: The Adventist Church expects the followers of Christ who are His disciples, who acquire the character of Christ, to show compassion and not commit violence. Can you help us understand the involvement of Adventists in military service, their participation in war, and the development of programs for Adventist military, knowing the environmental destruction, suffering, and death that wars cause?

"Early Adventism did not allow members to join the military, and two members were disfellowshipped for joining northern forces in the U.S. Civil War." Over time, however, this noncombatant stance has softened and is no longer a requirement of being a member in good standing. The Adventist material here reflects these early commitments:

Ellen White, in the 1860s, called for Seventh-day Adventists to not enter the Civil War even though she and most others supported the cause of the North. She also gave advice to those who would refuse military service despite the state's call, even in the threat of capital punishment. "I was shown that God's people, who are His peculiar treasure, cannot engage in this perplexing war, for it is opposed to every principle of their faith. In the army they cannot obey the truth and at the same time obey the requirements of their officers. There would be a continual violation of conscience. Worldly men are governed by worldly principles . . . . But God's people cannot be governed by these motives."[2]

Ellen White in her writings also highlights the formation of the character of Christ in the life of the believer and opposes the use of force.

"When He gives you the mind of Christ, your will becomes as His will, and your character is transformed to be like Christ's character."

"In the heart renewed by divine grace, love is the principle of action. It modifies the character, governs the impulses, controls the passions, subdues enmity, and ennobles the affections."[3]

"The kingdom of Christ does not and cannot bear any resemblance to the kingdoms of the world. In the kingdom of Christ there is no instrument of coercion. In it force has no place. The gospel of Him who gave His life for the life of the world is a gospel of peace. It is the Saviour's grace, His love, His tender compassion, that breaks every barrier down."[4]

"Before the final visitation of God's judgments upon the earth there will be among the people of the Lord such a revival of primitive godliness as has not been witnessed since apostolic times."[5]

Answer 6: The Adventist response to military service varies greatly from believer to believer and from one part of the world to another. Especially in the United States, many Adventists do not follow the injunction of James White and other pioneers of the movement to avoid serving in the military. The quoted material in the question represents our official stance.

This varied response is probably puzzling to those from a Mennonite background for whom this matter has played such a vital role in their tradition. The following dimensions of the Adventist response perhaps will shed some light.

- Avoidance of military service, while important, has never been one of the "pillars" of Adventist teaching. It has never been included among the Fundamental Beliefs of the church. Adventists very early decided that, while officially advocating avoidance of military service, this is an area to be left to the individual's conscience.

- Over the course of Adventist history large numbers of Adventists, perhaps the majority of those conscripted, have refused to bear arms. Some have been imprisoned, some have given their lives.

- The biggest schism (though comparatively not large) that the church has suffered arose out of this question. During World War I some Adventist leaders in Germany, caught up in patriotic fervor, advocated compliance with the state in military service. The argument that ensued eventually resulted in the formation of the Reformed Seventh-day Adventist Church which continues to this day. In general, Adventists in Europe still avoid military service and are critical of the course followed by many American Adventists.

- Especially in the United States, the church promoted a stance of "conscientious cooperation"—military service without the bearing of arms. The Church developed a Medical Cadet Corps to prepare young men to serve in medical capacities. One Adventist non-combatant, Desmond Doss, was awarded the Congressional Medal of Honor for heroic conduct on the field of battle (he saved the lives of more than 50 wounded comrades).

- With the ending of the draft in the United States, the issue of military service receded into the background. The Medical Cadet Corps was discontinued. At the same time, more and more Adventists began to enlist—perhaps viewing the military as a path to better themselves. Along with this trend there developed interest in chaplaincy ministry: Adventists began to see the military as a field of service where they could help needy men and women in difficult, sometimes desperate, situations. Adventist chaplains became widely respected and sought after by the military; some, like Vice-Admiral Barry Black, rose to positions of high rank.

I write from personal experience. As a young man growing up in Australia I stood in court before a magistrate to argue that I should not be required to carry arms. In "boot camp" I was one among only a few who did not have a rifle. I spent most of the time working in the military hospital or the officers' mess.

These conversations are especially helpful to Adventists in this area. They remind us of our past and call into question some of the developments and trends among us.

About the Role of Women

Question 7: According to the Scriptures, men and women were created in the image and likeness of God. This means that the two reflect the image of God and therefore men and women are equal before God. According also to the Scripture, gifts are handed out by the Holy Spirit without distinction of gender. However, there are some biblical texts where women are asked to be silent which reflect the patriarchal context in which these biblical texts were written.

We also have considerable evidence in the Gospels and the Pauline letters of the important role of women in the movement of Jesus in the early Church. Jesus broke the culture mores of His era and included women in His ministry. In the Pauline letters the Apostle Paul recognizes some of his sisters as collaborators and apostles jointly with him. In the Seventh-day Adventist Church, Ellen White, as a woman and as a prophet, surpassed the female role in her patriarchal culture and was, and is, a genuine and prominent religious figure.

How do we understand that women are not ordained as shepherdesses, although in practice they minister as shepherdesses in Adventist churches? How do we understand gender relations in the Church in the context of the teachings of the Scriptures that men and women were created equal before God, that Jesus included women in His ministry on earth, and that the role of women was very important in the early Church?

Answer 7: Generally, Adventists will agree that both man and woman were created in the image of God and also that they receive the gifts of the Holy Spirit without distinction. They see and appreciate the ministry of women today using these various gifts. They will also accept and applaud the place of women collaborating in the ministries of Jesus and Paul, although the awareness of the kind of participation by some biblical women such as Phoebe and Junia is limited. And they do accept Ellen White as having authority to teach and to lead the church.

Challenges have arisen from several quarters:

- Conservative Cultural Environment. Adventists faced criticism from culture in the early days when not only Ellen White but a number of other women preachers and ministers held accepted leadership roles in the Adventist Church. These women acted on the basis of a recognition of the leading and gifting of the Holy Spirit and were defended by the leaders of the Church. There is no record of women actually being ordained, however. Ellen White herself chose not to accept ordination in North America; however, we do have a copy of an ordination certificate given her by the

Australian church. For a while Adventists persevered in their broad understanding of the role of women in the church; but because it was not a priority to preserve and perpetuate this recognition of women, it slowly began to erode. In the early 20th century many felt that there were really only two sides religiously—the liberal theologians who questioned the basic doctrines of Christianity and the fundamentalists who sought to preserve them. While Adventists did not join the fundamentalist side (as they are good Swiss-type thinkers and adverse to joining either side), they viewed them generally as in the right. The fundamentalist view of the place of women in the early days was also supported by the general culture so that the weight of inertia in the environment pulled toward lessening acceptance of women in leadership. Thus, as the Adventist message traveled around the world, we did not speak with a clear, consistent voice about the ministry of women. Thus people of other world cultures which placed women in a subservient role were not challenged to rethink their culture in this area in light of the fundamental message of Scripture.

- Biblical interpretation. The testimony of Scripture on this is-sue is not as immediately obvious as those of us who believe in the place of women in pastoral ministry and in Women's ordination sometimes begin to think. Because Adventists see all Scripture as inspired, they do not easily ascribe Scriptures with which we are uncomfortable to mistaken cultural notions. We would look at historical-cultural backgrounds, rhetoric, etc., to understand what the biblical author is seeking to accomplish with his words, but for us the inten-tion of the biblical writer is inspired no matter how poorly it fits with modern ideas. (e.g. We would ask the cultural and situational reasons why Paul said women should be silent in church, rather than to suggest that Paul was wrong because he was a child of his culture.) This means we have to work through the puzzling passages carefully. Two challenges in Scriptural interpretation have slowed progress:

a. It is easy and natural for the average person to use proof-texting assuming the immediate transparency of every text rather than carefully considering the intention of a writer and the whole realm of genre and literary, historical, and scriptural context.

b. One way fundamentalists, and with them sometimes Adventists, have spoken of proper biblical interpretation is to say that we must take the Bible literally. Although almost no one applies this maxim *literally* across the board, many of those who are attracted by it have not recognized this.

• Acceptance of a cultural misunderstanding about the nature of ordination. It seems to be an odd anomaly that Adventists could accept the authority and leadership of Ellen White on one hand while still opposing the ordination of women. In addition, many Adventists who do not accept the ordination of women do accept women in pastoral ministry. At the root of this contradiction is the reality that Adventists as a whole have not given close attention to the meaning of ordination. Thus the implications of ordination that were existent in the churches and cultures from which they came are still assumed at a gut level by many members. This is obviously a particular challenge in predominately Catholic countries.

The situation today:

• The church has since the 1970s been "studying" this issue. Early on public debate was discouraged while General Conference commissions studied the issue. Ordination for women local elders was voted in 1972. The question of women's ordination as pastors came to a vote at the GC Session in 1990 and was strongly voted down by the world church, particularly by delegations from Latin American and Africa. In 1995 a request from the North American Division to allow each division to make the decision as to whether to ordain women was also voted down.

• At other levels of the church since 1990, the North American Division (NAD), the Trans-European Division (TED), and others have attempted to do whatever they could outside of ordination to encourage women called to pastoral ministry. The number of women pastors has increased steadily to a current number of over 100 in the NAD. They receive a credential as a commissioned minister which allows them to do almost everything the ordained pastor does (with the exception of organizing or disbanding a church, ordaining local elders, and being president of a conference). Several conferences, instead of holding ordination services for their ministers, hold ordination-commissioning services. Individual male pastors have refused to accept ordination asking to receive commissioning instead. A small number of local churches have held their own ordination services for their women pastors. The Seventh-day Adventist Theological Seminary at Andrews University issued a book, entitled *Women in Ministry*, supporting women in pastoral ministry and ordination. Most women pastors appreciate the work of those advocating for them and hope for soon progress in this area, but place their focus on simply doing with joy the work God has called them to do.

- There are really two key dilemmas that the world church faces in relation to this issue. One is the biblical interpretation issue discussed above. The other is a polity issue that can be summarized as: Justice versus Unity. The difficult question is which is the higher value: 1) Justice to women and the recognition of individual human rights which is a basic expectation of the western world and thus key both to our conformity to Christ and to our witness; and 2) the unity of Christ's body, the church, and the offense of the brother, recognizing that Jesus and the apostles did not immediately advocate directly for this and other aspects of needed social change. Many of us strongly in favor of women's ordination agonize over this dilemma.

- At the 2011 Annual Council of the church's Executive Committee, the North American Division and the Trans-European Division requested approval of a change to policy that would not require an individual to be ordained in order to serve as conference president. This request was denied. Not long afterward, in an unprecedented move, the NAD Executive Committee voted to nevertheless go ahead with this initiative, due to legal issues based on the fact that the divisions do not have a legal constituency. At this moment, close to ten conference/union Executive Committees in the NAD and the TED—who do not have a constituency—have voted to go ahead and ordain women, and others have called special constituency meetings to consider the issue. We find ourselves in a crucial time in the history of the Adventist Church.

ENDNOTES

[1] A Bible Conference for some 300 of the Church's teachers will convene in Jerusalem in June 2012.

[2] Ellen G White, *Testimonies for the Church*, vol 1, 361. Jeff Boyd, "Seventh-day Adventist's Anabaptist Heritage," paper presented in the class: Anabaptist History and Theology, in AMBS, Elkhart, Indiana, December 2011.

[3] Ellen G White, *Steps to Christ*, (Hagerstown, Maryland: Review and Herald Publishing Association, 1892), 59.

[4] Ellen G White, "Christ's Method of Imparting Truth," in *Manuscript Releases*, vol 21, no 1531, (Washington DC: Ellen G White Estate, 1993), 152.

[5] Ellen G White, *The Great Controversy*, 1888 edition, 464.

Frequently Asked Questions:

Adventist Questions/ Mennonite Answers

Questions about Hermeneutics

Question 1: How do Mennonites relate to the role of Christian tradition (Creeds, Church Fathers, etc.) in their interpretation of Scripture?

Answer 1: I have addressed this question to some degree in the longer document. To summarize:

- There is no one answer, given that Mennonites/Anabaptists vary widely in their interpretations of Scripture, which would include their use of historical documents and creeds.
- There is no formal, systematic, or intentional desire to deny the profound truths of the historic creeds. Nor is there formal or systematic alignment with one or the other of the early Church Fathers.
- The Anabaptists assumed that they understood and practiced the traditions of the faith more accurately and faithfully than what the Christendom church was doing.

Their argument was not with the historic creeds; it was with the many ways that they felt the Church has found to defend its non-adherence to the implications of these creeds for the Christian life and the life of the Church.

- There is a suspicion in Anabaptism that the Christendom church misappropriated the historic creeds as tools to ignore the truths of Scripture. The 16 century's broadly-based call to *sola scriptura*, which the Anabaptists shared, was not fundamentally a critique of the creeds. It was an insistence that the creeds could not replace the normative authority of Scripture for the life and practice of obedience and faith.

- The Anabaptists did not develop their own set of creeds to replace the historic traditions of the Church. They called the Church to be faithful to what it said it believed.

Question 2: What role do Mennonite historical documents play in their hermeneutics?

Answer 2: Mennonites have ploughed the Anabaptist historical soil very deeply in their attempts to understand the origins of the Anabaptist faith and its relevance for today. Many of the early writings have been discovered, translated, and published. The library of historical documents is indeed very large. These function today, as they did then, as plumb-lines, as check-points for new understandings that claim to be better. But they are not straight-jackets. Mennonite history has demonstrated the willingness of the church to adjust, change, adapt, ignore, nuance, and shift any portion of historical understandings that stands in the way of contemporary preferences.

Because of the polygenetic origins of the Anabaptist movements, there is always enough material for ongoing debates for the faith and practice of the church.

There have been dozens of official Confessions approved during the five centuries of the movement. A few of these carry a sense of obligated respect for the ongoing articulation of belief, more so in one region or the other.

Perhaps the two most notable or well-known are the *Schleitheim Confession* (1527), coming very early in the Swiss Anabaptist experience and, a bit later, the *Dordrecht Confession* (1632) reflecting the Dutch Mennonite experience.

In addition to the Confessions that have dotted the experience of the Mennonite churches are any number of "statements" that have been passed regarding particular themes, ethical or doctrinal. Mennonites have attempted to speak authoritatively to the current issues of the day, but the "authority" of the speech has proved to be subject to change, as the contexts have changed.

We should, perhaps, mention the *Ausbund* (1534) and the *Martyr's Mirror* (1662) as historical documents that have had remarkable and ongoing impact on the Mennonite identity to this day.

The *Ausbund* was the first Swiss hymnbook, over 800 pages long. It chronicled the life of martyrdom, faithfulness, and suffering by means of song. It is said to be written by Anabaptist prisoners in the castle of Passau, from 1535-1540. This book continues to be used today as the primary (or only) hymnal in some of the Amish traditions.

The *Martyr's Mirror* is similarly remarkable. It too is a very thick volume, documenting the stories of Anabaptist martyrs in the first century and a half of the Anabaptist movement. It too has achieved a certain obligated prominence in the libraries and homes of segments of Mennonites, especially those of Swiss origin.

A more recent effort to revive and articulate the foundational relevance of the Anabaptist vision is *The Anabaptist Vision* by Harold S Bender. He delivered this as a speech to the American Historical Society in New York City on December 28, 1943. Bender, at the time, was the acting President of Goshen College and was leading the Civilian Public Service effort for conscientious objection. The impact of this brief speech has been enormous around the world. In it, Bender identifies three basic tenets of Anabaptism: discipleship to Jesus; the church as a community of believers; and an ethic of love and non-resistance. It is difficult to overstate the shaping influence of this speech on the renewal of Anabaptist identity for the next six decades.

We would be amiss to not mention an even more recent work by a student of Bender, namely John Howard Yoder's *Politics of Jesus*

(1972). This work has had a very significant influence in ecumenical dialogue and in shaping contemporary Mennonite identity. This, along with Yoder's other writings, has had a very significant impact in Mennonite and ecumenical circles around the world.

None of these documents has achieved "creedal" status in the experience of the church. All of them have had extraordinary impact in shaping identity, purpose, and vocation as the church has continued its march through changing times.

Question 3: What role do the works of Menno Simons play in Mennonite theology, hermeneutics, and practice today? Are his writings continually translated into modern languages?

Answer 3: The works of Menno Simons could also be included in the previous answer, as could any number of other Anabaptist writers on the 16th century.

Simons' works are there. They are not considered as authoritative, but they are considered important touchstones in the Mennonite march toward faithfulness. Simons had some interesting perspectives, specifically on the Virgin birth, that were not then and are not now broadly accepted. His overall depth of work on thinking through the implications of being the church, being disciples of Jesus, and interacting with his contemporaries are masterpieces and continue to be consulted. Portions, if not all, of his voluminous writings have been translated into most languages where there are Anabaptist churches.

About Nonviolence and Law Enforcement

Question 4: How did peace and non-violence come to be so central in Mennonite theology, praxis, and self-understanding?

Answer 4: The initial stance of the Anabaptists was one of "defenselessness" in obedience to Jesus' command in the Sermon on the Mount, specifically Matthew 5:38-48. It was not like modern pacifism, which is often rooted in a philosophical ethical objection to violence, most especially war. Many pacifists base their stance on a very positive and optimistic anthropology. That was not the case with the Anabaptists. Their chief concern was to be the true church, and that meant identification with a suffering Christ, who went to the cross in love for his enemies. The ability to join him in suffering was rooted in the personal experience of regeneration. To join the church was thus often a decision to become vulnerable to suffering.

The experience of persecution and rejection produced in many instances a separated communal life, marked frequently by moving to where authorities exempted Mennonites from participation in war. Even then, the stance remained "defenselessness" rather than "non-violence." It was not questioned that Christ would come in judgment on the godless and the violent, or that God's sovereignty extended over governments that had, according to Romans 13, responsibility to reward good and punish evil. The distinction between church and world meant that what might be the responsibility of the governing authorities—bearing the sword—cannot be the responsibility of those who choose to follow the Jesus who told Peter to put away the sword, and rather to turn the cheek.

World Wars I and II were a wake-up call to the church to attend to the state of this conviction, since in WWII roughly half of Mennonite men went into the military. This led to what has been called the "recovery of the Anabaptist vision," a central feature of which was "nonresistance."

Since then, under the impact of the Vietnam war and the resistance to it, the civil rights movement (King and Gandhi), international experience (MCC), the writings of John Howard Yoder, and great receptivity to Mennonite teaching and writing in the area of peacemaking in the wider world, a marked shift has taken place from "non-resistance" or "defenselessness" as practiced within a church/world dichotomy to peacemaking and pacifism, buttressed increasingly by a stance of nonviolence with Jesus as model (often along with King and Gandhi) rather than ecclesiology and discipleship (*Nachfolge*).

There is thus today a debate among Mennonites, even if not always explicitly joined, about whether violence is rooted in sin or social realities, including lack of education about better methods, that is, about whether the solution to violence is the gospel and conversion or getting the world to be less violent through organized activism and education, to put it in starkest terms. The old "dualism" of church vs. world has little hold on many contemporary Mennonites. For an increasing number peacemaking and nonviolence are more crucial than being a part of the church. Indeed for many that has come to be the primary meaning of "Anabaptism." Christian doctrines such as the atonement, most especially if understood as Jesus dying for us by the will of God, have increasingly come under review, and in some cases, under attack because it is deemed to participate in "redemptive violence."

In many circles Mennonites have become known and know themselves as a "peace people." We face the challenge of anchoring our understanding of peace in a Christ who is our peace, and who calls us unambiguously to love enemies because God loved us and invites us to participate in that enemy love (Matthew 5; Romans 5; Ephesians 2).

Question 5: How do Mennonites relate to local law enforcement measures?

Answer 5: Historically Mennonites were respectful of the authorities, and understood the role of authorities, specifically the state, through the lens of Romans 13:1-7. That also means that when governments do not do the right thing, or demand the wrong thing, that Mennonites have believed they "need to obey God rather than the government" (Acts 5:29), and suffer the consequences. When the laws of the state do not contravene what are deemed to be the clear teaching of Scripture, then Mennonites are to obey the government, to pay taxes, etc.

Along with the "political awakening" mentioned above, came the question of whether to pay "war taxes." Is that not a way governments conscript us, when they don't need our bodies but do need our money? This has been a significant debate, and continues to be.

More recently, the issue of whether Mennonites can participate in policing has emerged with some urgency (whether with respect to local law enforcement or in contexts of intervention [e.g., R2P, "Responsibility to Protect"]). John Howard Yoder is often invoked in that he made a distinction between policing and war making.

There has been significant scholarly activity around "policing" in recent years. An important participant is Gerald W Schlabach (idem, ed., *Just Policing, Not War: An Alternative Response to World Violence* [Collegeville, MN: Liturgical Press, 2007]), a Mennonite who has recently become Roman Catholic, with participants in the volume from RC, Protestant, and Mennonite traditions. The volume is, significantly, dedicated to both Pope John Paul II and John Howard Yoder. Another example is the Spring 2008 issue of the *Conrad Grebel Review*, focused on "Mennonites and Policing: An Ongoing Conversation."

My own disquiet, expressed in the CGR issue under the title "Ecclesiology and Policing: Who Calls the Shots?", is that when ecclesiology is weak, when soteriology is social transformation, then this openness to policing, most especially when put forward as a model for military intervention (R2P) becomes, I fear, the slippery slope Niebuhr already greased decades ago. Is this "Just War" light?

Even so, new questions are being raised that put pressure on these questions. Development and relief workers in contexts of conflict are experiencing the importance of state institutions in order, for example, to get food aid to vulnerable people. Churches that are drawing people to faith are finding both police and military personnel responding to the gospel. How to answer the question of Christians and policing, broadly or narrowly conceived, will continue to be a matter of some urgency, as Mennonites are more and more "in the world" struggling also more and more to know what it means to be "not of it."

Question 6: Is it alright for other Christians to use strong measures to keep peace and enforce laws in a community where Mennonites live?

Answer 6: Historically we recognized that other Christians participated in both law enforcement and war. But there was a sense that it was not fully faithful to the teachings of Jesus. One senses this ambivalence more in Menno Simons than in the clearer rejection of this option in the *Schleitheim Confession*.

Cooperation in the missionary movement with Christians from other traditions who were nevertheless passionate in their efforts to reach persons for Christ had the effect of relegating nonresistance or "defenselessness" to a Mennonite "distinctive" not really at the core of the gospel.

In keeping with the narrative given above, the more recent raising of nonviolence to a core characteristic of Anabaptism, and thus to what it means to be a Mennonite, has led for some to a new kind of estrangement from other church traditions. They are seen as "Constantinian," and thus betray or at least compromise the teaching of Jesus regarding peace. For others, however, it has led to a very energetic effort to get other Christians to agree. It is an essential component to many interactions with both evangelical and "mainline" church communities. A celebrated recent example is German Mennonite theologian Fernando Enns' success at moving the WCC to declare and implement the just completed *Decade to Overcome Violence*. Violence is sadly still among us, but the church bodies represented in the WCC have taken a severely critical stance regarding the doctrine of the Just War in recent documents emerging from the *Decade*.

At the same time, in circles within the Mennonite community strongly oriented to practical and social peacemaking, the church/world dichotomy is not particularly determinative, and so the lines are drawn differently than they once were. There is great suspicion of letting others do the "dirty work" for us, while we get to stay "pure." As the discussions around policing illustrate, we are struggling to find our way ethically and theologically.

Short Bios of Dialogue Participants

Dr Bert B Beach was born in Switzerland from American missionary parents. Living in different European countries led him to speak five languages fluently. He was educated in Switzerland, France and the United States, completing his education by obtaining a doctorate in history from the University of Paris. His career has spanned half a century of leadership in Adventist education, church administration, religious liberty, and interchurch relations. He has directed or participated in numerous dialogs with various Christian churches and religious bodies. He is the author of six books and has written some two hundred articles. He is keen on building bridges of faith, friendship, and freedom.

During 32 years of active duty service (and four years in the reserves) in the US Army, **Chaplain (Colonel) Gary R Councell** continued active pastoral care of church/chapel congregations, completed a year of Clinical Pastoral Education (parish model) and earned a master's degree in counseling. He is a graduate of the military's Senior Service School (USAWC) and was assigned to the Office of the Chief of Chaplains (HQDA-DACH) for more than six years. His "ministry of presence" served people of all religious faiths or no faith by sharing God's love, grace and hope in circles often less accessible to pastors or overlooked by churches. As an Adventist chaplain, he was "courageous in spirit and compassionate in service," assisting soldiers in resolving issues around accommodation of religious practice, including conscientious objection (I-A-O and 1-O). He wrote the published essay, "Seventh-day Adventists and Military-related Service." Chaplain Councell assumed duties on December 1, 2005 as Director of Adventist Chaplaincy Ministries (ACM) in the General Conference of Seventh-day Adventists.

Dr Denis Fortin is professor of theology at the Seventh-day Adventist Theological Seminary, Andrews University, Berrien Springs, Michigan, and until recently served as dean (2006-2013). Born in Quebec City, Canada, Fortin received a Bachelor of Arts degree in pastoral ministry from Canadian University College, Alberta, in 1982. He earned a Master of Divinity from the Seventh-day Adventist Theological Seminary of Andrews University in 1986 and a Doctorate in Theology (PhD) from the Université Laval, Quebec, in 1995. He has served on the Faith and Order Commission of the National Council of the Churches of Christ in the USA, and on numerous committees for the Seventh-day Adventist Church. Fortin has authored a number of publications on Adventist history and theology. In 2004 he published *Adventism in Quebec: The Dynamics of Rural Church Growth, 1830-1910* (Andrews University Press). He is co-editor of the *Ellen G. White Encyclopedia* (Review and Herald, 2014).

Dr John Graz grew up in a home where his father was Protestant and his mother was Catholic. He became an Adventist when he was 18 years old, studied Theology in the French Seminary of Collonges near Geneva, and completed his Doctorate in History at the Sorbonne University in Paris. Dr Graz served as a pastor and church administrator for many years. He is currently director of the Public Affairs and Religious Liberty Department for the world headquarters of the Seventh-day Adventist Church. He is also Secretary General of the International Religious Liberty Association and has organized numerous congresses, festivals, symposiums, and meetings of experts on behalf of religious freedom. He has written several books and numerous articles which have been translated into many languages.

Dr William G Johnsson was born in Australia and he earned a degree in chemical technology before attending Avondale College, where he met his wife Noelene. Johnsson earned his PhD in theology from Vanderbilt University. He served as a missionary to India at Vincent Hill School and Spicer College. From 1975 to 1980 he taught New Testament classes at the Seventh-day Adventist Theological Seminary at Andrews University. In 1979 Johnsson was elected the first president of the Adventist Society for Religious Studies. From 1982 to 2006 he was editor of the *Adventist Review*, and he was founding editor of *Adventist World*, an international journal for Seventh-day Adventists. Johnsson has written more than 20 books and 1,000 articles. He currently represents the Seventh-day Adventist Church in Interchurch and Interfaith Relations. On May 6, 2007, Johnsson was the graduate commencement speaker at Andrews University, where he received an honorary doctorate.

Dr Peter Landless is a medical doctor who trained in South Africa, the country of his birth. During his first term of mission service, he completed a specialty in family medicine. In this same period he was ordained as a minister of the gospel. He subsequently specialized in internal medicine and then cardiology. Throughout this time he worked with mission outreach and pastoral work as well as pursuing an academic career in medicine (clinical work, teaching and research). Since 2001 he has served the global Seventh-day Adventist Church as an associate director of the department of Health Ministries. In October 2013, he was elected to serve as the Director of the Health Ministries department. He is also the executive director of the International Commission for the Prevention of Alcoholism and Drug Dependency (ICPA), a non-governmental organization with a UN (United Nations) Charter.

Bishop Danisa Ndlovu grew up in a Christian home. His maternal grandmother as well as his mother, both strong and committed Christians, had a great influence in his being a committed and faithful disciple of Christ. He accepted Christ as Lord and Saviour of his life at a very tender age and was baptized under the Brethren in Christ Church (BICC) as a teenager. He sensed the call of Christ to ministry after he rededicated his life to Christ on Good Friday in 1976. The same year he enrolled for a two-year Advanced Diploma in Theology at Ekuphileni Bible Institute. Danisa did his undergraduate studies at Daystar University College in Nairobi, in 1988. He is also a graduate of Ashland Theological Seminary, in Ohio, USA. In between his studies and after his graduate studies Danisa has served his denomination, the Brethren in Christ Church, in various leadership roles. He currently serves the church as Bishop. Bishop Ndlovu, in addition to his denominational responsibilities, is currently the President of Mennonite World Conference (MWC).

Dr Teresa Reeve is an associate professor of New Testament at the Seventh-day Adventist Theological Seminary at Andrews University. Born and raised in British Columbia, Canada, she originally studied Elementary Education and earned an MA in Developmental and Educational Psychology, working with various church entities in developing materials and providing training in the areas of child and family ministries. After completing an MDiv at Andrews University, she earned a PhD in Christianity and Judaism in Antiquity at the University of Notre Dame. Her special research interests are in Luke-Acts, and in New Testament social ethics. Teresa has served on several interdenominational dialogues and is currently a member of the Biblical Research Institute Committee and the Theology of Ordination Study Committee for the Seventh-day Adventist Church.

Dr Valerie G Rempel is Associate Dean of Fresno Pacific University Biblical Seminary where she holds the J B Toews Chair of History and Theology and serves as Director of the Center for Anabaptist Studies. She studied at the Mennonite Brethren Biblical Seminary before completing her doctoral studies in church history and theology at Vanderbilt University, Nashville, Tennessee. Dr Rempel has served on Mennonite Brethren and inter-Mennonite boards and is currently a member of the Faith and Life Commission of Mennonite World Conference.

Dr Henk Stenvers grew up in Amsterdam, The Netherlands in a Mennonite family. He was baptized in the Mennonite congregation in Amsterdam when he was 19 years old. He studied medicine at the University of Amsterdam. Henk worked in medicine for 20 years, mainly as general practitioner. Since early in his studies he was active for the church in youth work and later as member of different boards, local and national. From 1998 until 2002 he followed a lay-course in Mennonite Theology. Since 2002 he works as general secretary for the Dutch Mennonite Church. He is also involved in Mennonite World Conference since 2003 and is at present secretary of the Deacons Commission of MWC.

Dr Robert J Suderman is Canadian. He has dedicated his career to the life and health of the church. He has earned undergraduate degrees in History and Education; a Masters of Arts in Religion, and a ThD in Bible. He has served as teacher in Bolivia and Colombia, and has been invited as a resource person in leadership education in 36 countries around the world. He is the former General Secretary of Mennonite Church Canada, and presently serves as the Secretary for the Peace Commission of Mennonite World Conference. Robert is married to Irene, and together they have 3 sons, and 5 grandchildren. They live in New Hamburg, Ontario, Canada.

Patricia Urueña Barbosa is from Colombia, South America. She has completed her Master's Degree in Theology and Pedagogy. Patricia is a missionary working with Mennonite Mission Network in Ecuador for 14 years. She has been co-writer of several publications with the Latin American Council of Churches (CLAI), has taught at several theological institutions, including the branch of theology of the Latin American Biblical University in Ecuador, the South American Seminar in Ecuador and the Mennonite Biblical Seminary of Colombia. Currently she and her husband are serving as National Coordinators of Ministries of the Ecuador Mennonite Partnership.

Dr Thomas R Yoder Neufeld is Professor Emeritus of Religious Studies (New Testament) at Conrad Grebel University College at the University of Waterloo. Born in Canada in 1947, he grew up in German-speaking Europe. Tom studied in Canada and the United States, graduating with a Master of Divinity in 1973, and a Doctor of Theology in New Testament in 1989, both at Harvard Divinity School. After serving as a hospital and prison chaplain, and as congregational pastor, he began teaching in 1983, retiring at the end of 2012. Dr Thomas R Yoder Neufeld serves both his local congregation and the wider church as teacher and preacher. Among his publications are *Ephesians* (Believers Church Bible Commentary;

Herald Press, 2002), *Recovering Jesus: the Witness of the New Testament* (Brazos, 2007), and, most recently, *Killing Enmity: Violence and the New Testament* (Baker Academic, 2011), published in the UK as *Jesus and the Subversion of Violence: Wrestling with the New Testament Evidence* (SPCK, 2011). Tom is a member of the Mennonite World Conference General Council, as well as of the MWC Faith and Life Commission.